Growing up Fast and Furious

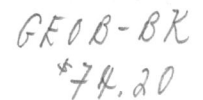

Growing up Fast and Furious

Reviewing the impacts of violent and sexualised media on children

Editors

Wayne Warburton

Danya Braunstein

THE FEDERATION PRESS
2012

Published in Sydney by
   The Federation Press
   PO Box 45, Annandale, NSW, 2038.
   71 John St, Leichhardt, NSW, 2040.
   Ph (02) 9552 2200. Fax (02) 9552 1681.
   E-mail: info@federationpress.com.au
   Website: http://www.federationpress.com.au

National Library of Australia
Cataloguing-in-Publication entry
   Growing up fast and furious: Reviewing the impacts of violent and sexualised media on children / Wayne Warburton and Danya Braunstein, editors

   Includes index.
   ISBN 978 186287 823 5 (pbk)

   Mass media and children.
   Mass media and teenagers.
   Mass media and youth.

302.23083

© The Federation Press except Chapters 6 (© Cordelia Fine) and 11 (© Alan Hayes).

This publication is copyright. Other than for the purposes of and subject to the conditions prescribed under the Copyright Act, no part of it may in any form or by any means (electronic, mechanical, microcopying, photocopying, recording or otherwise) be reproduced, stored in a retrieval system or transmitted without prior written permission. Enquiries should be addressed to the publisher.

Typeset by The Federation Press, Leichhardt, NSW.
   Printed by Griffin Press, Adelaide, SA.

Contents

Foreword vii
Acknowledgements xiii
About the authors xiv

1. Growing up fast and furious in a media saturated world 1
   Wayne Warburton

2. Children and media violence: Behavioural and neurological effects of viewing violence 34
   John P Murray

3. The impact of violent video games: An overview 56
   Craig A Anderson and Wayne A Warburton

4. How does listening to Eminem do me any harm? What the research says about music and anti-social behaviour 85
   Wayne Warburton

5. The internet as "fast and furious" content 116
   Ed Donnerstein

6. Messages, minds and mental contamination 129
   Cordelia Fine

7. The impact of sexualisation – Knowing and seeing too much 145
   Louise Newman

8. Children, media and ethics 159
   Emma Rush

9. There oughta be a law: The (potential) role of law and regulation in slowing down and calming down 175
   Elizabeth Handsley

10. Media and social policy: Towards an evidence-based approach to content regulation 197
Danya Braunstein, Julia Plumb and Wayne Warburton

11. A two-edged sword? The place of the media in a child friendly society 220
Alan Hayes and Carole Jean

Index 237

Foreword

L Rowell Huesmann

As a psychologist and media researcher who has been studying the effects of violence in the mass media for over 40 years, it is a great pleasure to be able to write the Foreword to this volume. Given the many reviews of the literature on violent media that have been published over the past 40 years or so, some might question the need for another book on the topic. However, recent events have shown that even supposedly intelligent people still fail to grasp the danger to society that is posed by the explosion of violent and sexualised media to which our youth and children are being exposed.

On 27 June 2011 the United States Supreme Court ruled that a State government could not ban retailers from selling violent video games to minors. The direction of the decision was not unexpected given the composition of the court and long-standing broad interpretation by American courts of the First Amendment to the US Constitution. However, the competing opinions offered by the justices to justify their rulings provide interesting insights into the struggles even intelligent laymen have had in piecing together the vast body of research in the area into a coherent one.

The California law only prohibited direct sales to minors of violent games. The games could still be purchased by an adult for the minor, but, just as minors cannot attend R-rated movies without an accompanying adult, they could not buy a violent game by themselves. The California law defined the violent games to be prohibited from sale to minors as those in which the range of options available to the player included "killing, maiming, dismembering or sexually assaulting an image of a human being in a way that was patently offensive, appealed to minors' deviant or morbid interests, and lacked serious literary, artistic, political or scientific value". This language was adopted from previous State laws restricting pornography – laws that the Supreme Court had upheld years ago. However, Justice Anthony Scalia, often considered to be the conservative intellectual star of the court, rejected the parallel in the majority opinion that he authored. He wrote: "Because speech about violence is not obscene, it is of no consequence that California's statute mimics the New York statute regulating obscenity-for-minors that we upheld". Considering that the first dictionary definition of "obscenity" is "offensive to decency" and the third definition is "disgusting," it is hard to understand how an intelligent person who understood what was in many violent video games could adopt this position. However, Scalia went on to write that "disgust is not a valid basis for restricting expression" even to minors. His conservative colleague, Justice Thomas, took him to task for the intellectual sloppiness of the position for a strict constructionist, and wrote:

> [T]he freedom of speech as originally understood, does not include a right to speak to minors (or a right of minors to access speech) without going through the minors' parents or guardians.

More challenging to the popular perception of Scalia as an intellectual, however, are the misunderstandings and misinterpretations of the scientific research on the topic that he revealed in his opinion. It is clear from what he wrote that he neither read the original research nor was aware of the extent. He wrote that the existing studies

> do not prove that violent video games cause minors to act aggressively (which would at least be a beginning). Instead, nearly all of the research is based on correlation, not evidence of causation, and most of the studies suffer from significant, admitted flaws in methodology.

Any dispassionate reader of the original scientific literature of the past 50 years knows that Scalia's conclusion is patently false and an embarrassment to both him and a court that is supposed to examine evidence carefully.

In contrast to Scalia, his colleague, Supreme Court Justice Breyer, obviously did take the time to read the original research and reached a quite different conclusion about the research and about what the decision should have been. In a dissenting opinion he wrote:

> Social scientists, for example, have found causal evidence that playing these games results in harm. Longitudinal studies, which measure changes over time, have found that increased exposure to violent video games causes an increase over the same period.

Even more impressive is that Breyer, in contrast to Scalia, actually saw the importance of the fact that established psychological learning theory and media effects theory explained why media violence and video game violence would teach youth to behave aggressively. He wrote:

> Video games can help develop habits, accustom the player to performance of the task, and reward the player for performing that task well. Why else would the Armed Forces incorporate video games into its training?

It is clear from this case that the effects of violent and sexualised mass media on children and youth are still not well understood by a substantial segment of the public. While the body of scientific literature demonstrating and explaining the deleterious effects has burgeoned, public opinion has not followed along. One reason is that many with vested interests in violent media (because of monetary investments or because of investments in their own self-images as users) bombard the public with glib arguments about no effects. If these vested interests can influence Justice Scalia and the US Supreme Court, they can certainly influence a large segment of the public, However, another reason for the disconnect between public opinion and research may be because we need more reviews of the research, theory and appropriate conclusions, along with appropriate policy recommendations, presented in forums that are accessible to the general public and in language that is understandable to the public. This book can serve that role.

The first part of the book provides cogent review of much of the empirical evidence that indicts media violence as a cause of increased aggression in the observer. Wayne Warburton's overview and John Murray's review of some key older studies, along with recent studies using modern biosocial investigation methods, make important information readily accessible to those with little background in the field. Similarly, the Anderson and Warburton chapter on violent video games provides a clear exposition of the most recent empirical research and theoretical interpretation of the effects of violent video games. In Chapter 4 Warburton then turns to reviewing the effects of music and music lyrics on both prosocial and antisocial behaviour. Music is an unappreciated but particularly powerful tool for influencing humans because the human mind is uniquely capable of forming enduring connections between music and whatever is associated with it (eg, violence or sex); so that the music may prime thoughts, ideas and behaviours after only a few exposures. In his Chapter 5, Donnerstein explores the impact of the internet on youth and children both as a source for access to the more traditional mass media (films, TV shows, video games) and as a new window on the world that makes access to potentially harmful material much easier for youth. In particular, Donnerstein focuses on the internet as a powerful new tool for sexual socialisation, and focuses on new communication media within the internet as potential promoters of both non-sexual cyber bullying and sexual cyber bullying. Louise Newman, in Chapter 7, expands on Donnerstein's discussion of the impact of sexual material on the internet to discuss more generally the sexualisation of youth and the role of the media in such sexualisation, as well as the effects that restrictiveness on the distribution in the mass media of sexual themes and displays might have on child development. Finally, Cordelia Fine, in Chapter 6, provides a stimulating overview of the roles that advertisements in the mass media – and particularly highly sexualised advertisements – play in altering children's self images and behaviour.

These reviews of what we know about the effects of violent and sexualised media on youth are followed by four interesting chapters concerning policy and ethical implications that derive from our understanding of how these kinds of media change youths' behaviours and ways of thinking. Emma Rush provides the unique perspective of a philosophical ethicist on issues of media effects and media regulation. Are principles or consequences more important? Is it more ethical to empower children or to protect them? What is the most ethical balance between allowing freedom of expression and protecting children from harm? Rush also correctly (I think) notes that the media literacy movement promoted by so many as an alternative to regulation is not proven to be effective and is not likely to be as effective as regulation. Elizabeth Handsley follows with a chapter that exposes very clearly the difficulties of formal government regulation of violent and sexual media in societies that value free expression. Danya Braunstein and her colleagues follow this with a chapter in which they make a strong plea to base regulation on empirical evidence rather than political or even ethical positions. The evidence is in, they correctly point out, so let's base regulation on the evidence that is in, and let's do it now!

In the final chapter, Alan Hayes expands on this perspective by pointing out the multiply-determined nature of aggressive and violent behaviour that needs to be addressed if real reductions in violence are to be obtained. Violence in the media is a factor in promoting aggression just as ethnic stereotypes in the media promote racism, and presenting slim and fat people promotes norms that may promote anorexia or obesity. However, the mass media is not the only factor or even the most important factor in promoting these problems. Hayes correctly argues that we need to focus more on the factors that make some people more susceptible to these influences, and others less susceptible, if we are to have a media policy that promotes a child friendly society.

In sum, the essays in this book are the kinds of essays that are needed to move the public toward a better understanding of the effects that media can have and the kinds of policies that might ameliorate those effects. They represent an important contribution to the field.

Rowell Huesmann
September 2011

Acknowledgements

Special thanks to The Hon Greg Donnelly, MLC, who provided a significant financial contribution to make this book a reality.

Thanks to the Australian Council on Children and the Media (ACCM) and the Children and Families Research Centre (CFRC), Macquarie University for their assistance and cooperation with organising the conference, the presentations from which formed the intellectual basis of this book.

It is important to note that the views and opinions expressed in this book are solely those of the authors, and do not represent the views of the Australian Council on Children and the Media, the Children and Families Research Centre, or Macquarie University.

About the authors

Craig A Anderson

Craig Anderson, PhD, Stanford University, 1980, is Distinguished Professor of Psychology and Director of the Center for the Study of Violence at Iowa State University. He is President of the International Society for Research on Aggression. He has been awarded Fellow status by the American Psychological Society and the American Psychological Association. Anderson's 150+ publications span a wide range of areas, including judgment and decision-making; depression, loneliness and shyness; personality theory and measurement; and attribution theory. He is one of the most widely cited scholars in social psychology textbooks. In recent years, his work has focused on the development of a General Aggression Model designed to integrate insights from cognitive, developmental, personality, and social psychology. His pioneering work on video-game violence has led to consultations with educators, government officials, child advocates, and news organisations worldwide. He has published over 150 works, most in top scientific outlets. Oxford University Press recently published his book on *Violent Video Game Effects on Children and Adolescents* (2007).

Danya Braunstein

Danya Braunstein is a Psychologist, Media Consultant and Researcher. She specialises in the clinical treatment of emotional regulation and impulse control, including effects of developmental traumas, conduct disorders and personality disorders. She has conducted experimental research into aggressive behaviour, and evaluative research for clinical treatment programs. This follows a successful media career, where she worked with multi-awarded and top rated TV series, including *Australian Idol*, *The Biggest Loser Australia*, and children's programming. She specialised in conducting in-depth character interviews, storyline development and systems management. These series have been broadcast in Australia and internationally.

Ed Donnerstein

Ed Donnerstein is Professor of Communication at the University of Arizona. His major research interests are in mass-media violence, as well as mass media policy. He has published over 225 scientific articles in these general areas and serves on the editorial boards of a number of academic journals in both psychology and communication. He was a member of the American Psychological Association's Commission on Violence and Youth, and the APA Task Force on Television and Society. He is a Past-President of the International Society for Research on Aggression. In 2008 he received the American Psychological Association Division 46 Award for Distinguished Scientific Contributions to Media Psychology. In addition, he was primary research site director for the National Cable Television Associations 3.5 million-dollar project on TV violence. He served as Dean of the College of Social and Behavioral Sciences at the University of Arizona from 2002-2009. He was also Dean of Social Sciences at the University of California-Santa Barbara as well as the Rupe Chair in the Social Effects of Mass Communication.

ABOUT THE AUTHORS

Cordelia Fine

Cordelia Fine is an Associate Professor in the Centre for Ethical Leadership at the Melbourne Business School, University of Melbourne. Her interdisciplinary research interests include moral psychology, the social psychology and neuroscientific investigation of gender, neuroethics and marketing ethics. Cordelia Fine is the author of *A Mind of Its Own: How Your Brain Distorts and Deceives* and *Delusions of Gender: The Real Science Behind Sex Differences*.

Image credit: Dean Cambray

Elizabeth Handsley

Elizabeth Handsley is a Professor of Law at Flinders University in Adelaide, South Australia. She has degrees in French and law from the University of New South Wales and in law from Northwestern University in Chicago. Over her career her research has spanned a number of fields, including feminist analysis of tort law, separation of judicial power and various aspects of media law, including defamation, contempt and regulation for the protection of children. In the latter field her work has focused on food advertising. Elizabeth has been closely involved in the activities of the Australian Council on Children and the Media since 1999, and was elected President in 2010. In her advocacy work she has co-authored numerous submissions to inquiries and reviews and given countless media interviews. In December 2010 she was one of six experts invited to address the Standing Committee of Attorneys-General on classification of computer games.

ABOUT THE AUTHORS

Alan Hayes

Professor Alan Hayes is the Director of the Australian Institute of Family Studies, being appointed in September 2004. He also holds a professorial appointment at Macquarie University. He is currently a member of the Family Law System Reference Group, the *Building a Civil Justice Evidence Base* Reference Group, the Chief Justice's Family Law Forum, the Australian Government's Longitudinal Studies Advisory Group (LSAG), the Work and Family Roundtable, the National Advisory Board of the Family Law Section, Law Council of Australia, and an inaugural member of the APS200 Leadership Forum. He has research and policy interests in the pathways children and their families take through life, and the role of families in supporting and sustaining development across life, from infancy and early childhood. Much of his work has focused on disadvantage, with a longstanding interest in prevention and early intervention. The impact of relationship breakdown on children is a particular interest.

Carole Jean

Carole has a BA (Hons) and Graduate Diploma in Librarianship, both from Monash University. She has worked as a Librarian at the Australian Institute of Family Studies for the past 20 years, providing reference and information services to AIFS researchers and the general public.

xvii

ABOUT THE AUTHORS

L Rowell Huesmann

After gaining his PhD at Carnegie-Mellon University in 1969, L Rowell Huesmann held positions at Yale University and the University of Illinois at Chicago before moving in 1992 to the University of Michigan, Ann Arbor, where he is Amos N Tversky Collegiate Professor of Communication Studies and Psychology and Director of the Research Center for Group Dynamics at the Institute for Social Research. He is past president of ISRA, the International Society for Research on Aggression and has been editor-in-chief of its journal *Aggressive Behaviour*, since 2004. He was the recipient in 2005 of the American Psychological Association's award for Distinguished Lifetime Contributions to Media Psychology. He has made key theoretical and empirical contributions to understanding the development of aggressive behaviour, focussing on aggressive scripts and social learning processes. He is also one of the leading scholars on media violence effects on aggression and has been a principal researcher in the famous Columbia County Longitudinal Study that began in 1960 and the Cross National Television Study that began in 1977.

John Murray

John P Murray, PhD, is a Research Fellow in the Department of Psychology at Washington College; an Emeritus Professor of Developmental Psychology in the School of Family Studies and Human Services at Kansas State University; and a Visiting Scholar in the Center on Media and Child Health at Children's Hospital Boston, Harvard Medical School. He has conducted research on children's social development for almost 40 years – starting in 1969 as a Research Coordinator for the Surgeon General's Scientific Advisory Committee on Television and Social Behavior at the National Institute of

Mental Health, in Washington. His recent research projects are focused on children and violence and include studies mapping children's brain activations – using functional Magnetic Resonance Imaging (fMRI) – while the youngsters view violent and nonviolent videos, and studies of youth growing up in war zones and conflict areas. Dr Murray has published 14 books and about 90 articles on the social development of children and youth. His recent book – *Children and Television: Fifty Years of Research* (Norma O Pecora, John P Murray & Ellen A Wartella, editors) – was published by Erlbaum Publishers in 2007.

Louise Newman

Louise Newman is Professor of Developmental Psychiatry and Director of the Monash University Centre for Developmental Psychiatry & Psychology. In January 2011 she was appointed as a Member in the General Division of the Order of Australia. She is a practising infant psychiatrist with expertise in the area of disorders of early parenting and attachment difficulties in infants. She has undertaken research into the issues confronting parents with histories of early trauma and neglect. Her current research is focusing on the evaluation of infant-parent interventions in high-risk populations, the concept of parental reflective functioning in mothers with borderline personality disorder and the neurobiology of parenting disturbance.

Julia Plumb

Julia Plumb has worked with Dr Warburton since early 2009 on a variety of research projects, including studies examining the effects of aggressive and antisocial media on adults and children, maladaptive thought-patterns in children from abusive homes, and theories of control and power in domestic violence. Completing her honours degree in Psychology at Macquarie University in 2011, Julia is the recipient of multiple Department of Psychology Prizes, and was recently awarded the Macquarie Higher Studies Scholarship. In 2012, she is to receive the Australian Psychological Society (APS) Prize in Psychology, the Vice-Chancellor's Commendation for Academic Excellence, and the University Medal for Psychology. In addition to aggression and media effects, Julia's key interests in psychology are personality disorders, the neurobiology/neuropharmacology of mental illness and addiction, and the burgeoning field of neuroplasticity.

Emma Rush

Dr Emma Rush is a lecturer in philosophy and ethics at Charles Sturt University (<www.csu.edu.au>). She was the lead author of two papers on the sexualisation of children released by the Australia Institute in 2006 (<www.tai.org.au>). These papers prompted considerable public debate, ultimately leading to a Senate Inquiry into the issue. Emma continues to write and speak about the issue of the sexualisation of children to academic, professional and general audiences. Within applied ethics, Emma's other research area is environmental ethics. She also works more broadly across the area of professional ethics, teaching undergraduate and postgraduate students in human services and health.

Wayne Warburton

Dr Wayne Warburton is a lecturer in developmental psychology with the Department of Psychology and is the Deputy Director of the Children and Families Research Centre at Macquarie University (Sydney). Wayne is also a registered psychologist, and represents the interests of telecommunications consumers on the Telecommunications Industry Ombudsman's governing council. Wayne has a strong research interest in media effects, primarily comparing the impact of violent visual versus auditory media and examining the effect of violent lyrics versus aggressive tone in violent music. Wayne also has a research interest in media depictions of aggression as a means of controlling one's environment, the development of stable aggressive patterns of thought through media exposure, and video game and screen addictions. Along with other authors from this volume (Craig Anderson, Rowell Huesmann and Ed Donnerstein) Wayne is a co-author of the *Statement on video game violence* used as expert testimony in the Gruel amicus curiae brief, in the US Supreme Court Case of *Schwarzenegger and Brown v Video Software Dealers Association and Entertainment Software Association* (Docket # 08-1448) in which the State of California sought reinstatement of a law prohibiting the sale of violent video games to minors. Wayne is passionate that research evidence should be used more widely to inform public policy.

Chapter 1

Growing up fast and furious in a media saturated world

Wayne Warburton

A media-saturated world? It sounds melodramatic, but a quick look at the facts suggests otherwise. In the United States, children aged 8–18 are exposed to an average of almost 11 hours of media each day and spend more time "learning from" media than from teachers at school. Australian kids are a few hours behind, but still have considerable exposure. And this does not even take into account other incidental exposure to media, such as to advertising on roadside signs, products, tee shirts and other media experienced in subtle ways that are not measured in surveys. Clearly, media such as television, movies, music, video games, advertising and the internet have a strong influence on the development of children. For this reason, knowledge about the ways that media can impact on children and adolescents is an important resource for parents, paediatricians, psychologists, policy-makers, students, teachers and other professionals who work with children. With this in mind, the aim of this book is to provide up-to-date information about the influence of mass media on children in two important areas – media violence and the premature sexualisation of children.

There are two aspects to this book that should make it particularly helpful to those with an interest in children's welfare and development. The first is that the chapters are written by people from a variety of backgrounds – psychology, law, media production, paediatric psychiatry and sociology among others. The second is that this book is evidence-based. This is particularly important, because, as Rowell Huesmann (2010) has noted, there is a general public perception that the issue of whether media can impact on people's behaviour is undecided. This disturbs me somewhat, as there are a number of media effects that are very well researched and where there is a strong consensus amongst the vast majority of researchers. We hope that by presenting a series of chapters that provide a summary of the research evidence to date, this book will assist readers to judge the evidence for themselves.

Before we dive into the facts and figures, there is one more point that should be made. In terms of aggressive behaviour or the premature sexualisation of children, mass media is just one of many influences on children, and is just one of the many "risk factors" for negative outcomes. None of the authors would claim that media is the only factor, or even the most important factor, that can influence children's sexual development and levels of aggression. Readers are therefore cautioned not to over-interpret the media influences described in this book. Having said this, it is also important that readers don't underestimate the importance of these findings. Although media is just one of many influences in our children's lives, it is a powerful and pervasive influence and one that we can do something about, from parenting, to professional practice, to the making of policies and laws.

Media saturation

How much?

Let's start by looking at the US statistics, as these figures are more recent than the Australian data and were collected after an explosion in the take-up of media technologies such as mp3 players and other portable media devices. Rideout and colleagues (2010) have undertaken the most recent and most comprehensive survey. On an average day, a child aged 8–18 in the United States spends around 4.5 hours watching television, 2.5 hours listening to music, 1.25 hours playing video games, half an hour watching movies and 1.5 hours on a computer (see Table 1). These activities can overlap, such as listening to music while surfing the internet. Total average daily media exposure, excluding screen use at school and mobile phone use, adds to 10.75 hours, with 7 hours and 38 minutes of actual time elapsing. Around 66 per cent of 8–18-year-olds have a mobile phone, as do 85 per cent of 15–18-year-olds, and for these children and adolescents a further 1.5 hours per day are spent texting and another half hour talking on their phones.

Table 1: Average daily media use figures: Australia vs United States

Media type	US, 2009, 8–18-year-olds Rideout et al (2010)		Australia, 2007, 8–17-year-olds ACMA (2007)		Australia, 2009, Internet users (NITR, 2010)[#]	
	Hours	Minutes	Hours	Minutes	Hours	Minutes
Total exposure	10	45*	–		8	42±
% multi-tasking	29%		–		–	
Total hours per day	7	38*	5	8[∂]	–	
Television and DVD	4	29	2	18	3	44[†]
Movies		25	–		–	
Music/Radio	2	31		35	1	16
Internet radio	–		–			40
Video games	1	13		39	–	
Computer	1	29	1	17	–	
Online/internet use					2	18
Mobile phone	2	8		19		32
Print		38	–			41

* Not including mobile phone use
† Includes television, videos and videos on personal computers
∂ Does not include print media or movie attendance
Average use across all internet users in Australia
± Does not include video game playing or movie attendance. The 2010 data reveal a further increase of 12 minutes per day using the internet; 5 minutes using television and 5 minutes using radio.

In terms of violent content, Huston et al (1992) estimated that by the age of 18, US children have witnessed, on average, 200,000 acts of violence and 8000 murders on television alone. Television content has increased in violence since then, and more recent media such as video games can involve participating in hundreds of virtual murders per hour. For these reasons, the 1992 study probably underestimates the average current exposure of children to media violence to a significant extent, and more recent estimates of up to 40,000 murders seem closer to the mark (eg, Crenshaw & Mordock, 2005; Gullotta et al, 2005).

In Australia, the most recent comprehensive study of children's media habits was undertaken by the Australian Communications and Media Authority (ACMA) in 2007. This study reveals that Australian children spend less time with media than do American children, at around 5 compared to 7.5 hours per day, but that this figure represents 49 per cent of their discretionary time (see Table 1 for a comparison with US data). On an average day in 2007, Australian children watched more than 2.25 hours of television and spent 39 minutes playing video games, 35 minutes listening to music, 19 minutes using a mobile phone and 1.25 hours on the computer, primarily using the internet. It is noteworthy that 100 per cent of children sampled watched television, 96 per cent used a computer at home and 94 per cent played video games. Amongst children, mobile phone take-up numbers in 2007 were similar to those for the United States in 2009, with 54 per cent of 8–17-year-olds and 90 per cent of 15–17-year-olds owning a mobile phone. It is also interesting that the television timeslot most watched by 8–17-year-olds in Australia was 6.00 pm to 9.00 pm, with 3.00 pm to 6.00 pm being the next most popular. Clearly, Australian children viewed a lot of television content produced for adults.

Australians had strongly embraced technology by 2007, with 98 per cent of Australian households with children under 18 owning a computer, 91 per cent having internet access and 76 per cent having broadband access (broadband figures now exceed 80 per cent). By 2010, mobile internet use had reached 50 per cent penetration for the first time, 8 per cent of Australians used tablet computers such as i-pads (expected to reach 50% by 2016) and 70 per cent had accessed audio or video online (LeMay, 2012; Neilson Internet and Technology Report, 2011). Internet users are also substantial consumers of all media. According to the 2010 *Neilson Internet and Technology Report*, the average Australian internet user in 2009 was exposed to 8 hours and 42 minutes of media per day, not including video games or movies, with a further increase found in 2010 (see Table 1). When comparing the Australian and US data for children, it should be noted that the three year difference in data collection may be important. The US data found a substantial 2.2 hour increase in average daily media consumption between 2004 and 2009, primarily due to a large increase in the ownership of mp3 players, mobile phones and laptop and tablet computers. As there has been a similarly large increase in the take-up of such technologies in Australia in recent years, it is likely that the media exposure of Australian children has also risen significantly since 2007.

Who? Differences by age, gender, ethnicity and socio-economic status

According to Rideout and colleagues (2010), US boys 8–18 consumed around 1 hour per day more media than US girls, with most of this coming from greater use of video games. Media use increased with age from 7.8 hours per day for 8–10-year-olds to 11.3–11.8 hours per day for 11–18-year-olds, with use peaking marginally in the 11–14 age group. Black and Hispanic youth consumed around 4.5 hours more media per day than white youth (13.0 v 8.3 hours per day) and this disparity had doubled for black youth and quadrupled for Hispanic youth over the five years before the study. There were no ethnic differences in how much time parents allowed their children to spend with media, but parents of white children were more likely to impose controls on content. Children whose parents had a college or higher education level spent 1.5 hours less per day consuming media than children of parents with lower education levels. Interestingly, a 2004 study by Amy Jordan found that parents with a higher socio-economic status (SES) were more likely to have rules about how much time their children spent with media but fewer rules about content, and parents with a lower SES had more rules about media content than about amount of time spend with media.

In Australia, boys also consume more media than girls, especially video games (an additional 30 minutes per day), and are more likely to have media and communication devices in their bedroom. Girls spend more time on mobile phones (21 v 13 minutes per day) and on social networking activities such as e-mail and facebook (38 v 28 minutes per day). In Australia there is a more linear increase in media use with age than is found in the United States. Whereas 8–11-year-olds spend 40 per cent of their leisure time consuming media, this rises to 60 per cent for 15–18-year-olds. This is especially true for computer and internet use which rises from 10 minutes per day (3–4-year-olds) to internet use of 30 minutes per day at 9–11, 1.5 hours at 12–14 and 2.4 hours at 15–17. The one exception to this linear age trend is video game playing, which, as in the United States, peaks at around 11–13 years of age.

In Australia there are no documented differences in children's media use according to ethnicity, but households where a language other than English is spoken are more likely to have multiple computers in the home, computers with internet access in children's bedrooms and hand-held games, but are less likely to have a television, games console or DVD player in a child's bedroom. In terms of socio-economic status, families at all income levels tend to have a full array of media devices (ACMA, 2007), but children of higher SES families spend less time watching television and more time reading (Rutherford et al, 2009). Higher SES households are less likely to have a television in children's bedrooms but are more likely to have a computer with internet access in the child's bedroom (ACMA, 2007).

Where is media being accessed?

There are two important factors relevant to where media is accessed for modern Australian children. The first is that there has been a strong recent convergence of media to internet-based platforms, and particularly mobile internet-capable i-devices. The rollout of the Australian high-speed National Broadband Network (NBN) should further accelerate convergence. This shift is exemplified in the change from 1999 US television data, where 8–18-year-olds spent 3 hours and 5 minutes per day watching live television, 27 minutes watching DVDs and 14 minutes watching time-shifted (that is, pre-recorded) television. By 2009 live television viewing had dropped to 2 hours 39 minutes per day and DVD viewing was similar at 32 minutes, but time-shifted viewing had increased to 22 minutes, online viewing to 24 minutes, i-pod viewing to 16 minutes and mobile phone viewing to 15 minutes (Rideout et al,

2010). That is, even though there was a 26 minute drop in the daily viewing of television sets, there was 1 hour and 3 minute increase in viewing by alternate modes (many broadband-mediated) and a half hour increase overall.

Secondly, media is now more portable and there is access for children in multiple places within and outside the home. Table 2 (see over page) shows a comparison of US and Australian data for media ownership and the location of media appliances within homes. What is clear is that the average household in both countries is well serviced for media appliances, but that Australian children are much less likely to have access to media in their own bedrooms. What is yet to be clarified is the degree to which portable media access will make bedroom access for children less relevant in coming years. Media content can be accessed online via mobile phones and on laptop, netbook and tablet computers. Much media content can also be downloaded to mp3 players. Some video games, including violent games like Grand Theft Auto IV, are also available in i-phone downloadable versions. This means that it is becoming increasingly difficult for parents to monitor their children's media consumption, either for duration or content.

Why? What is so appealing about media to children?

The traditional theory as to why children (and adults) are so drawn to media is *gratification theory*, which suggests that individuals use media to meet their psychological needs, such as the need for information, entertainment, social interaction, and mastery and control (see Calvert & Kotler, 2003). In addition, media such as video games can be very "absorbing", thus reducing the level of worrying thoughts and unpleasant feelings in the conscious mind and replacing them with immersion into the virtual world. More recently, researchers have become interested in what needs are met by social network sites such as Facebook and information sharing sites such as You Tube. Research by Shao (2009) suggests that such sites are used more for entertainment than as sources of information, and there is some suggestion that such sites meet a need for self-expression as well as for social interaction.

Table 2: Media per household and source*

Media Source or location	US 2009[†]	Australia 2007[#]
Appliances per household		
Television sets	3.8	2.8
DVD players	2.8	1.7
Computers	2.0	1.8
Video game consoles	2.3	1.0
CD players	2.2	–
Radios	2.5	–
mp3 players	–	1.5
Mobile phones	–	2.9
In children's bedrooms		
Computer	36%	18%
Internet access	33%	9%
Television	71%	20%
Video game console	50%	10%
In cars		
Portable DVD or TV	37%	–

* Blank spaces indicate an item not measured in that survey
[†] Rideout et al, (2010)
[#] ACMA (2007); Screen Australia, (2007).

A recent study of Grade 5 and 6 children in Canada revealed that the top three reasons children gave for watching television and playing video games were:
1. for entertainment;
2. to spend time with family; and
3. because they were bored. (He et al, 2010)

Adolescents report primarily turning to media when there is little else to do and they are bored. Adolescents are also more likely to choose media that matches their current mood, unlike adults who tend to use media to improve their mood (Carpentier et al, 2008). A survey of over 4000 Finnish youth aged 12–18 found that electronic gaming was particularly important for social communication for boys. The survey also revealed that motives change as children age, with older compared to younger adolescents using gaming more for entertainment, to relax and to escape their worries, and less to develop new gaming skills or to experience different roles and worlds (Wallenius et al, 2009).

What? The positive and negative impacts of media on children

Research has shown that media can have both short-term and long-term effects on children. Typically, short-term effects are tested through either experiments, which can demonstrate a causal link between exposure to certain types of media (for example, violent versus non-violent) and an immediate outcome (such as subsequent aggressive behaviour), or observational studies in "real world" settings. Longer term effects are determined in studies that examine the correlation between people's media habits and typical behaviours, and in longitudinal studies that follow a group of people over a period of time and examine changes to both their media habits and outcomes such as aggression.

The overall conclusion from research of all types is that media is a powerful tool and a powerful teacher. It is the subject matter taught that is crucial. Exposure to pro-social, age-appropriate and helpful media can have a very positive impact on child development, and exposure to anti-social, violent, frightening and age-inappropriate media can have a range of negative effects on children in both the short- and long-term.

Positive impacts

Pro-social and helping behaviour

Mares and Woodard (2005) looked at the average findings of 34 studies that tested the positive effects of television on children's social interactions. Overall, the studies found that children who watched pro-social content on television behaved significantly more helpfully or held significantly more helpful attitudes than others, both in experimental settings and at home. Gentile and colleagues (2009) ran a series of studies showing that pro-social video game playing was linked with pro-social behaviours and attitudes in both the short- and long-term (more in Chapter 3). Recently, there has been a resurgence of interest in pro-social media effects, and a lot of new findings are expected between now and 2020.

Education

The benefits of educational television have been well researched, but are age-dependant. The American Academy of Pediatrics has advised its members to recommend no screen time for children under two years, as there is no evidence of any benefit to children of this age, but there are several studies linking media exposure to language delay in children under two (AAP, 2009; Tanimura et al, 2007). Age-appropriate educational television has been linked with improved scores on vocabulary tests and enhanced achievement in reading and mathematics in children three and older (Rutherford et al, 2009; see also Schmidt & Anderson, 2007). These effects also seem to be cumulative. A large scale longitudinal study in the United States found that 5-year-olds who primarily viewed educational television shows during their preschool years were more successful in school 10 years later, even when statistically removing the influence of parental socio-economic status and children's prior intelligence scores (Anderson et al, 2001). Video games have also been used effectively to teach maths and reading, to teach pilots how to fly, soldiers how to use weapons and surgeons how to use laparoscopic surgical techniques (Swing et al, 2010; see also Gentile & Gentile, 2008, on video games as a teaching aid).

Spatial cognition, coordination and fine motor skills

Improvements in spatial cognition and fine motor skills are primarily found in research on video game playing (see Bailey et al, 2010; Swing et al, 2010 for reviews). These are dealt with in more detail in Chapter 3.

Pain management

Television, video games and music have all been successfully used to distract or soothe children during painful procedures, thereby reducing anxiety and perceived levels of pain (Nilsson, 2008; Schmitt et al, 2011; Standley, 1995; Weiss et al, 2011). It should be noted, though, that distracting media seem to be less effective for helping younger children manage pain (Weiss et al, 2011).

Social networks

A range of media can be used as tools for social interaction. Children can talk about media with their friends and can use media to interact with friends through social networking sites, text messages, mobile phones, chat rooms, internet blogs, skype and multi-player online games. In addition, some types of media can be central to an identity. For example, music preferences are important to a child's developing identity and self-image from early adolescence on (Roe, 1996). Media that helps children and teenagers develop a *positive* self-identity can have a positive impact on healthy development.

Negative impacts

Links with poor general health

In a survey of over 20,000 American and Canadian students in grades 6–10, screen-based media use (SBM) was negatively related to most positive health indices and positively related to several of the negative health indicators (Iannotti et al, 2009). In both countries, SBM was positively correlated with health complaints, physical aggression, cigarette smoking and alcohol use. SBM was also modestly but consistently associated with individual perceptions of poorer quality of life and quality of family relationships. The one exception was that screen-based media use was positively related to the quality of peer relationships (Iannotti et al, 2009).

Sleep deficits

There is a growing literature linking media use with sleep deficits and sleep disturbances. A recent review of 36 papers investigating the relationship between sleep and electronic media in school-aged children/adolescents revealed that delayed bedtime and shorter total sleep time were the sleep problems most consistently related to media use (Cain & Gradisar, 2010). For example, a study of more than 1000 Australian 10–13-year-olds found that those who were exposed to the most screen time received less nightly sleep than their peers (Olds et al, 2006). Another study of adolescents found that watching three or more hours of television per day was associated with sleep problems that persisted into early adulthood (Johnson et al, 2004) and a more recent study found that children who multi-task less with media get more sleep on school nights (Calamaro et al, 2009). Violent content, bedroom access to television, and evening media use have also been linked to sleep problems in younger children aged 3–5 (Garrison et al, 2011). Indeed, television viewing and the playing of computer games in the two hours leading up to bedtime seem to be particularly problematic, having now been linked with sleep disturbances (Paavonen et al, 2006), poorer quality sleep (Dworak et al, 2007), resistance to going to bed, difficulty falling asleep and less sleep time overall (Owens et al, 1999).

Less time undertaking healthy activities

This is a contested area of research, and rightly so, as the studies have been inconsistent at best (Vandewater et al, 2007). Given that children in the United States spend 7.5 hours per day with media, it seems logical that this should come at the expense of physical activities. However a number of studies have found no association between physical activity and television viewing (eg, Rideout et al, 2010; Robinson & Killen, 1995; Vandewater et al, 2007) and the 2007 ACMA study in Australia found that children aged 8–17 reported being involved in more physical activity compared to the 1995 survey, despite an increase in overall media use.

Addiction

Video game addiction is a serious and growing problem that is covered in more detail in Chapter 3 (see Griffiths, 2008; King, Delfabbro & Griffiths, 2010; Weinstein, 2010). There is also a growing concern that a variety of other screen-based activities may be addictive and new evidence is just emerging that this may be the case. However a lack of conclusive research evidence precludes too much being said in an evidence-based volume such as this. Those with an interest in child development should keep a watch for further developments around this issue.

Mental health problems

High consumption of media has been associated with unhappiness, problems in social adjustment, post-traumatic stress disorder (PTSD) and anxiety- and depression-related disorders (de Leeuw et al, 2010; Rideout et al, 2010; Singer et al, 1998). For example, a recent Australian study of 925 adolescents found that high overall media use was associated with poorer behaviour, health status and health-related quality of life. High video game use was also associated with poor global health, depression and anxiety (Mathers et al, 2009). In addition, violent and frightening media have been linked with anxiety, fears, sleep disturbances, PTSD, long-term phobias and avoidant behaviours, and occasionally with effects so strong they have resulted in hospitalisation (Buzzuto, 1975; Cantor, 2006; 2009; Cantor & Omdahl, 1991; Mathai, 1983; Simons & Silveira. 1994). In addition, sexualised media can have a negative effect on identity formation and have been linked with disorders such as bulimia and anorexia nervosa (see Chapter 7 for a more detailed analysis).

Attention deficits and education problems

These are dealt with in more detail in Chapter 3. In brief, there is growing research evidence linking levels of television exposure and video game exposure with attention deficits in children (Chan & Rabinowitz, 2006; Swing et al, 2010). There are also links between levels of media consumption and poorer school performance (eg, Gentile et al, 2004; Rideout et al, 2010). These may be due simply to the displacement of study time with media time, but it is also possible that other effects such as reduced attentional ability may play a part. More research is needed to clarify if this is the case.

Unhealthy lifestyle choices

There is considerable research with youth linking media exposure and substance use, and alcohol and cigarette advertising to alcohol use and smoking (AAP, 2010; Anderson et al, 2009; Strasburger, 2010). For example, a recent study with a large representative sample of year 9–12 students across 50 US States found clear links between watching three or more hours of television per day, or playing three or more hours of video games per day, and various risky behaviours, including using alcohol before age 13, lifetime heroin and illegal injection-drug use, current cocaine use, marijuana use and physical fighting (Denniston et al, 2011). A longitudinal study of American youth aged between 10–15 years had similar findings. Adolescents who watched more than four hours of television per day were 5 to 6 times more likely to have started smoking in the following two years than those who watched less television, even when gender, maternal education, household poverty and child aptitude test scores were taken into account (Gidwani et al, 2002).

Although, as noted, there is little evidence linking high media use to low activity levels, there are clear links, worldwide, between levels of media use and obesity (eg, Strasburger, 2009). For example, a huge survey of 137,593 youth aged 10–16 years from 34 (mainly) European countries found that television viewing times were higher for overweight compared to normal weight youth (Janssen et al, 2005). Another comprehensive longitudinal study of around 1000 New Zealand children measured the number of hours of television viewing and Body Mass Index (BMI) from ages 3 to 26. The study found that high levels of television viewing during childhood (ages 5–15) were associated with overweight, poor cardiorespiratory fitness, raised cholesterol and increased cigarette smoking at age 26, even after adjusting for gender, socio-economic status, parental BMI and BMI at age 5 years. This study suggests that excessive television viewing during childhood is likely to have long-term detrimental consequences for adult health (Hancox et al, 2004; Hancox & Poulton, 2006).

Interestingly, Australian studies have found mixed results. The ACMA (2007) study found that many children consume a substantial portion of their daily energy intake whilst watching television, much of it from salty or sugary snacks, and a study by Hesketh and colleagues (2007) found a positive association between screen time and BMI 3 years later. However Burke and colleagues (2006) found positive links between media use and overweight for boys but not girls. Wake et al (2003) found no such link when other factors (such as parental BMI) were taken into account, and Hardy et al (2009) found no consistent link between screen time and lower fitness levels. Although the Australian findings are inconsistent, the evidence for links between media consumption and obesity is strong enough that the American Academy of Pediatrics (2011) has issued a policy statement that concludes "media clearly play an important role in the current epidemic of childhood and adolescent obesity. The sheer number of advertisements that children and adolescents see for junk food and fast food have an effect. So, too, does the shift away from good nutritional practices that increased media screen time seems to create" (p 203). Overall, the evidence seems strong enough to warrant serious concern about the long-term health effects of excessive media use.

Fear, anxiety and phobias

There is a large body of work by Joanne Cantor and others showing that children's exposure to frightening media (including violent media) can have significant short- and long-term effects on children (Cantor, 2003; 2006; Cantor & Omdahl, 1991). Importantly, these differ by the child's age. Younger children are "concrete" thinkers and make judgements based on the obvious characteristics of a situation. They are more afraid of media portrayals of creatures with obviously frightening characteristics such as monsters and witches, despite the low likelihood of encountering such creatures in real life (Cantor, 1994; 1996; 2001; 2003; 2006; Cantor et al, 1986). In addition, because younger children cannot yet think in abstract terms, they may think that an event seen repeatedly on television is actually a series of new events of a similar type occurring again and again. This means that repeated coverage of natural disasters can have a particularly traumatic effect on younger children.

As children develop the capacity to empathise with others (starting around the age of 4) and to understand abstract concepts (at around ages 7–8), they start to become less afraid of creatures and situations that cannot realistically harm them, but become more afraid in response to media portrayals of situations they can imagine resulting in personal harm to them, or their family or friends, such as news coverage of natural disasters or portrayals of death within a family (Cantor, 1994; 1996; 2001; 2003; 2006; Cantor et al, 1986). Children are especially likely to become upset if some aspect of what they see reminds them of their *own* family and friends.

These fears can be short term (for example, Owens and colleagues (1999) found that 9 per cent of kindergarten to 4th grade children had nightmares related to their television viewing at least once a week) but can persist into adulthood and affect the way people think and respond to others. Most research suggests that between 25 and 35 per cent of adults have a significant fear that originated from childhood exposure to frightening media (eg, Harrison & Cantor, 1999).

Susceptibility to persuasion by advertising

Children and adolescents of all ages are vulnerable to the influences of advertising (see Chapter 6), and younger children (that is, those under eight-years-old) are particularly vulnerable because they (a) learn more easily from incidental/irrelevant information at the periphery of their mental focus than do adolescents or adults, (b) find it harder to distinguish between advertisements and other media content, (c) learn quickly from media content and are able to recognise brands even if they don't understand the message of an advertisement, and (d) tend to believe that advertisements are truthful (see Rutherford, 2009 for a brief review). To give one example, Borzekowski and Robinson (2001) found that children between the ages of 2 and 6 who watched videos with embedded food commercials were significantly more likely to choose the advertised food item from a pair of similar products, even with only one or two exposures to the advertisement.

Detriment to family relationships

An interesting 16-year study of 3000 children in New Zealand by Richards et al (2010) found that time spent viewing television and time spent playing on a computer were linked with poorer attachment to parents. Given that the core of attachment relationships involves beliefs about one's self worth and the trustworthiness of others (eg, Bowlby, 1980; Shaver & Mikulincer, 2005), it is not surprising that media use, which is linked with distrust and fear (Anderson et al, 2003; Cantor, 2003; 2006; Donnerstein et al, 1994), would undermine key attachment beliefs as well as take up time that could be spent in warm and supportive interactions with one's caregivers, family and peers.

Prejudice and misogyny

On purely theoretical grounds one would expect children to internalise and adopt attitudes and beliefs experienced in the mass media (both positive and negative), through the processes of imitation, incidental learning, explicit learning and acculturation (Anderson et al, 2003; Gerbner et al, 1994). There are many examples of media containing prejudiced, stereotyped or misogynistic content that could influence children. In the violent video game Grand Theft Auto (GTA), players can solicit prostitutes, have sex with them and then kill them to retrieve their money. Given that 56 per cent of US children aged 8–18 played GTA in a large recent poll (Rideout et al, 2010), and GTA has been imitated in real life on a number of occasions (see Chapter 3), it seems very likely that even young children would implicitly and explicitly learn attitudes from video games like GTA, including misogynistic attitudes about women. It is also noteworthy that video games have markedly less female characters (findings range from 3–20 per cent: see Beasly & Standley, 2002; Braun & Girouz, 1989), often stereotype women as props, bystanders, damsels in distress or victims (Smith, 2006), have mostly white characters and heroes, and tend to portray minority characters as athletes, street thugs, victims and criminals (Jansz & Martis, 2007).

There are similar findings from studies of television content, although the percentages are a little less striking and representations of women also included low-status jobs and domestic chores (eg, see Signorelli, 2001). Extreme misogyny is also evident in many rap and heavy/death metal songs (see Chapter 4 for more detail). A number of studies have also shown that childhood exposure to stereotyped material in media can increase both gender stereotyping (O'Bryant

& Corder-Bolz, 1978) and traditional gender-role attitudes (Morgan, 1987), but that exposure to non-traditional programming can lead to decreases in stereotyping (Nathanson et al, 2002). The evidence thus shows, as would be predicted by theory, that media can have both a positive and a negative effect on children's beliefs and attitudes towards others.

Premature sexualisation of children

This is covered in detail in Chapters 7 and 8 and will be covered only briefly here. There is now evidence that (a) media is a key medium by which children learn about sex (Pardun et al, 2005), (b) that age-inappropriate sexual content in media is linked with early sexual activity and teenage pregnancy (Strasburger et al, 2009), and (c) that premature or inappropriate exposure to sexualised material can have a negative impact on various mental health issues in children (see Chapter 7 for details). For example, in a study of 1000 12–14-year-olds in the United States, exposure to sexual content in music, movies and television was associated with accelerated teenage sexual activity and a doubling of the likelihood of early intercourse (Brown et al, 2006). Another study of ~1500 US 12–17-year-olds found that teenagers who listened to "sexually degrading" music (that is, which focused on casual sex and women as sex objects) were more likely to have advanced sexual activity or early intercourse, even when 18 other variables linked to early intercourse were accounted for in the data analysis (Pardun et al, 2005; see also Collins, et al, 2004). In addition, exposure to age-inappropriate sexual material in the media is associated with disturbances to sexual identity development and eating disorders (among other psychological problems).

Aggressive behaviour

This is the focus of Chapters 2–5 in this volume (Chapter 2 describes 60 years of research on television violence and provides brain imaging data; Chapter 3 focuses on video game violence and details several theories about the processes by which exposure to media violence increases aggressive behaviour; Chapter 4 reviews the research examining links between violent music and aggression; and Chapter 5 examines issues around violence and aggression online as well as cyber-bullying). Studies on media violence are numerous – over 1000 on television violence and several hundred on video game effects alone. Evidence converges across the multiple study types already noted (experimental, correlational, longitudinal, observational), and across races and populations, to suggest several key impacts of violent media:

a. an increase in aggressive behaviour;
b. an increase in beliefs normalising aggressive behaviour;
c. an increase in "behavioural scripts" that involve solving conflict with aggression;
d. beliefs around the notion that the world is more dangerous than it really is and that others want to harm you; and
e. emotional desensitisation to violence and decreased physiological arousal when exposed to violence. (Engelhardt et al, 2011; Krahé et al, 2011; see also Anderson et al, 2003; 2010; Donnerstein et al, 1994; Gentile, 2003; Strasburger et al, 2009 for reviews of these effects)

Is the "jury still out" regarding links between media and aggression?

In my view, the evidence that exposure to violent media increases the likelihood of aggressive behaviour in children, and for these other impacts of violent media on children, is compelling. However, as already noted, there is a common public perception that among media violence researchers there is little consensus about these effects. Although it is true that some findings have been ambiguous, and there are even findings of no effect at times, I think it is important to provide some perspective around this debate.

In my experience the vast majority of scholars who are actively undertaking research in this area accept these effects as demonstrated. Indeed, Ed Donnerstein, a prominent media violence researcher for more than three decades (and the author of Chapter 5 in this volume) has stated that "the evidence for these links is as strong as that for the contribution of any other studied contributor to community violence. The task of psychologists is no longer to demonstrate an effect, but to tease out its complexities and develop processes of remediation and amelioration" (Donnerstein, 2011).

Nevertheless, there are a small number of academics who dispute these effects (some of whom are funded by, or work in, industries that produce or promote violent media). These researchers appear (a) to be given a disproportionate amount of media coverage, and (b) to have a disproportionate impact on public views. In working out which viewpoint has the most credibility in terms of research, a recent study by Sacks and colleagues (2011) is instructive.

In the United States, a case was filed in the Supreme Court – *Schwarzenegger and Brown v Video Software Dealers Association and Entertainment Software Association* (Docket # 08-1448). In essence this case involved the State of California appealing to the Supreme Court to be able to reinstate laws under which video game retailers who allowed underage children to purchase games could be penalised, much as is the case with cigarettes and alcohol. Several amicus curiae (friend of the court) briefs were filed, including one submitted by Counsel of Record Steven F Gruel (the Gruel brief) and one submitted by Counsel of Record Patricia A. Millett (the Millett brief). The Gruel brief included a statement outlining the scientific evidence for violent video game effects along the lines already noted. This statement was prepared by 13 researchers described by Sacks and colleagues as "the top media-effects researchers" from various countries, including several authors from this volume – Craig Anderson, Ed Donnerstein, Rowell Huesmann and Wayne Warburton. The statement (which is reproduced in full in Chapter 3) was signed by 102 other scholars. The Millett brief put forward the view that there is no evidence for violent video game effects on children and was signed by 82 scholars, medical scientists, and industry representatives, owners or agents.

Given that the Millett brief has 82 signees (vs 115) and has attracted a lot of publicity, it could appear at face value that there is a reasonably even division amongst scholars in this area. Sacks and colleagues (2011) questioned whether the 82 Millett brief signees were all bona fide scholars with a track record of media violence research, and compared the credentials of the two groups. They found that the Gruel authors and signees (who wrote that the established research findings had demonstrated a link between violent media exposure and aggression), as a group, had vastly more research expertise in the areas of violence, aggression and media effects than did the Millett signees (see Table 3). One noteworthy finding was that the Gruel brief authors had published 338 times as many articles on media effects in "top tier" scientific journals.

Table 3: Comparison of publication records of Gruel brief authors and signees with Millet brief signees: Ratio of publications

	Gruel authors vs Millett signees	Gruel signees vs Millett signees
Media-effects articles in top tier journals	338:1	48:1
Peer-reviewed articles of original research on violence or aggression	28:1	14:1
Articles on violence or aggression	18:1	8:1
Have published one peer-reviewed article on aggression or violence	100% vs 17%	60% vs 17%
Have published one peer-reviewed article on media violence	100% vs 13%	37% vs 13%

They concluded that "although the Millett brief states that its signatories have 'extensive experience with the research regarding the effects on individuals of media violence, including violence in video games', this assertion is wholly unsupported by their scholarly publication records" (p 11).

This provides some evidence that even though there may appear to be a significant group of scholars and researchers who do not accept the evidence for the effects of violent media on children, this group is probably a small minority and includes very few researchers who are actively studying and publishing about media violence effects. In contrast, most of the active media violence researchers tend to have a convergent belief that increased exposure to violent media can increase the likelihood of aggressive thoughts, feelings and behaviours, and have a substantial research and publication record on which to base these opinions.

How does violent media impact children and youth?

Early research in this area centred on findings that children will imitate aggressive models in the media, especially if those models are admired, heroic, attractive, high-status, or rewarded for their aggression (see Bandura 1965; 1973; Bandura, et al, 1961; 1963a, 1963b). Soon after, researchers examined other ways in which children learn from media, either through seeing aggression rewarded (or not punished), or through associating aggression with common situations (see Chapter 3 in this volume, for a much more detailed description). It is now well-demonstrated that exposure to media in which aggression is portrayed as rewarded, or where aggression is not punished, increases the likelihood of aggressive behaviour in children (Anderson et al, 2003).

Another approach that emphasises learning arose later and became quite influential – Cultivation Theory (Gerbner et al, 1994). According to this approach, media is omnipresent in Western culture and, over time, exposure acculturates consumers of the media to the attitudes and beliefs of the media world, with greater exposure leading to greater acculturation (that is, people's own attitudes and beliefs align more and more with those that they see and hear in media).

Perhaps the most helpful way of thinking about the underlying psychological processes by which children learn from media is found in the neo-associationist approach of Berkowitz (1989; 1993). This, and subsequent influential approaches such as the General Aggression Model (Anderson & Bushman, 2002; see Chapter 3), assume an underlying neural network of concepts in semantic memory (Collins & Loftus, 1975). According to this approach, when people experience something new, clusters of neurons are set aside to recognise that thing again. These clusters are called "nodes", and humans have nodes for all sorts of objects, feelings and concepts. Nodes are heavily interconnected in the brain's "neural network", and the wiring of those connections is determined by experience. Nodes for objects, sensations, feelings and ideas that are activated together (that is, experienced together) become "wired" together in the brain, and this wiring becomes more robust with more frequent activation. In addition, activation of one node "spreads" to the nodes that are wired to it, with the most strongly connected nodes themselves becoming partially or fully activated as well (Collins & Loftus, 1975).

Substantial groups of nodes that are frequently activated together can become very strongly wired together into a "knowledge structure" (or "schema" or "script"), and activating one or more nodes from that structure will automatically activate the whole structure. For example, after visiting a supermarket a number of times, one does not need to actively think through the process of shopping there. Activating one or more of the nodes from the group of nodes wired together around the supermarket concept (for example, by seeing the supermarket logo), will partially or fully activate the supermarket knowledge structure (for example, the person will be aware there should be a swinging gate at the front left, trolleys lined up nearby, fruit and vegetables next, milk and dairy at the back and so on). Activation occurs automatically and the knowledge structure guides our expectations and behaviours, often operating out of conscious awareness (that is, much of what happens occurs on "automatic pilot").

If someone experiences a lot of aggression or violence, either in their real life or through mass media, it can be presumed that they develop a neural network which includes a lot of concepts around the notion of aggression or violence, a number of knowledge structures (schemas or scripts) that involve solving conflict with aggression or responding with aggression in various situations, and multiple cues (triggers such as seeing a weapon or being "given the finger") that can activate those knowledge structures. When these schemas or scripts are frequently activated, they can become chronically accessible – that is, they are partially activated much of the time, are easily brought to full activation by small triggers in the environment and thus have a disproportionate influence on how a person actually behaves.

This "neural network" concept is an important one because it illustrates that the "you are what you eat" principle applies to our brain and mind as well as our body. Just as our body changes in response to what we eat, the brain wires up according to what we experience. And if what we experience involves a lot of aggression and violence, our neural network will reflect those experiences, just as eating 3 kilograms of unclarified fat a day would be reflected in our arteries and the functioning of our organs.

Advice for practitioners, professionals and parents

How can parents and practitioners help to protect children from some of the negative impacts of media exposure? The first way is to encourage "healthy eating" of media in children – that is, to use media in moderation and have regard to its content. In practical terms this may mean:

(a) Parents restricting hours of media consumption ("limit setting"), which can be effective in both reducing hours of media exposure (Carlson et al, 2010) and reducing aggressive behaviour (Gentile et al, 2004);

(b) Parents co-viewing media or co-listening to media with their children, especially violent and sexualised media, and active interaction with children during media use;

(c) Parents restricting access to violent, sexualised or inappropriate content, and encouraging children to choose instead media with age-appropriate and pro-social and/or educational content;

(d) Talking to children about media that they have seen (for example, Nathanson, 1999, found that children whose parents speak negatively about violence on television are less aggressive. However, when parents make no comment about violence on television, their children are more aggressive than average). This is also important for sexualised media, where unhelpful ideas can be challenged;

(e) Being aware of the factors that enhance the negative impact of violent media on children:
- Violence that is followed by a lack of consequences or a reward is more likely to be imitated than violence that is punished;
- Violence used to exact justice and punish the "bad guys" is more likely to encourage aggression;

- Children who identify with violent characters are more likely to be negatively influenced by media violence;
- Seeing realistic violence may increase aggression where there is no realistic negative consequence for the perpetrator or victim (see Barlett & Rodeheffer, 2009; Gentile, Saleem & Anderson, 2007; Huesmann et al, 2003);

(f) Being aware of factors that do and do not decrease the negative effects of media violence on children:
- If the victim of violence displays pain and suffering or if the perpetrator seems to be punished, children are less likely to behave aggressively afterwards;
- There is no evidence that fantasy or cartoon violence is harmless. Even unrealistic media violence encourages aggressive thoughts, emotions and behaviours;
- It is not only angry, hostile children, or children from low socio-economic backgrounds, who are negatively influenced by violent media. Studies have shown that even children with low hostility personalities, and from all socioeconomic backgrounds, become more aggressive after exposure to violent media;
- Studies show that girls are just as influenced by media violence as boys (see Anderson et al, 2003; Gentile, Saleem & Anderson, 2007; Huesmann et al, 2003);

(g) Being aware of the influence of sexualised media on children and taking positive steps to reduce exposure and challenge unhelpful media messages about sexualisation with balanced, helpful and developmentally appropriate information;

(h) Being aware that the American Academy of Pediatrics (AAP: 2010) recommends no screen media exposure for children under 2 and a maximum of 1–2 hours per day for children over this age (see also the television viewing guidelines from the Division of Paediatrics in the Royal Australasian College of Physicians: McDowell et al, 1999);

(i) Keeping sources of media, including televisions, games consoles and internet-capable computers, out of children's bedrooms (AAP, 2001);

(j) Being a good role model with your own media use and encourage alternatives such as reading and sport (AAP, 2010).

References

AAP (American Academy of Pediatrics) (2001). Policy statement – Children, adolescents and television. *Pediatrics, 107,* 423–426.

AAP (2009) Policy statement – Media violence. *Pediatrics, 124,* 1495–1503.

AAP (2010) Policy statement – Children, adolescents, substance abuse, and the media. *Pediatrics, 126,* 791–799.

AAP (2011). Children, adolescents, obesity and the media. *Pediatrics, 128,* 201–208.

ACMA (Australian Communications and Media Authority) (2007). *Media and communications in Australian families 2007. Report of the media and society research project.* Accessed 7 March 2012, <http://www.acma.gov.au/webwr/_assets/main/lib101058/media_and_society_report_2007.pdf>.

ACMA (2010). *Trends in media use by children and young people. Insights from the Kaiser Family Foundation's Generation M2 2009 (USA), and results from the ACMA's media and communications in Australian families 2007.* Accessed 7 March 2012, <www.acma.gov.au/.../trends_in_media_use_by_children_and_young_people.doc>.

Anderson, CA, Berkowitz, L, Donnerstein, E, Huesmann, LR, Johnson, J, Linz, D, Malamuth, N, & Wartella, E (2003). The influence of media violence on youth. *Psychological Science in the Public Interest, 4,* 81–110.

Anderson, CA, & Bushman, BJ (2002). Human aggression. *Annual Review of Psychology, 53,* 27–51.

Anderson, P, de Bruijn, A, Angus, K, Gordon, R, & Hastings, G (2009). Impact of alcohol advertising and media exposure on adolescent alcohol use: A systematic review of longitudinal studies. *Alcohol and Alcoholism, 44(3),* 229–243.

Anderson, DR, Huston, AC, Schmitt, KL, Linebarger, DL, & Wright, JC (2001). Early childhood television viewing and adolescent behavior: The recontact study. *Monographs of the Society for Research on Child Development (Vol 66).* Malden MA: Blackwell Publishing.

Anderson, CA, Shibuya, A, Ihori, N, Swing, EL, Bushman, BJ, Sakamoto, A, Rothstein, HR, & Saleem, M (2010). Violent video game effects on aggression, empathy, and prosocial behavior in Eastern and Western countries. *Psychological Bulletin, 136,* 151–173.

Bailey, K, West, R, & Anderson, CA (2010). A negative association between video game experience and proactive cognitive control. *Psychophysiology, 47,* 34–42.

Bandura, A (1965). Influence of models' reinforcement contingencies on the acquisition of imitative responses. *Journal of Personality and Social Psychology, 1,* 589–595.

Bandura, A (1973). *Aggression: A social learning analysis.* Englewood Cliffs, NJ: Prentice Hall.

Bandura, A, Ross, D, & Ross, SA (1961). Transmission of aggression through imitation of aggressive models. *Journal of Abnormal and Social Psychology, 63,* 575–582.

Bandura, A, Ross, D, & Ross, SA (1963a). A comparative test of the status envy, social power, and secondary reinforcement theories of identificatory learning. *Journal of Abnormal and Social Psychology, 67,* 527–534.

Bandura, A, Ross, D, & Ross, SA (1963b). Imitation of film-mediated aggressive models. *Journal of Abnormal and Social Psychology, 66,* 3–11.

Barlett, C, & Rodeheffer, C (2009). Effects of realism on extended violent and nonviolent video game play on aggressive thoughts, feelings, and physiological arousal. *Aggressive Behavior, 35,* 213–224.

Beasley, B, & Standley, TC (2002). Shirts vs. skins: Clothing as an indicator of role stereotyping in video games. *Mass Communication and Society, 5*, 279–293.

Berkowitz, L (1989). Frustration-aggression hypothesis: Examination and reformulation. *Psychological Bulletin, 106*, 59–73.

Berkowitz, L (1993). *Aggression: Its causes, consequences, and control*. New York: McGraw Hill.

Borzekowski, D and Robinson, T (2001). The 30-second effect: An experiment revealing the impact of television commercials on the food preferences of preschoolers. *Journal of the American Dietetic Association, 101, 1*, 42–46.

Bowlby, J (1980). *Attachment and loss, Vol 3: Loss*. New Scale PA: Lippincott.

Braun, CMJ, & Giroux, J (1989). Arcade video games: Proxemic, cognitive and content analyses. *Journal of Leisure Research, 21*, 92–105.

Brown, J, L'Engle?, K, Pardun, C, Guo, G, Kenneavy, K, & Jackson, C (2006). Sexy media matter: Exposure to sexual content in music, movies, television, and magazines predicts black and white adolescents' sexual behavior. *Pediatrics, 117*, 1018–1027.

Burke, V, Beilin, L, Durkin, K, Stritzke, W, Houghton, S, & Cameron, C (2006). Television, computer use, physical activity, diet and fatness in Australian adolescents. *International Journal of Pediatric Obesity, 1(4)*, 248–255.

Buzzuto, JC (1975). Cinematic neurosis following *The Exorcist*. *Journal of Nervous and Mental Disease, 161*, 43–48.

Cain, N, & Gradisar, M (2010). Electronic media use and sleep in school-aged children and adolescents: A review. *Sleep Medicine, 11(8)*, 735–742.

Calamaro, C, Mason, T, & Ratcliffe, S (2009). Adolescents living the 24/7 lifestyle: Effects of caffeine and technology on sleep duration and daytime functioning. *Pediatrics, 123*, e1005-e1010.

Calvert, SL, & Kotler, JA (2003). Lessons from children's television: The impact of the Children's Television Act on children's learning. *Applied Developmental Psychology, 24*, 275–335.

Cantor, J (1994). Confronting children's fright responses to mass media. In D Zillman, B Jennings & AC Huston (eds), *Media, Children and the family* (pp 139–150). Hillsgate, New Jersey: Lawrence Erlbaum Associates.

Cantor, J (1996). Television and children's fear. In TM MacBeth (ed), *Tuning in to young viewers* (pp 87–115). Thousand Oaks, California: Sage.

Cantor, J (2001). The media and children's fears, anxieties, and perceptions of danger. In DG Singer & JL Singer (eds), *Handbook of children and the media* (pp 207–221). Thousand Oaks, California: Sage.

Cantor, J (2003). Media and fear in children and adolescents. In DA Gentile (ed), *Media violence and children* (pp 185–203). Westport, Connecticut: Praeger.

Cantor, J (2006). Why horror doesn't die: The enduring and paradoxical effects of frightening entertainment. In J Bryant & P Vorderer (eds), *Psychology of entertainment* (pp 315–327). London: Routledge.

Cantor, J (2009). Fright reactions to mass media. In J Bryant & M-B Oliver (eds), *Media effects: Advances in theory and research* (pp 287–303). New York: Routledge.

Cantor, J, & Omdahl, BL (1991). Effects of fictional media depictions of realistic threats on children's emotional responses, expectations, worries, and liking for related activities. *Communication Monographs, 58,* 384-401.

Cantor, J, Wilson, BJ, & Hoffner, C (1986). Emotional responses to a televised nuclear holocaust film. *Communication Research, 13,* 257-277.

Carlson, S, Fulton, J, Lee, S, Foley, J, Heitzler, C, & Huhman, M (2010). Influence of limit-setting and participation in physical activity on youth screen time. *Pediatrics, 126,* e89-e96.

Carpentier, FRD, Brown, JD, Bertocci, M, Silk, JS, Forbes, EE, & Dahl, RE (2008) Sad kids, sad media? Applying mood management theory to depressed adolescents' use of media. *Media Psychology, 11,* 143-166.

Chan, PA, & Rabinowitz, T (2006). A cross-sectional analysis of video games and attention deficit hyperactivity disorder symptoms in adolescents. *Annals of General Psychiatry, 5,* 16.

Collins, AM, & Loftus, EF (1975). A spreading activation theory of semantic processing. *Psychological Review, 82,* 407-428.

Collins, RL, Elliott, MN, Berry, SH, Kanouse, DE, Kunkel, D, Hunter, SB, & Miu, A (2004). Watching sex on television predicts adolescent imitation of sexual behaviour. *Pediatrics, 114,* e280-e289.

Crenshaw, DA, & Mordock, JB (2005). *Understanding and treating the aggression of children: Fawns in gorilla suits.* Lanham, MD: Jason Aronson.

de Leeuw, JR, de Bruijn, M, de Weert-van Oene, GH, Schrijvers, AJ (2010). Internet and game behaviour at a secondary school and a newly developed health promotion programme: a prospective study. *BMC Public Health, 10,* 544. doi:10.1186/1471-2458-10-544.

Denniston, MM, Swahn, MH, Feldman Hertz, M, & Romero, LM (2011). Associations between electronic media use and involvement in violence, alcohol and drug use among United States high school students. *Western Journal of Emergency Medicine, 12,* 310-315.

Donnerstein, E (2011). *The mass media as a risk factor for aggression in children and adolescents.* Invited paper presented at the 2nd Australian Conference on Children and the Media, Sydney, Australia, March.

Donnerstein, E, Slaby, RG, & Eron, LD (1994). The mass media and youth aggression. In LD Eron, JH Gentry, & P Schlegel (eds), *Reason to hope: A psychosocial perspective on violence and youth* (pp 219-250). Washington DC: American Psychological Association.

Dworak, M, Schierl, T, Bruns, T, & Strüder, HK (2007). Impact of singular excessive computer game and television exposure on sleep patterns and memory performance of school-aged children. *Pediatrics, 120,* 978-985.

Engelhardt, CR, Bartholow, BD, Kerr, GT, & Bushman, BJ (2011). This is your brain on violent games: Neural desensitization to violence predicts increased aggression following violent video game exposure. *Journal of Experimental Social Psychology, 47,* 1033-1036.

Garrison, M, Liekweg, K, & Christakis, D (2011). Media use and child sleep: The impact of content, timing and environment. *Pediatrics, 128,* 29-35.

Gentile, DA (ed) (2003). *Media violence and children: A complete guide for parents and professionals.* Westport CT: Praeger.

Gentile, DA, Anderson, CA, Yukawa S, Ihori, N, Saleem, M, Ming, LK, Shibuya, A, Liau, AK, Khoo, A, & Sakamoto, A (2009). The effects of prosocial video games on prosocial behaviors: International evidence from correlational, experimental, and longitudinal studies. *Personality and Social Psychology Bulletin, 35*, 752–763.

Gentile, DA, & Gentile, JR (2008). Violent video games as exemplary teachers: A conceptual analysis. *Journal of Youth and Adolescence, 9*, 127–141.

Gentile, DA, Lynch, PJ, Ruh Linder, J, & Walsh, DA (2004). The effects of violent video game habits on adolescent hostility, aggressive behaviors, and school performance. *Journal of Adolescence, 27*, 5–22.

Gentile, DA, Saleem, M, & Anderson, CA (2007). Public policy and the effects of media violence on children. *Social Issues and Policy Review, 1*, 15–61.

Gerbner, G, Gross, L, Morgan, M, & Signorelli, N (1994). Growing up with television: The cultivation perspective. In J Bryant & D Zillmann (eds), *Media effects* (pp 17–41). Hillsdale NJ: Erlbaum.

Gidwani, PP, Sobol, A, DeJong, W, Perrin, JM, & Gortmaker, SL (2002). Television viewing and initiation of smoking among youth. *Pediatrics, 110*, 505–508.

Griffiths, M, (2008). Internet and video game addiction. In C Essau (ed), *Adolescent addiction: Epidemiology, assessment and treatment* (pp 231–267). San Diego CA: Elsevier.

Gullotta, TP, Adams, GR, & Ramos, JM (eds) (2005). *Handbook of adolescent behavioral problems: Evidence-based approaches to prevention and treatment*. New York: Springer.

Hancox, RJ, Milne, BJ, & Poulton, R (2004). Association between child and adolescent television viewing and adult health: a longitudinal birth cohort study. *Lancet, 364*, 257–262.

Hancox, R, & Poulton, R (2006). Watching television is associated with childhood obesity: But is it clinically important? *International Journal of Obesity, 30*, 171–175.

Hardy, L, Dobbins, T, Denney-Wilson, E, Okely, A, & Booth, M (2009). Sedentariness, small-screen recreation, and fitness in youth. *American Journal of Preventive Medicine, 36(2)*, 120–125.

Harrison, K, & Cantor, J (1999). Tales from the screen: Enduring fright reactions to scary media. *Media Psychology, 1(2)*, 97–116.

He, M, Piche, L, Beynon, C, & Harris, S (2010). Screen-related sedentary behaviors: children's and parents' attitudes, motivations, and practices. *Journal of Nutrition Education and Behaviour, 42*, 17–25.

Hesketh, K, Wake, M, Graham, M, & Waters, E (2007). Stability of television viewing and electronic game/computer use in a prospective cohort study of Australian children: relationship with body mass index. *International Journal of Behavioral Nutrition and Physical Activity, 4*, 60.

Huesmann, LR (2010). Nailing the coffin shut on doubts that violent video games stimulate aggression: Comment on Anderson et al (2010). *Psychological Bulletin, 136*, 179–181.

Huesmann, LR, Moise-Titus, J, Podolski, C, & Eron, L (2003). Longitudinal relations between children's exposure to TV violence and their aggressive and violent behavior on young adulthood. *Developmental Psychology, 39*, 201–221.

Huston, A, Donnerstein, E, Fairchild, H, Feshback, ND, Katz, PA, Murray, JP, Rubinstein, EA, Wilcox, BL, & Zuckerman, D (1992). *Big world, small screen: The role of television in American society*. Lincoln: University of Nebraska Press.

Iannotti, RJ, Kogan, MD, Janssen, I, Boyce, WF (2009). Patterns of adolescent physical activity, screen-based media use, and positive and negative health indicators in the U.S. and Canada. *Journal of Adolescent Health, 44,* 493–499.

Janssen, I, Katzmarzyk, PT, Boyce, WF, Vereecken, C, Mulvihill, C, Roberts, C, Currie, C, & Pickett, W (2005). Health behaviour in School-Aged Children Obesity Working Group. Comparison of overweight and obesity prevalence in school-aged youth from 34 countries and their relationships with physical activity and dietary patterns. *Obesity Review, 6,* 123–132.

Jansz, J, & Martis, RG (2007). The Lara phenomenon: Powerful female characters in video games. *Sex Roles, 56,* 141–148.

Johnson JG, Cohen, P, Kasen, S, First, MB, & Brook, JS (2004). Association between television viewing and sleep problems during adolescence and early adulthood. *Archives of Pediatric and Adolescent Medicine, 158,* 562–568.

Jordan, AB (2004). The role of media in children's development: An ecological perspective. *Journal of Developmental and Behavioral Pediatrics, 25,* 196–206.

King, DL, Delfabbro, PH, & Griffiths, MD (2010). Cognitive behavioural therapy for problematic video game players: Conceptual considerations and practice issues. *Journal of CyberTherapy and Rehabilitation, 3,* 261–274.

Krahé, B, Möller, I, Huesmann, LR, Kirwil, L, Felber, J, & Berger, A (2011). Desensitization to media violence: Links with habitual media violence exposure, aggressive cognitions, and aggressive behaviour. *Journal of Personality and Social Psychology, 100,* 630–646.

LeMay, R. (2012). Apple Australia sold 1 million iPads in 2011. Article in Delimiter. com, 15 February. Accessed April 2 at: http://delimiter.com.au/2012/02/15/apple-australia-sold-1-million-ipads-in-2011/

Mares, ML, & Woodard, EH (2005). Positive effects of television on children's social interactions: A meta-analysis. *Media Psychology, 7,* 301–322.

Mathai, J (1983). An acute anxiety state in an adolescent precipitated by viewing a horror movie. *Journal of Adolescence, 6,* 197–200.

Mathers, M, Canterford, L, Olds, T, Hesketh, K, Ridley, K, & Wake, M (2009). Electronic media use and adolescent health and well-being: Cross-sectional community study. *Academic Pediatrics, 9,* 289–290.

McDowell, M, Weddell, C, & Baur, L (1999). *Getting in the picture: A parent's and carer's guide for the better use of television for children.* Sydney: Division of Paediatrics, Royal Australasian College of Physicians.

Morgan, M (1987). Television, sex-role attitudes, and sex-role behavior. *Journal of Early Adolescence, 7,* 269–282.

Nathanson, AI (1999). Identifying and explaining the relationship between parental mediation and children's aggression. *Communication Research, 26,* 124–143.

Nathanson, AI, Wilson, BJ, McGee, J, & Sevastian, M (2002). Counteracting the effects of female stereotypes on television via active mediation. *Journal of Communication, 52,* 922–937.

Nilsson, U (2008). The anxiety- and pain-reducing effects of music interventions: A systematic review. *AORN Journal, 87,* 780–807.

NITR (Nielson Internet and Technology Report) (2011). *Australian Internet and Technology Report, 2011.* Sydney: Nielson Company.

O'Bryant, SL, & Corder-Bolz, CR (1978). The effects of television on children's stereotyping of women's work roles. *Journal of Vocational Behavior, 12*, 233–244.

Olds, T, Ridley, K, & Dollman, J (2006). Screenieboppers and extreme screenies: the place of screen time in the time budgets of 10–13 year-old Australian children. *Australian and New Zealand Journal of Public Health, 30*, 137–142.

Owens, J, Maxim, R, McGuinn, M, Nobile, C, Msall, M, & Alario, A (1999). Television-viewing habits and sleep disturbance in school children. *Pediatrics, 104*, 27.

Paavonen, E, Pennonen, M, Roine, M, Valkonen, S and Lahikainen, A (2006). TV exposure associated with sleep disturbances in 5- to 6-year-old children. *Journal of Sleep Research, 15, pp* 154–161.

Pardun, CJ, L'Engle, KL, & Brown, JD (2005). Linking exposure to outcomes: Early adolescents' consumption of sexual content in six media. *Mass Communication and Society, 8*, 75–91.

Richards, R, McGee, R, Williams, S, Welch, D, & Hancox, R (2010). Adolescent screen time and attachment to parents and peers. *Archives of Pediatrics and Adolescent Medicine, 164*, 258–262.

Rideout, VJ, Foehr, UG, & Roberts, DF (2010). *Generation M2: Media in the lives of 8-18 year olds*. Merlo Park CA: Henry J Kaiser Foundation.

Robinson TN, & Killen JD (1995) Ethnic and gender differences in the relationships between television viewing and obesity, physical activity and dietary fat intake. *Journal of Health Education, 26*, S91–S98.

Roe, K (1996). Music and identity among European youth: Music as communication. In P Rutten (ed), *Music in Europe* (pp 85–97). Brussels: European Music Office. Accessed 4 August 2011, <http://www.icce.rug.nl/~soundscapes/DATABASES/MIE/Part2_chapter03.shtml>.

Rutherford, L, Bittman, M, & Biron, D (2009). *Young Children and the media*. Perth: Australian Research Alliance for Children and Youth.

Sacks, DP, Bushman, BJ & Anderson, CA (2011). Do violent video games harm children? Comparing the scientific amicus curiae 'experts' in Brown v. Entertainment Merchants Association. *Northwestern Law Review, 106*, 1–12. Accessed 7 March 2012, <http://www.law.northwestern.edu/lawreview/colloquy/2011/15/LRColl2011n15PollardSacks>.

Schmidt, M, & Anderson, D (2007). The impact of television on cognitive development and educational achievement. In N Pecora, D Murray & E Wartella (eds), *Children and television: Fifty years of research* (pp 65–84). Mahwah, New Jersey: Lawrence Erlbaum.

Schmitt, YS, Hoffman, HG, Blough, DK, Patterson, DR, Jensen, MP, Soltani, M, Carrougher, GJ, Nakamura, D, & Sharar, SR (2011). A randomized, controlled trial of immersive virtual reality analgesia, during physical therapy for pediatric burns, *Burns, 37*, 61–68.

Screen Australia website (March 2011). *Archive: Free-to-air TV: Audiences: By age*. Accessed 2 March 2011, <http://www.screenaustralia.gov.au/research/statistics/archftvviewage.asp>.

Screen Australia website (March 2011). *Audiovisual markets – Cinema. Audiences: Roy Morgan data: Age profile*. Accessed 20 March 2011, <http://www.screenaustralia.gov.au/research/statistics/ wcrmageprofile.asp>.

Screen Australia website (March 2011). *Audiovisual markets – Cinema. Audiences: Roy Morgan data: Attendance patterns by age.* Accessed 10 March 2011, <http://www.screenaustralia.gov.au/research/statistics/wcrmagepattern.asp>.

Screen Australia website (March 2011). *Archive: Media and communication devices: Household penetration and children's access.* Accessed 15 March 2011, <http://www.screenaustralia.gov.au/research/statistics/archaumcapenetration.asp>.

Screen Australia website (March 2011). *Archive: Game players: Children.* Accessed 15 March 2011, <http://www.screenaustralia.gov.au/research/statistics/archnmgameplaykids.asp>.

Screen Australia (2007). *Penetration of, and access to, selected media and communication devices in households with children, 1995 and 2007.* Accessed 21 April 2011, <http://www.screenaustralia.gov.au/research/statistics/archaumcapenetration.asp>.

Shaver, PR, & Mikulincer, M (2005). Attachment theory and research: Resurrection of the psychodynamic approach to personality. *Journal of Research in Personality, 39,* 22–45.

Shao, G (2009). Understanding the appeal of user-generated media: A uses and gratification perspective. *Internet Research, 19,* 7–25.

Signorelli, N (2001). Television's gender role images and contribution to stereotyping. In DG Singer & JL Singer (eds), *Handbook of children and the media* (pp 341–258). Thousand Oaks CA: Sage.

Simons, D, & Silveira, MR (1994). Post-traumatic stress disorder in children after television programmes. *British Medical Journal, 308,* 389–390.

Singer, MI, Slovak, K, Frierson, T, & York, P (1998). Viewing preferences, symptoms of psychological trauma, and violent behaviors among children who watch television. *Journal of the American Academy of Child and Adolescent Psychiatry, 37,* 1041–1048.

Smith, SL (2006). Perps, pimps and provocative clothing: Examining negative content patterns in video games. In P Vorderer & J Bryant (eds), *Playing video games* (pp 57–75). Mahwah NJ: Lawrence Erlbaum.

Standley, J (1995). Music as a therapeutic intervention in medical and dental treatment: Research and clinical applications. In T Wigram, B Saperston & R West (eds), *The art and science of music therapy: A handbook.* Langhorne US: Harwood Academic.

Strasburger VC (2009). Why do adolescent health researchers ignore the impact of the media? *Journal of Adolescent Health, 44,* 203–205.

Strasburger, V (2010). Policy statement – Children, adolescents, substance abuse, and the media. *Pediatrics, 126,* 791–799.

Strasburger, VC, Wilson, BJ, & Jordan, AB (2009). *Children, adolescents, and the media* (2nd ed). Thousand Oaks, CA: Sage.

Swing, EL, Gentile, DA, Anderson, CA, & Walsh, DA (2010). Television and video game exposure and the development of attention problems. *Pediatrics, 126,* 214–221.

Tanimura, M, Okuma, K, & Kyoshima, K (2007). Television viewing, reduced parental utterance, and delayed speech development in infants and young children. *Archives of Pediatric and Adolescent Medicine, 161,* 618–619.

Vandewater, E, Rideout, V, Wartella, E, Huang, X, Lee, J and Shim, I (2007). Digital childhood: Electronic media and technology use amongst infants, toddlers and preschoolers. *Pediatrics, 119,* 1006–1015.

Wake, M, Hesketh, K, & Waters, E (2003). Television, computer use and body mass index in Australian primary school children. *Journal of Paediatrics and Child Health, 39,* 130–134.

Wallenius, M, Rimpelä, A, Punamäki, R, & Lintonen, T (2009). Digital game playing motives among adolescents: Relations to parent–child communication, school performance, sleeping habits, and perceived health. *Journal of Applied Developmental Psychology, 30,* 463–474.

Weinstein, AM (2010). Computer and video game addiction – a comparison between game users and non-game users. *The American Journal of Drug and Alcohol Abuse, 36,* 268–276.

Weiss, KE, Dahlquist LM, & Wohlheiter, K (2011). The effects of interactive and passive distraction on cold pressor pain in preschool-aged children. *Journal of Pediatric Psychology.* doi: 10.1093/jpepsy/jsq125.

Chapter 2

Children and media violence: Behavioural and neurological effects of viewing violence

John P Murray

We know a great deal about the behavioural and attitudinal changes associated with viewing violence. Indeed, there is a long history of research on this topic, dating from the 1950s through to the present. Much of this research was focused on the impact of viewing violence on television (see Murray, 1973; Pecora et al, 2007) and, more recently, studies of video game violence (Vorderer & Bryant, 2006).

The addition of studies of brain activation patterns while viewing video game violence (see Murray et al, 2006; Strenziok, et al, 2010; 2011; Wang et al, 2009) provide insights into the ways in which viewers "process" violence and enhance our understanding of the nature of video game violence effects. So, what do we know about the behavioural and neurological effects of viewing violence? Is there a basis for speculating that viewing video violence, or participating in the entertainment violence of video games, can produce neurological patterns, stored images and guides for behaviour that might increase the likelihood of violent acting-out among youngsters? Might these actions become somewhat automatic by having this aggressive repertoire frequently "triggered" by threats in the social context? Can this lead to people becoming "thoughtless vigilantes" who quickly respond to provocations with violence by leaning on the limbic system and other fast-reacting brain structures while bypassing the prefrontal cortex and rational decision-making that weighs the consequences of actions?

This chapter is designed to provide a review of the long history of research on behavioural effects of violence viewing and integrate the emerging evidence from neurological studies. We begin with the early research and concerns that set the stage for investigations of media violence.

Early Research and Social Concerns

The early studies of television's influence began almost simultaneously in England and the United States and Canada in the mid-1950s. They were designed to take advantage of the regulated introduction of the new medium. Later studies – in the 1970s – would revisit these issues and this research strategy when television was being introduced into isolated communities in Australia (Murray & Kippax, 1977; 1978; 1979) and Canada (Williams, 1986; MacBeth, 1996).

In England, a group of researchers at the London School of Economics and Political Science, under the direction of Hilde Himmelweit, a Reader in Social Psychology, began the first study of children's television viewing patterns while television was still relatively new (only three million television sets were installed in the 15 million households in England). This study was proposed by the Audience Research Department of the British Broadcasting Corporation (BBC) but was conducted by independent researchers. The research, begun in 1955, was published in a 1958 report, *Television and the Child: An Empirical Study of the Effect of Television on the Young* (Himmelweit et al 1958). The American and Canadian study was conducted by Wilbur Schramm and his colleagues in communications at Stanford University. This project began in 1957 and was published in a 1961 report, *Television in the Lives of Our Children* (Schramm et al, 1961).

The British and American/Canadian surveys provided a very important benchmark for understanding the broad and general effects of television on children. For example, Himmelweit, et al, noted: "We have found a number of instances where viewers and controls differed in their outlook; differences which did not exist before television came on the scene. There was a small but consistent influence of television on the way children thought generally about jobs, job values, success, and social surroundings" (pp 17–18). With regard to aggression, these correlational studies did not support an association. Himmelweit and her colleagues noted:

> We did not find that the viewers were any more aggressive or maladjusted than the controls; television is unlikely to cause aggressive behaviour, although it could precipitate it in those few children who are emotionally disturbed. On the other hand, there was little support for the view that programmes of violence are beneficial; we found that they aroused aggression as often as they discharged it. (p 20)

The conclusions of Schramm and colleagues included the observation that those Canadian and American children who had high exposure to television and low exposure to print were more aggressive than those with the reverse pattern. Thus, the early correlational studies or surveys identified some areas of concern about television violence and set the stage for more focused investigations.

First Experimental Studies

Moving beyond these 1950s surveys, there was another set of studies that emerged in the early 1960s – not surveys or correlational studies but experimental studies that were addressed to cause and effect relationships in the television-violence/aggressive-behaviour equation. These initial experiments were conducted by Albert Bandura, at Stanford University, who studied preschool age children, and Leonard Berkowitz, at the University of Wisconsin, who worked with college-age youth. In both instances, the studies were experimental in design, which meant that subjects were randomly assigned to various viewing experiences with all other environmental influences held constant. Therefore the results of this manipulated viewing could be used to address the issue of causal relationships between viewing and behaviour. The early Bandura studies, such as "Transmission of Aggression through Imitation of Aggressive Models" (Bandura et al, 1961) or "Imitation of Film-mediated Aggressive Models" (Bandura et al, 1963), were set within a social learning paradigm and were designed to identify the processes governing the ways that children learn by observing and imitating the behaviour of others. In this context, therefore, the studies used stimulus films (videotape was not generally available) back projected on a simulated television screen, and the behaviour of children was observed and recorded in a playroom setting immediately following the viewing period. Children who viewed models whose behaviour was aggressive themselves behaved more aggressively than children who viewed non-aggressive models. Despite the structured nature of these studies, Bandura's research was central to the debate about the influence of media violence. Moreover, the work of Berkowitz and his colleagues, such as "Effects of Film Violence on Inhibitions against Subsequent Aggression" (Berkowitz & Rawlings, 1963) or "Film Violence and the

Cue Properties of Available Targets" (Berkowitz & Geen, 1966), studied the simulated aggressive behaviour of youth and young adults following the viewing of segments of violent films, such as a Kirk Douglas boxing film, *The Champion*. The demonstration of increased willingness to use aggression against others following viewing further fuelled the debate about the influence of media violence.

Concern about the influence of television violence began as early as the start of this new medium. The first Congressional hearings were held in the early 1950s (United States Congress, 1952; 1955). At these early hearings, developmental psychologist Eleanor Maccoby (1954) and sociologist Paul Lazarsfeld (1955) presented testimony that relied upon some early studies of violence in films, such as the 1930s report, *Boys, Movies and City Streets* (Cressey & Thrasher, 1933) to outline a necessary program of research on the issue of television violence and its effects on children.

As the 1960s progressed, concern in the United States about violence in the streets and the assassinations of President John F Kennedy, Martin Luther King, Jr and Robert Kennedy stimulated continuing interest in media violence. In response, several major government commissions and scientific and professional review committees were established, from the late 1960s through the 1990s, to summarise the research evidence and public policy issues regarding the role of television violence in salving or savaging young viewers.

The Five Principal US Commissions

The five principal US commissions and review panels – the National Commission on the Causes and Prevention of Violence (Baker & Ball, 1969); the Surgeon General's Scientific Advisory Committee on Television and Social Behaviour (1972; Murray, 1973); the National Institute of Mental Health (1982) Television and Behaviour Project; the Group for the Advancement of Psychiatry (1982) Child and Television Drama Review; and the American Psychological Association Task Force on Television and Society (Huston, et al, 1992) – have been central to setting the agenda for research and public discussion.

In 1982, the National Institute of Mental Health (NIMH) published a 10 year follow-up of the 1972 Surgeon General's study. The two volume report (National Institute of Mental Health, 1982; Pearl et al, 1982), collectively titled *Television and Behaviour: Ten Years of Scientific Progress and Implications for the Eighties*, provided a reminder of the breadth and depth of knowledge that has accumulated on the issue of television violence. In this regard, the NIMH staff and consultants concluded:

> After 10 more years of research, the consensus among most of the research community is that violence on television does lead to aggressive behaviour by children and teenagers who watch the programs. This conclusion is based on laboratory experiments and on field studies. Not all children become aggressive, of course, but the correlations between violence and aggression are positive. In magnitude, television violence is as strongly correlated with aggressive behaviour as any other behavioural variable that has been measured. (p 10)

In 1986, the American Psychological Association (APA) empanelled a Task Force on Television and Society to review the research and professional concerns about the impact of television on children and adults. The nine psychologists assigned to this committee undertook reviews of relevant research, conducted interviews with television industry and public policy professionals, and discussed concerns with representatives of government regulatory agencies and public interest organisations. The final report, entitled *Big World, Small Screen: The Role of Television in American Society* (Huston et al, 1992) included the following observation about television violence:

> American television has been violent for many years. Over the past 20 years, the rate of violence on prime time evening television has remained at about 5 to 6 incidents per hour, whereas the rate on children's Saturday morning programs is typically 20 to 25 acts per hour. There is clear evidence that television violence can cause aggressive behaviour and can cultivate values favoring the use of aggression to resolve conflicts. (p 136)

The extent of concern – both social and scientific – is demonstrated by the fact that over the past half century, about 1000 reports have been published on the issue of television violence (Murray, 1980; Pecora et al, 2007). Of course, only a small percentage of these thousands of pages represent original studies or research reports, but there is an extensive body of research on the impact of television violence. Nevertheless, the research history is best described in terms of the nature of the research approaches: correlational research and the special case correlational research longitudinal studies that are sometimes called cross-lagged panel studies.

Correlational Research

The demonstration of a relationship between viewing and aggressive behaviour is a logical precursor to studies of the causal role that television violence may play in promoting aggressive behaviour. In the typical correlational studies that followed the Himmelweit et al (1958) and Schramm et al (1961) studies, such as those conducted for the Surgeon General's research program (eg, Dominick & Greenberg, 1972), the researchers found consistent patterns of significant correlations between the number of hours of television viewed or the frequency of viewing violent programs and various measures of aggressive attitudes or behaviour. Also, another study, Atkin and colleagues (1979) found that heavy television-violence viewers were more likely to choose physical and verbal aggressive responses to solve hypothetical interpersonal conflict situations (that is, 45 per cent of the heavy-violence viewers chose physical/verbal aggressive responses v 21 per cent of the low-violence viewers). Similarly, a further study in this genre (Walker & Morley, 1991) found that adolescents who reported enjoying television violence were more likely to hold attitudes and values favourable to behaving aggressively in conflict situations.

In another approach, a large database, the Cultural Indicators Project, has been used to explore the relationship between television portrayals and the viewer's fearful conception of the world. In a series of studies begun in the 1960s, George Gerbner and his colleagues at the University of Pennsylvania (Gerbner, 1970; Gerbner at al, 1994) have tracked public perceptions of society in relation to the respondent's extent of television viewing. Of relevance to the violence issue, these researchers have identified differences in the risk-of-victimisation perceptions, described as the "mean world syndrome" effect, of light v heavy viewers. The heavy viewers (usually five or more hours per day) are much more fearful of the world around them than are light viewers (about two or fewer hours per day). When questioned about their perceptions of risk, heavy viewers are much more likely to overestimate (that is, greater than the FBI crime reports for their locale would suggest) the chance that they will be the victim of crime in the ensuing six months, have taken greater precautions by changing the security of their homes or restricting their travels at night and are generally more fearful of the world. As Gerbner et al (1994) note:

> We have found that long-term exposure to television, in which frequent violence is virtually inescapable, tends to cultivate the image of a relatively mean and dangerous world ... in which greater protection is needed, most people cannot be trusted, *and most people are just looking out for themselves*. (p 30, italics added)

Special-Case Correlational Research (Longitudinal Studies)

Studies such as the early surveys clearly demonstrate that violence viewing and aggressive behaviour are related but they do not address the issue of cause-and-effect. And yet, there are some special-case correlational studies in which "intimations of causation" can be derived from the fact that these studies were conducted over several time periods. There have been three major "panel" studies: A study funded by CBS (Belson 1978), one funded by NBC (Milavsky et al, 1982) and the third funded by the Surgeon General's Committee and NIMH (Lefkowitz et al, 1972; Huesmann et al, 1984; Huesmann & Eron, 1986).

The CBS study (Belson, 1978) was conducted in England with 1565 youths who were a representative sample of 13–17-year-old males living in London. The boys were interviewed concerning the extent of their exposure to a selection of violent television programs (broadcast during the period 1959 through 1971 and rated by members of the BBC viewing panel for level of violence) as well as each boy's level of violent behaviour as determined by his report of how often he had been involved in any of 53 categories of violence over the previous six months. The degree of seriousness of the acts reported by the boys ranged from only slightly violent aggravation, such as taunting, to more serious and very violent behaviour such as: "I tried to force a girl to have sexual intercourse with me"; "I bashed a boy's head against a wall"; "I burned a boy on the chest with a cigarette while my mates held him down"; and "I threatened to kill my father". Approximately 50 per cent of the 1565 boys were not involved in any violent acts during the six-month period. However, of those who were involved in violence, 188 (12 per cent) were involved in 10 or more acts during the six-month period. When Belson compared the behaviour of boys who had higher exposure to televised violence to those who had lower exposure (and had been matched on a wide variety of possible contributing factors), he found that the high-violence viewers were more involved in serious interpersonal violence.

The NBC study (Milavsky et al, 1982) was conducted over a three-year period from May 1970 to December 1973 in two cities, Fort Worth and Minneapolis. Interviews were conducted with samples of second- to sixth-grade boys and girls and a special sample of teenage boys. In the elementary school sample, the information on television viewing and measures of aggression were collected in six time periods over the three years. The aggression measure consisted of peer ratings of aggressive behaviour based on the work of Eron and his colleagues (Eron et al, 1971). In the teenage sample there were five waves of interviews over the three years and the aggression measures were self-report rather than peer-reported aggression. In summarising the results of this study, the authors concluded: "On the basis of the analyses we carried out to test for such a causal connection there is no evidence that television exposure has a consistently significant effect on subsequent aggressive behaviour in the [elementary school] sample of boys". (Milavsky, et al, 1982, p 482). Similar null findings were reported for the elementary school girls and the teenage boys. However, re-analyses of these data by Kenny (1984) and Cook and his associates (Cook et al, 1983) have concluded that there are small but clear causal effects in the NBC data and that these effects become stronger when analysed over longer time periods through successive waves of interviews.

Finally, one of the longest panel studies, 22 years, is the work of Leonard Eron and his colleagues (Eron, 1963; Lefkowitz et al, 1972; Eron, 1982; Huesmann et al, 1984; Huseman & Eron, 1986). In the initial studies, conducted for the Surgeon General's investigation of television violence (Lefkowitz, et al, 1972), the researchers were able to document the long-term effects of violence viewing by studying children over a 10-year period from age 8 to age 18. At these two time periods, the youngsters were interviewed about their program preferences and information was collected from peer ratings of aggressive behaviour. The violence levels of their preferred television programs and other media and measures of aggression across these two time periods suggested the possibility that early television violence viewing was one factor in producing later aggressive behaviour. In particular, the findings for 211 boys followed in this longitudinal study demonstrated that television violence at age 8 was significantly related to aggression at age 18 (r=.21) and the 8-year-old violent television preferences were significantly related to aggression at age 18 (r=.31) but television violence preferences at age 18 were not related to aggressive behaviour at the earlier time period, age 8 (r=.01). Furthermore, in a follow-up study, when these young men were age 30, the authors found a significant correlation (r=.41) between television violence levels at age 8 and serious interpersonal criminal behaviour (for example, assault, murder, child abuse, spouse abuse, rape) at age 30 (Huesmann et al, 1984).

Behavioural to Neurological – Connections

Research conducted over the past 50 years leads to the conclusion that televised violence does affect viewers' attitudes, values and behaviour (Hearold, 1986; Murray, 1994; Paik & Comstock, 1994). In general, there seem to be three main classes of effects – aggression, desensitisation and fear:

- Aggression: Heightened levels of viewing televised violence can lead to increases in aggressive behaviour and/or changes in attitudes and values favouring the use of aggression to solve conflicts;
- Desensitisation: Extensive violence viewing may lead to decreased sensitivity to violence and a greater willingness to tolerate increasing levels of violence in society;
- Fear: Extensive exposure to television violence may produce the "mean world syndrome" in which viewers overestimate their risk of victimisation.

Although the body of research on the effects of viewing television violence is extensive and fairly coherent in demonstrating systematic patterns of influence, we know surprisingly little about the processes involved in the production of these effects. Although we know that viewing televised violence can lead to increases in aggressive behaviour or fearfulness and changed attitudes and values about the role of violence in society, it would be helpful to know more about how these changes occur in viewers.

To set the context for the continuing research – within the broad framework of a social learning paradigm – we know that changes in behaviour and thoughts can result from observing models in the world around us, be they parents, peers, or other role models, such as those provided by mass media. The processes involved in "modelling" or imitation and vicarious learning of overt behaviour were addressed in social learning theories in the 1960s (Bandura, 1962; 1965; 1969; Berkowitz 1962; 1965) but we need to expand our understanding of the neurological processes that might govern the translation of the observed models into thoughts and actions.

As a start in this new direction, both Bandura (1994) and Berkowitz (1984) have provided some theoretical foundations for the translation of communication "events" into thoughts and actions. Bandura's "social-cognitive" approach and Berkowitz's outline of a "cognitive-neoassociation" analysis posit a role for emotional arousal as an affective tag that may facilitate lasting influences. As Bandura (1994) notes: "People are easily aroused by the emotional expressions of others. Vicarious arousal operates mainly through an intervening self-arousal process. ... That is, seeing others react emotionally to instigating conditions activates emotion-arousing thoughts and imagery in observers" (p 75). With regard to aggression, we know that viewing television violence can be emotionally arousing (eg, Cline et al, 1973; Osborn & Endsley, 1971; Zillman, 1971; 1982) but we lack direct measures of cortical arousal or activation patterns in relation to violence viewing.

The pursuit of neurological patterns of cortical arousal in violence viewing would likely start with the amygdala because it has a well-established role in the control of physiological responses to emotionally arousing or threatening stimuli (Damasio, 1994; 1999; Kosslyn & Koenig, 1995; LeDoux, 1996; LeDoux & Hirst, 1986; Ornstein, 1997; Panksepp, 1998; Steward, 2000). Indeed, a National Research Council (1993) report from the Panel on the Understanding and Control of Violent Behaviour, concludes:

> All human behaviour, including aggression and violence, is the outcome of complex processes in the brain. Violent behaviours may result from relatively permanent conditions or from temporary states. ... Biological research on aggressive and violent behaviour has given particular attention to the following in recent years: ... (2) functioning of steroid hormones such as testosterone and glucocorticoids,

especially their action on steroid receptors in the brain; ... (6) neurophysiological (that is, brain wave) abnormalities, particularly in the temporal lobe of the brain; (7) brain dysfunctions that interfere with language processing or cognition. (pp 115-116)

Thus, one suggestion for further research on the impact of media violence is to assess some of the neurological correlates of viewing televised violence. In particular, the use of videotape violent scenes can serve as the ideal stimulus for assessing activation patterns in response to violence. These neurobiological studies hold the key to understanding the ways in which children might respond to seeing violence in entertainment and this might also be the key to thinking about the desensitisation to violence, or what some might describe as a "drugging" effect on the developing child. To assess this possibility, we (Murray et al, 2006) embarked on an initial study of children's brain activations while the youngsters viewed violent and non-violent video program material. We reasoned that there may be similarities between the ways humans respond to the threats of physical violence in the real world and the neurobiological response to so-called "entertainment" violence.

Beginnings of brainmapping

We can begin our quest with some notions and expectations drawn from previous research suggesting that we might find the "threat recognition" system – involving the limbic system and right hemisphere of the brain – as an area that will be activated while viewing video violence. The development of hypotheses about violence viewing and brain activation, however, needs to start with research on physiological arousal (eg, Osborn & Endsley, 1971; Zillmann, 1982; Zillmann & Bryant, 1994) and link this to cortical arousal (Davidson et al, 1990; Davidson & Tomarken, 1989; Ekman, & Davidson, 1993; 1994; Ekman et al, 1990).

In our pilot study (Murray, 2001; Murray et al, 2006), we found that both violent and nonviolent viewing activated brain regions implicated in aspects of visual and auditory processing. In contrast, however, viewing television violence selectively recruited right precuneus, right posterior cingulate, right amygdala, bilateral hippocampus and parahippocampus, bilateral pulvinar, right inferior parietal and prefrontal and right premotor cortex. Thus, television violence viewing appears to activate brain areas involved in arousal/attention, detection of

Figure 1: Composite brain activation patterns of eight children viewing video violence

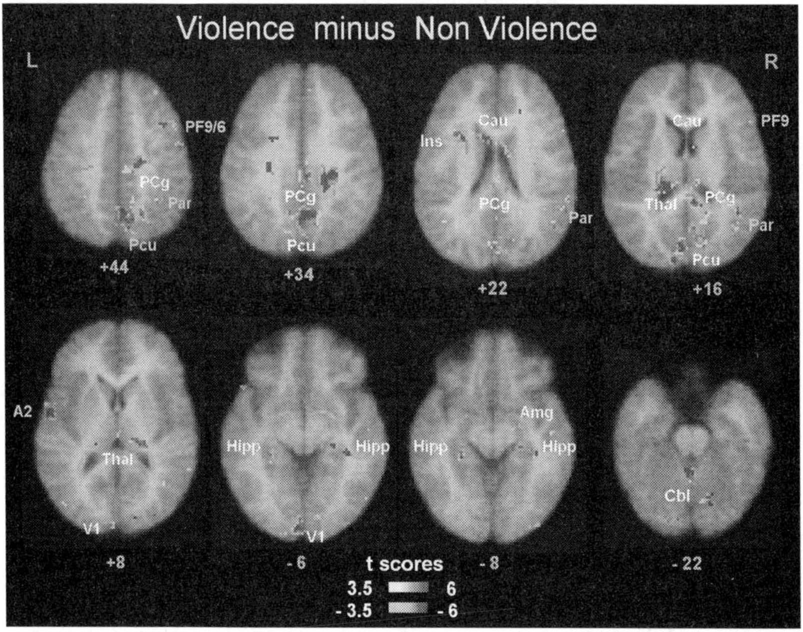

(see Murray et al, 2006)

threat, episodic memory encoding and retrieval, and motor programming. These findings are displayed in Figure 1, showing the significant contrasts between Violence Viewing and Non-Violence Viewing by brain lobe/region in the xyz stereotaxic atlas coordinates (Talairach & Tournoux, 1988).

It can be seen that the Regions of Interest (ROI) of the composite activations of eight children, combined in adjusted Talairach space, include the amygdala, hippocampus and posterior cingulate. These areas are important because they are likely indicators of the perception of threat and possible long-term memory storage of the threat-event (particularly, these patterns are similar to the memory storage of traumatic events by Post Traumatic Stress Disorder patients). These activation patterns demonstrate that video violence viewing selectively activates right hemisphere and some bilateral areas, which collectively suggests significant emotional processing of video violence. Furthermore, this is the sort of evidence that indicates a bypassing of the frontal cortex and its function to plan and rationally decide on a course of action. Therefore, this pattern of brain processing of media violence might lead to behaviour typical of a "thoughtless vigilante" who acts reflexively and seems unaware of the consequences of his or her actions.

Our continuing research at Harvard Medical School, Children's Hospital Boston, is designed to address these questions about violence viewing in a more robust study that employs a larger and more differentiated sample of children who have had differing experiences with violence (for example, children who are identified as high or low in aggressive tendencies and children who have been victims of abuse). We will continue to use the methods and procedures that were demonstrated to be effective in the pilot study – we will conjoin measures of physiological arousal (for example, GSR, heart rate) with neuroimaging techniques (for example, functional Magnetic Resonance Imaging(fMRI)) to track the emotional and neurological processes involved in viewing televised violence. We anticipate finding clear differences in the three groups of children, with the victims of violence – the abused youngsters – being most responsive to viewing media violence and the aggressive youngsters being the least responsive to the entertainment violence; this is the desensitisation effect that results from extensive violence viewing and acting out the violence witnessed in the entertainment world of film, television and video game violence. In the past five or six years, there has been a great expansion in research interest in the connection of behavioural and neurological patterns related to video violence viewing. In particular, interest has focused on the role of the prefrontal cortex in mediating or moderating the violence viewing and aggression relationships. Several recent papers have provided new insights on this fascinating area of research.

Exploring the Prefrontal Cortex

The most ambitious program of research in this area is the work of a group at the University of Indiana Medical School (eg, Kronenberger et al, 2005; Mathews et al, 2005; Wang et al, 2009). In their early research, the team focused on the issue of frontal lobe activation in aggressive and nonaggressive adolescents while viewing video violence in an MRI. In one of the early studies (Kronenberger et al, 2005), the Indiana team examined the relationship between media violence exposure in television and video games in aggressive v non-aggressive adolescents. They interviewed 27 adolescents (13–17 years) diagnosed as Disruptive Behaviour Disorders (DBD) with aggressive features and 27 Controls who were matched for age, gender and IQ, concerning their exposure to violence on television and video games. The results indicated that the DBD-aggressive youngsters had higher aggregate media violence exposure, higher exposure to video game violence and higher parent-reported exposure to television violence than their matched Controls. Indeed, exposure to television violence tended to be accompanied by exposure to video game violence. Moreover, the relation between media violence and DBD was *not* due to the effects of gender or IQ, both of which can be correlated with aggression.

This initial finding encouraged the team to pursue the possible links between playing a violent video game and brain activation patterns. In the next study (Mathews et al, 2005), the team used fMRI to explore frontal lobe activation in aggressive and nonaggressive adolescents. In an initial visit, subjects were given diagnostic assessments and media violence interviews. Twenty-eight Aggressive adolescents (adolescents with DBD with aggressive features) and 43 Nonaggressive Control adolescents were given a semi-structured interview concerning media violence exposure and a Media Violence Exposure Index (MEVI) was constructed for each adolescent. In the second visit, the adolescents were presented with an executive functioning task (the Counting Stroop (CS) task) while in the MRI scanner. Of the Aggressive DBD students, 19 successfully completed the CS task at 70 per cent or better accuracy. These 19 DBD adolescents were matched (on age, gender and IQ) with 19 Controls who also completed the CS task successfully. Analysis of the fMRI scans showed differences in executive processing patterns in the DBD adolescents when compared to the Controls. The main area of interest was the dorsolateral prefrontal cortex (DLPFC), the anterior cingulate cortex (ACC), inferior frontal gyrus (IFG) and the middle frontal gyrus (MFG). The results demonstrated sharp differences between the Aggressive teens and the Controls – the entire Control group showed significant activation of the ACC, left MFG and Left IFG, while the Aggressive teens showed activation only in the MFG, bilaterally. The main conclusion from this analysis is that, frontal lobe activation is reduced in aggressive (DBD) teens and this is reinforced by the finding that even in the Control subjects, those with high media violence exposure demonstrated similar reduced prefrontal activation, rather like the Aggressive teens. Thus, the authors conclude that high media violence exposure alters brain activation patterns in both aggressive and control subjects and is responsible for reduced prefrontal control and executive function processing. That is, exposure to media violence is linked to a reduction in activation of the part of the brain used to control and inhibit behaviour, think through consequences and plan for the future.

As a follow-on to these findings, the Indiana team (Wang et al, 2009) conducted a study showing that even a short-term exposure to a violent video game changes both the frontal cortex and limbic system functioning in adolescents. In this case, the adolescents played a violent or nonviolent video game 10 minutes before an fMRI scan that involved measures of executive functioning (the CS task). The adolescents (13–17 years) were screened for any history of neurologic or psychiatric disorders and 44 youngsters were selected on the basis of absence of pathology. The random assignment to two groups of 22 teens assigned to play either a violent video game ("Medal of Honor") or a nonviolent video game ("Need for Speed") ensured that the groups did not differ on age, IQ or gender. All youngsters were interviewed about their media violence exposure (MEM) and were given 30 minutes training in learning and practicing to play whichever game has been assigned. On the following visit, the youngsters played their assigned game for 30 minutes, immediately before (within 10 minutes of) the fMRI scans. The subjects were given two tasks in the MRI: the traditional CS task, a measure of executive functioning and attentional control; and the Emotional Stroop task, involving emotion-laden violent and nonviolent words which are likely to activate the limbic system, particularly the amygdala. The results demonstrated that the youngsters who played the violent video game (Medal of Honor) showed more activity in the amygdala (right) and less activation in the medial prefrontal cortex (MFPC) while the teens who played the nonviolent game (Need for Speed) demonstrated activations of the prefrontal cortex, the ACC and the DLPFC. Indeed, there was a distinct uncoupling of activation with the amygdala in the nonviolent video game group. Thus, the study demonstrates that even short-term involvement with violent video game playing can significantly alter neural circuitry in the execution of cognitive and emotional tasks during fMRI scans.

Other researchers, Kelly and colleagues (2007) have shown that repeated exposure to media violence is associated with diminished response in the frontolimbic network. In particular, repeated exposure to violent media (but not exposure to other active but nonviolent media) results in reduced right lateral orbitofrontal cortex (ltOFC) and a decreased interaction with the amygdala. Thus, even short term exposure to violent media can result in diminished responsiveness in the part of the brain network that is associated with regulating reactive, aggressive responses.

Furthermore, in a series of studies by Jordan Grafman and his team at the National Institutes of Health (Strenziok et al 2010; 2011), the researchers have found that repeated viewing of aggressive videos resulted in desensitisation to violence and an increased likelihood of behaving aggressively due to decreased impulse control in these teen-aged viewers. Using fMRI as well as skin conductance (sometimes called galvanic skin response or GSR), the investigators found that repeated viewing of violent video segments resulted in a downward linear adaptation in skin conductance responses with increasingly aggressive videos. In addition, they found that areas of the brain, including the left lateral orbitofrontal cortex (LOFC) and the right precuneus and the inferior parietal lobules on both sides of the brain (bilateral) showed downward activation patterns in a linear fashion as viewing of violence continued and expanded in aggressiveness. The conclusions from these several studies indicate that "aggressive media activates an emotional-attention network that has the capability to blunt emotional responses through reduced attention with repeated viewing of aggressive media contents, which may restrict the linking of the consequences of aggression with an emotional response [desensitisation] and therefore potentially promotes aggressive attitudes and behavior" (Strenziok, et al, 2010, p 10).

Conclusions

So, what have we learned about neurological and behavioural correlations in relation to media violence? Clearly, we are in the beginning stages of this line of inquiry, but we begin to see the patterns of potential influence. It is possible that repeated exposure to media violence may lead to changes in both the prefrontal cortex and limbic system interactions, and that these may disrupt the processing of aggressive, emotion-laden information. The result may be an increase in aggressive behaviour and/or the triggering of excessive aggression in response to provocation. The fact that aggressive and emotional arousing perceptions seem to be stored in the posterior cingulate gives rise to the possibility that these aggressive action patterns might become the automatic guide for social behaviour. Hence, we have the possibility of the production of "Thoughtless Vigilantes" and the clear threat to the social and intellectual development of children and youth.

References

American Academy of Pediatrics (2009). Council on Communications and Media policy statement – Media violence. *Pediatrics, 124(5)*, 1495–1503.

Anderson, DR, Bryant, J, Murray, JP, Rich, M, Rivkin, MJ, & Zillmann, D (2006). Brain imaging – An introduction to a new approach to studying media processes and effects. *Media Psychology, 8(1)*, 1–6.

Anderson, DR, Fite, KV, Petrovich, N, & Hirsch, J (2006). Cortical activation while watching video montage: An fMRI study. *Media Psychology, 8(1)*, 7–24.

Atkin, CK, Greenberg, BS, Korzenny, F, & McDermott, S (1979). Selective exposure to televised violence. *Journal of Broadcasting, 23(1)*, 5–13.

Baker, RK, & Ball, SJ (1969). *Mass media and violence: A staff report to the National Commission on the Causes and Prevention of Violence.* Washington, DC: United States Government Printing Office.

Bandura, A (1962). Social learning through imitation. In MR Jones (ed), *Nebraska symposium on motivation* (pp 211–269). Lincoln, NE: University of Nebraska Press.

Bandura, A (1965). Vicarious processes: A case of no-trial learning. In L Berkowitz (ed), *Advances in experimental social psychology*, vol 2. New York: Academic Press.

Bandura, A (1969). Social learning theory of identificatory processes. In DA Goslin (ed), *Handbook of socialization theory and research* (pp 213–262). Chicago: Rand McNally.

Bandura, A (1994). Social cognitive theory of mass communication. In J Bryant & D Zillmann (eds), *Media effects: Advances in theory and research* (pp 61–90). Hillsdale, NJ: Erlbaum.

Bandura, A, Ross, D, & Ross, SA (1961). Transmission of aggression through imitation of aggressive models. *Journal of Abnormal and Social Psychology, 63(3)*, 575–582.

Bandura, A, Ross, D, & Ross, SA (1963). Imitation of film-mediated aggressive models. *Journal of Abnormal and Social Psychology, 66(1)*, 3–11.

Belson, W (1978). *Television violence and the adolescent boy*. Farnborough, England: Saxon House, Teakfield Limited.

Berkowitz, L (1962). *Aggression: A social psychological analysis*. New York: McGraw-Hill.

Berkowitz, L (1965). Some aspects of observed aggression. *Journal of Personality and Social Psychology, 2,* 359-365.

Berkowitz, L (1984). Some effects of thoughts on anti- and prosocial influences of media events: A cognitive-neoassociation analysis. *Psychological Bulletin, 95,* 110-427.

Berkowitz, L, & Geen, RG (1966). Film violence and the cue properties of available targets. *Journal of Personality and Social Psychology, 3(5),* 525-530.

Berkowitz, L, & Rawlings, E (1963). Effects of film violence on inhibitions against subsequent aggression. *Journal of Abnormal and Social Psychology, 66 (5),* 405-412,

Buss, AH, & Warren, WL (2000). *Aggression Questionnaire – Manual*. Los Angeles, CA: Western Psychological Services.

Cline, VB, Croft, RG, & Courrier, S (1973). Desensitization of children to television violence. *Journal of Personality and Social Psychology, 27(3),* 360-365.

Comstock, G & Paik, H (1991). *Television and the American child*. San Diego, CA: Academic Press.

Cook, TD, Kendzierski, DA, & Thomas, SA (1983). The implicit assumptions of television research: An analysis of the 1982 NIMH report on Television and Behavior. *Public Opinion Quarterly, 47,* 161-201.

Cressey, PG, & Thrasher, FM (1933). *Boys, movies, and city streets*. New York: Macmillan.

Damasio, AR (1994). *Descartes' error: Emotion, reason, and the human brain*. New York: Putnam.

Damasio, AR (1999). *The feeling of what happens: Body and emotion in the making of consciousness*. New York: Harcourt Brace.

Davidson, RJ, & Tomarken, AJ (1989). Laterality and emotion: An electrophysiological approach. In F Boller & J Grafman (eds), *Handbook of neuropsychology* (pp 419-441). Amsterdam: Elsevier.

Davidson, RJ, Ekman, P, Saron, C, Senulis, J, & Friesen, WV (1990). Emotional expression and brain physiology I: Approach/withdrawal and cerebral asymmetry. *Journal of Personality and Social Psychology, 58,* 330-341.

Dominick, JR, and Greenberg, BS (1972). Attitude towards violence: The interaction of television exposure, family attitudes, and social class. In GA Comstock and EA Rubinstein (eds), *Television and social behavior* (Vol 3). Washington, DC: Government Printing Office.

Ekman, P, & Davidson, RJ (1993). Voluntary smiling changes regional brain activity. *Psychological Science, 4(5),* 342-345.

Ekman, P, & Davidson, RJ (1994). *The nature of emotion: Fundamental questions*. New York: Oxford University Press.

Ekman, P, Davidson, RJ, & Friesen, WV (1990). The Duchenne smile: Emotional expression and brain physiology II. *Journal of Personality and Social Psychology, 58,* 342-353.

Ekman, P, Liebert, RM, Friesen, W, Harrison, R, Zlatchin, C, Malstrom, EV, &Baron, RA (1972). Facial expressions of emotion as predictors of subsequent aggression. In GA Comstock, EA Rubinstein, & JP Murray (eds), *Television and social behaviour, Vol 5: Television's effects: Further explorations* (pp 22-58). Washington, DC: United States Government Printing Office.

Eron, L (1963). Relationship of TV viewing habits and aggressive behavior in children. *Journal of Abnormal and Social Psychology, 67,* 193-196.

Eron, L (1982). Parent child interaction, television violence and aggression of children. *American Psychologist, 27,* 197-211.

Eron, LD, Gentry, JH, & Schlegel, P (eds) (1994). *Reason to hope: A psychosocial perspective on violence and youth.* Washington, DC: American Psychological Association.

Eron, LD, Waqlder, LO, & Lefkowitz, MM (1971) *Learning of aggression in children.* Boston: Little, Brown.

Finkelhor, D, Turner, H, Ormrod, R, Hamby, S, & Kracke, K (2009, October). Children's exposure to violence: A comprehensive national survey. *Juvenile Justice Bulletin.* Washington: US Department of Justice.

Gadow, KD, & Sprafkin, J (1993). Television violence and children with emotional and behavioural disorders. *Journal of Emotional and Behavioural Disorders, 1(1),* 54-63.

Gerbner, G (1970). Cultural indicators: The case of violence in television drama. *Annals of the American Academy of Political and Social Science, 388,* 69-81.

Gerbner, G, Gross, L, Morgan, M, & Signorielli, N (1994). Growing up with television: The cultivation perspective. In Bryant, J, & Zillmann, D (eds), *Media effects: Advances in theory and research.* Hillsdale, NJ: Erlbaum.

Grimes, T, Vernberg, E, & Cathers, T (1997). Emotionally disturbed children's reactions to violent media segments. *Journal of Health Communication, 2(3),* 157-168.

Group for the Advancement of Psychiatry (1982). *The child and television drama: the psychosocial impact of cumulative viewing.* New York: Mental Health Materials Center.

Hasson, U, Nir, Y, Levy, I, Fuhrmann, G, & Malach, R (2004). Intersubject synchronization of cortical activity during natural vision. *Science, 303,* 1634-1640.

Hearold, S (1986). A synthesis of 1043 effects of television on social behaviour. In G Comstock (ed), *Public communication and behaviour* (Vol 1; pp 65-133). New York: Academic Press.

Himmelweit, HT, Oppenheim, AN, & Vince, P (1958). *Television and the child: An empirical study of the effects of television on the young.* London: Oxford University Press.

Huesmann, LR & Eron, LD (eds) (1986). *Television and the aggressive child: A cross-national comparison.* Hillsdale, NJ: Erlbaum.

Huesmann, LR, Eron, LD, Lefkowitz, MM, & Walder, LO (1984). Stability of aggression over time and generations. *Developmental Psychology, 20,* 1120-1134.

Hummer, TA, Wang, Y, Kronenberger, WG, Mosier, KM, Dunn, DW, & Mathews, BP (in press). Short-term violent video game play by adolescents alters prefrontal activity during cognitive inhibition. *Media Psychology.*

Huston, AC, Donnerstein, E, Fairchild, H, Feshbach, ND, Katz, PA, Murray, JP, Rubinstein, EA, Wilcox, B, & Zuckerman, D (1992). *Big world, small screen: The role of television in American society.* Lincoln, NE: University of Nebraska Press.

Kelly, CR, Grinband, J, & Hirsch, J (2007). Repeated exposure to media violence is associated with diminished response in inhibitory frontolimbic network. *PloS ONE, 2(12),* e1268.

Kenny, DA (1984). The NBC study and television violence. *Journal of Communication, 34(1),* 176-182.

Kosslyn, SM, & Koenig, O (1995). *Wet mind: The new cognitive neuroscience.* New York: Free Press.

Kronenberger, WG, Mathews, VP, Dunn, DW, Wang, Y, Wood, EA, Giauque, AL, Larsen, JJ, Rembusch, ME, Lowe, MJ, & Li, T-G (2005). Media violence exposure and executive functioning in aggressive and control adolescents. *Journal of Clinical Psychology, 61(6),* 725-737.

Kronenberger, WG, Mathews, VP, Dunn, DW, Wang, Y, Wood, EA, Larsen, JJ, Rembusch, ME, Lowe, MJ, Giauque, AL, & Lurito, JT (2005). Media violence exposure in aggressive and control adolescents: Differences in self- and parent-reported exposure to violence on television and in video games. *Aggressive Behaviour, 31*, 201–216.

Langleben, DD, Loughead, JW, Ruparel, K, Hakun, JG, Busch-Winokur, S, Halloway, MB, Strasser, AA, & Lerman, C (2009). Reduced prefrontal and temporal processing and recall of high "sensation value" ads. *NeuroImage, 46(1),* 219–225.

Lazarsfeld, PF (1955). Why is so little known about the effects of television and what can be done? *Public Opinion Quarterly, 19,* 243–251.

LeDoux, J (1996). *The emotional brain: The mysterious underpinnings of emotional life.* New York: Simon & Schuster.

LeDoux, JE, & Hirst, W (eds) (1986). *Mind and brain: Dialogues in cognitive neuroscience.* New York: Cambridge University Press.

Lefkowitz, M, Eron, L, Walder, L, & Huesmann, LR (1972). Television violence and child aggression: A follow up study. In GA Comstock & EA Rubinstein (eds), *Television and social behavior, vol 3. Television and adolescent aggressiveness.* Washington, DC: United States Government Printing Office.

Lim, S, & Reeves, B (2009). Being in the game: Effects of Avatar choice and point of view on psychophysiological responses during play. *Media Psychology, 12,* 348–370.

MacBeth, TM (1996). *Tuning in to young viewers: Social science perspectives on television.* Thousand Oaks, CA: Sage.

Maccoby, EE (1954). Why do children watch television? *Public Opinion Quarterly, 18,* 239–244.

Mathews, VP, Kronenberger, WG, Wang, Y, Lurito, JT, Lowe, MJ, & Dunn, DW (2005). Media violence exposure and frontal lobe activation measured by functional magnetic resonance imaging in aggressive and nonaggressive adolescents. *Journal of Computer Assisted Tomography, 29(3),* 287–292.

Matsuda, G & Hiraki, K (2006). Sustained decrease in oxygenated hemoglobin during video games in the dorsal prefrontal cortex: A NIRS study of children. *NeuroImage, 29(3),* 706–711.

Milavsky, JR, Kessler, RC, Stipp, HH, & Rubens, WS (1982). *Television and aggression: A panel study.* New York: Academic Press.

Murray, JP (1973). Television and violence: Implications of the Surgeon General's research program. *American Psychologist, 28(6),* 472–478.

Murray, JP (1980). *Television and youth: 25 years of research and controversy.* Boys Town, NE: The Boys Town Center for the Study of Youth Development.

Murray, JP (1993). The developing child in a multimedia society. In GL Berry & JK Asamen (eds), *Children and television: Images in a changing socio-cultural world* (pp 228–241). Newbury Park, CA: Sage.

Murray, JP (1994). The impact of televised violence. *Hofstra Law Review, 22(4),* 809–825.

Murray, JP (1998). Studying television violence: A research agenda for the 21st century. In JK Asamen & GL Berry (eds), *Research paradigms, television, and social behaviour* (pp 369–410). Thousand Oaks, CA: Sage.

Murray, JP (2000). Media effects. In AE Kazdin (ed), *Encyclopedia of Psychology* (Vol 5; pp 153–155). New York: Oxford University Press.

Murray, JP (2001). TV violence and brainmapping in children. *Psychiatric Times, 17(10),* 70–71.

Murray, JP, & Kippax, S (1977). Television diffusion and social behaviour in three communities: A field experiment. *Australian Journal of Psychology, 29(1),* 31–43.

Murray, JP, & Kippax, S (1978). Children's social behavior in three towns with differing television experience. *Journal of Communication, 28(1)*, 19–29.

Murray, JP, & Kippax, S (1979). From the early window to the late night show: International trends in the study of television's impact on children and adults. In L Berkowitz (ed), *Advances in experimental social psychology, vol 12* (pp 253–320). New York: Academic Press.

Murray, JP, Liotti, M, Ingmundson, P, Mayberg, HS, Pu, Y, Zamarripa, F, Liu, Y, Woldorff, M, Gao, J-H, & Fox, PT (2006). Children's brain response to TV violence: Functional magnetic resonance imaging (fMRI) of video viewing in 8-13 year-old boys and girls. *Media Psychology, 8(1)*, 25–37.

National Institute of Mental Health (1982). *Television and behavior: Ten years of scientific progress and implications for the eighties, vol 1, Summary report*. Washington, DC: United States Government Printing Office.

National Research Council (1993). *Understanding and preventing violence*. Washington, DC: National Academy Press.

Ornstein, R (1997). *The right mind: Making sense of the hemispheres*. New York: Harcourt Brace.

Osborn, DK, & Endsley, RC (1971). Emotional reactions of young children to TV violence. *Child Development, 42(1)*, 321–331.

Paik, H & Comstock, G (1994). The effects of television violence on antisocial behaviour: A meta-analysis. *Communication Research, 21(4)*, 516–546.

Panksepp, J (1998). *Affective neuroscience: The foundations of human and animal emotions*. New York: Oxford University Press.

Pearl, D, Bouthilet, L, & Lazar, J (eds) (1982). *Television and behaviour: Ten years of scientific progress and implications for the eighties, Vol 2, Technical reviews*. Washington, DC: United States Government Printing Office.

Pecora, N, Murray, JP, & Wartella, E (2007). *Children and television: Fifty Years of research*. Mahwah, NJ: Earlbaum.

Redcay, E, Dodell-Feder, D, Pearrow, MJ, Mavros, PL, Kleiner, M, Gabrieli, JD, & Saxe, R (2010). Live face-to-face interaction during fMRI: A new tool for social cognitive neuroscience. *Neuroimage, 50(4)*, 1639–1647.

Schramm, W, Lyle, J, & Parker, EB (1961). *Television in the lives of our children*. Palo Alto, CA: Stanford University Press.

Shinichiro, N, Miki, N, Nagamitsu, S, Nagano, M, Yamashita, Y, Takashimia, S, & Matsuishi, T (2006). Prefrontal cerebral blood volume patterns while playing video games: A near-infrared spectroscopy study. *Brain and Development, 28(5)*, 315–321.

Steward, O (2000). *Functional neuroscience*. New York: Springer.

Strasburger, VC (2009). Commentary – Why do adolescent health researchers ignore the impact of the media? *Journal of Adolescent Health, 44*, 203–205.

Strenziok, M, Krueger, F, Deshpaned, G, Lenroot, RK, van der Meer, E, & Grafman, J (2010). Fronto-parietal regulation of media violence exposure in adolescents: A multi-method study. *Social Cognitive and Affective Neuroscience, 5(1)*, 1–11.

Strenziok, M, Krueger, F, Heinecke, A, Lenroot, RK, Knutson, KM, vander Meer, E, & Grafman, J (2011). Developmental effects of aggressive behavior in male adolescents assessed with structural and functional brain imaging. *Social Cognitive and Affective Neuroscience, 6(1)*, 2–11.

Surgeon General's Scientific Advisory Committee on Television and Social Behavior (1972). *Television and growing up: The impact of televised violence*. Washington, DC: United States Government Printing Office.

Talairach, J & Tournoux, P (1988). *Co-planar stereotaxic atlas of the human brain*. New York: Thieme Medical Publishers.

Toga, AW, & Maziotta, JC (1996). *Brain mapping: The methods*. New York: Academic Press.

United States Congress, House Committee on Interstate and Foreign Commerce (1952). *Investigation of Radio and Television Programs, Hearings and Report*, 82nd Congress, 2nd session, 3 June–5 December 1952. Washington, DC: United States Government Printing Office.

United States Congress, Senate Committee of the Judiciary, Subcommittee to Investigate Juvenile Delinquency (1955). *Juvenile Delinquency (Television Programs)*, Hearings, 83rd Congress, 2nd session, 5 June–20 October 1954. Washington, DC: United States Government Printing Office.

Vorderer, P, & Bryant, J (2006). *Playing video games: Motives, Responses, and Consequences*. Mahwah, NJ: Erlbaum Publishers.

Vuilleumier, P, & Pourtois, D (2007). Distributed and interactive brain mechanisms during emotion face perception: Evidence from functional neuroimaging. *Neuropsychologia, 45(1),* 174–194.

Walker, KB, & Morley, DD (1991). Attitudes and parental factors as intervening variables in the television violence-aggression relation. *Communication Research, 8(2),* 41–47.

Wang, Y, Mathews, VP, Kalnin, AJ, Mosier, KM, Dunn, DW, Saykin, AJ, & Kronenberger, WG (2009). Short term exposure to a violent video game induces changes in frontolimbic circuitry in adolescents. *Brain Imaging and Behaviour, 3,* 38–50.

Weber, R, Ritterfield, U, & Mathiak, K (2006). Does playing violent video games induce aggression?: Empirical evidence of a functional magnetic resonance imaging study. *Media Psychology, 8(1),* 39–60.

Williams, TM (ed) (1986). *The impact of television: A natural experiment in three communities*. New York: Academic Press.

Wilmer, JB, Germine, L, Chabris, CF, Dhatterjee, G, Williams, M, Lokin, E, Nakayama, K, & Duchaine, B (2010). Human face recognition ability is specific and highly heritable. *Proceedings of the National Academy of Sciences, 107(11),* 5238–5241.

Zillmann, D (1971). Excitation transfer in communication-mediated aggressive behaviour. *Journal of Experimental Social Psychology, 7,* 419–434.

Zillmann, D (1982). Television viewing and arousal. In D Pearl, L Bouthilet & J Lazar (eds), *Television and behaviour: Ten years of scientific progress and implications for the eighties, Vol 2. Technical reviews* (pp 53–67). Washington, DC: United States Government Printing Office.

Zillmann, D, & Bryant, J (1994). Entertainment as media effect. In J Bryant & D Zillmann (eds), *Media Effects: Advances in theory and research* (pp 437–461). Hillsdale, NJ: Erlbaum.

Chapter 3

The impact of violent video games: An overview

Craig A Anderson and Wayne A Warburton

Parents often ask about the effects of violent video games on their children and teenagers. In most cases, they note that their "common sense" instinct is that too much exposure to violent video games must have some sort of negative effect on their children, but that they have read in the media that "the jury is still out" on violent media effects or that there is no convincing evidence that violent video game playing is harmful. Confusion around this conflict will often prompt them then to ask: "what does the scientific evidence really say?" In this chapter we show that the common sense view is backed up by a substantial body of recent scientific findings. Helpful and pro-social video game content has great potential for enhancing the lives of children and adolescents, but exposure to anti-social and violent video game content increases the likelihood of a range of negative outcomes, with greater exposure increasing the risk.

Video games have been around for nearly 50 years. Kirsch (2010) notes the first as being Spacewar (released in 1962), a game in which two spaceships battle to the death in space. Although the graphics were very simple compared to modern games, the theme of battling to the death is one that has endured through the ensuing five decades.

According to the most recent comprehensive poll by the Kaiser Foundation, American children aged 8–18 play an average of eight hours of video games per week, an increase of over 400 per cent from 1999 (Rideout, Foehr & Roberts, 2010). Playing is heaviest in the 11–14 age group, with boys outplaying girls more than 2.5 hours to 1. A recent study suggests that around 99 per cent of American boys play video games, along with 94 per cent of girls (Lenhart et al, 2008). It is common for US children and adolescents to play more than 20 hours per week and it is not uncommon for males to play 40 hours or more per week (Bailey, West & Anderson, 2010). On average, Australian 7–18-year-olds played somewhat less than their US counterparts in 2007 (4.7 hours per week: see ACMA, 2007), but this figure could have risen substantially in recent years if Australian children have followed the steep upward trend found in the latest US studies.

The types of games vary, but content analyses by Dill and colleagues (2005) show that the majority of top selling video games and children's favourite games contain violence, and often strong violence. More recently, *Call of Duty: Modern Warfare 2* grossed ~$USD 550 million in the first five days of its 2009 release, at that time more than any other entertainment product in history (movies included). Next on the list in 2009 was *Grant Theft Auto IV* (*GTA*), with ~$USD 500 million in five days. Even more recently (a year is a long time in the video game world) *Call of Duty: Black Ops* grossed $USD 360 million in a single day, breaking all records (Ortutay, 2010). According to Wikipedia, the massive multiplayer online game (MMOG) *World of Warcraft* has more than 12 million online subscribers and thus currently grosses more than $USD 180 million per month (at $15 per month per player). *GTA*, which is rated M17+ in the United States and involves such activities as going on murderous rampages, having sex with prostitutes and then murdering them to retrieve the money paid, has been played by 56 per cent of United States children aged 8–18 (Rideout et al, 2010). Clearly, a large number of children and adolescents are exposed regularly to video games with high levels of violence and anti-social themes. This makes it important for parents, educators and professionals who work with children to have some knowledge of their effects.

Before turning to the negative effects of violent video games however, it is important to stress that video games can have many helpful benefits. Here are just a few.

Helpful effects of video games

Pain management

Kirsch (2010) notes that various media, including video games, can be used to distract and relax children during painful medical procedures.

Coordination and spatial cognition

A number of studies reveal that video games which require the placement of objects within a screen (such as *Tetris*) can enhance the spatial cognition abilities of players (that is, the ability to mentally arrange and rotate objects in three dimensions). Indeed, video game playing has been linked with a wide array of visual and spatial skills, primarily through practice effects (see Green & Bavelier, 2006; Okagaki & Frensch, 1994; see also Bailey et al, 2010, for a review). In one study by Gopher, Weil and Bareket (1994), the flight performance of Israeli Air Force cadets who had been trained on the Space Fortress II video game was compared with the performance of an untrained group. The trained cadets performed better in almost all aspects of flight performance and as a result the game was incorporated into the Israeli Air Force training program.

Pro-social behaviour

Although this area of study is still in its infancy, there is mounting evidence that video games which model and involve participants in pro-social, helping behaviours can lead to increases in pro-social behaviour in the short and long term. Most notably, Gentile et al (2009) found that elementary school students exposed to pro-social video games were more helpful than those exposed to violent or non-social video games. In a second longitudinal study of Japanese children in grades 5, 8 and 11, exposure to pro-social video games at the start of the study was linked with increased pro-social behaviour some months later, even when the baseline pro-social tendencies of children were statistically removed. In a final study of Singaporean secondary school students, the amount of pro-social video game play experienced was correlated with helping behaviour, cooperation, sharing and empathy. A study by Greitemeyer and Osswald (2009) found that pro-social video game playing led to a short-term reduction in the tendency to see the world as hostile and an immediate reduction in anti-social thoughts.

Education

A considerable literature reveals video games to be a powerful teaching tool (eg, Barlett et al, 2009; Murphy et al, 2002; Swing & Anderson,

2008). They have been used to teach algebra (Corbett et al, 2001), biology (Ybarrondo, 1984), photography (Abrams, 1986), and computer programming (Kahn, 1999), to teach children how to manage diabetes (Lieberman, 2001; 2006) and to teach specific skills using simulators (for example, by Qantas pilots, NASA and the Air Force). Gentile and Gentile (2008) describe the educational advantages of using video games as teaching tools. These include the power of video games to engage children and to "encourage children to persevere in acquiring and mastering a number of skills, to navigate through complex problems and changing environments, and to experiment with different identities until success is achieved" (p 127).

Exercise

There has been a recent explosion in the popularity of video games that promote physical activity and exercise (that is, "Exergames"). Games such as *Wii Sports Heart Rate; Wii Fit; Wii Play; Wii FitPlus; Dance, Dance Revolution* and *Just Dance* seem to be part of a recent trend that has seen an increase in the availability and popularity of non-violent, helpful games.

Clearly, video games have considerable potential to enhance the lives of children and adolescents. Unfortunately, excessive video game playing, especially of violent video games, has the potential to impact children in a number of negative ways.

Harmful effects of video games

Video game addiction

In his moving biography, *Unplugged: My Journey into the Dark World of Video Game Addiction*, Ryan Van Cleave describes the way that a violent online game, *World of Warcraft*, dominated his life to such an extent that he was unable to function normally and was driven to the verge of suicide. Video game addiction is now taken so seriously by psychologists and psychiatrists that it was recently considered for inclusion in the fifth edition of the Diagnostic and Statistical Manual for Mental Disorders (DSM) as a diagnosable psychiatric disorder and has been lodged in its appendix to encourage further research. It is clear that many children play video games at a "pathological" level that causes damage to family, social, school or psychological functioning (see Anderson et al, 2012). For example, it has been found that 8.5 per cent of 8–18-year-old US video game players do so at pathological levels (Gentile, 2009). Similar studies have found figures of 11.9 per cent in Europe (Grusser et al, 2007), 8.7 per cent in Singapore (Choo et al, 2010), 10.3 per cent in China (Peng & Li, 2009) and 4 per cent for 12–18-year-olds in Norway (Johansson & Götestam, 2004), with a further 15.5 per cent "at risk".

As will be seen in the ensuing sections, the amount that children play video games is very important. Those who play excessively are not only at risk of a number of negative outcomes, they are also much more likely to be playing violent games (see Krahé & Möller, 2004).

Attention deficits

There are some studies linking the amount of time children spend playing video games to attention deficits, impulsivity and hyperactivity (see Bailey et al, 2010; Swing et al, 2010). For example, Gentile (2009) found that adolescents who used video games at pathological levels were nearly three times more likely to be diagnosed with Attention Deficit Disorder or Attention Deficit Hyperactivity Disorder than adolescents who played at non-pathological levels. In a landmark paper, Swing and colleagues (2010) examined the effect of video game playing on attention in elementary school children. They used a longitudinal study that statistically controlled for a range of other factors that could also lead to attention problems and found that amount of time spent playing video games predicted increases in teacher assessments of attention deficits in the children 13 months later. These results suggest that the children's level of video game playing played a causal role in their subsequent loss of attentional capacity.

Anderson et al (2012) believe that on theoretical grounds some video games should have less effect on attentional problems (for example, those that require controlled thought and planning) and that those which require constant reactive behaviours from players (a common feature of many violent first person shooting games for example) may be more problematic in terms of children developing attentional difficulties.

School performance

It is well established that spending longer hours playing video games is linked with poorer school performance for both children and adolescents (Anderson et al, 2007; Chan & Rabinowitz, 2006; Chiu et al, 2004; Cordes & Miller, 2000; Gentile, 2009; Gentile et al, 2004; Sharif & Sargent, 2006). One explanation for this is a simple displacement of time – hours spent playing video games eats into time that would normally be spent studying and reading. For example, in a study of 1491 youth between 10 and 19, gamers spent 30 per cent less time reading and 34 per cent less time doing homework (Cummings & Vandewater, 2007). It is also possible, however, that children who perform more poorly at school are also more likely to "spend more time playing games, where they may feel a sense of mastery that eludes them at school" (Anderson et al, 2012). Of course, another possibility is the that excessive gaming creates attention deficits, which in turn can lead to poorer school performance.

Increased aggression

Should we be concerned about children and adolescents playing violent video games? Can this lead to aggressive behaviour? Over 98 per cent of paediatricians in the United States have considered these questions and believe that excessive violent media exposure has a negative effect on childhood aggression (Gentile et al, 2004). Similarly, there is a consensus amongst the vast majority of violent video game researchers that too much exposure to violent video games increases the likelihood of aggressive thoughts, feelings and behaviours, leads to desensitisation to violence and also leads to decreases in pro-social behaviours and empathy (Anderson et al, 2010; Huesmann, 2010). There are, however, a small number of researchers who dispute this evidence and it seems that the views of this small minority have had a large impact on public perceptions (Anderson & Gentile, 2008; Dill, 2009). In this section of the chapter we will broadly examine the arguments for this view and then review the scientific evidence that does find violent video game effects. In this way, we hope that readers can judge the evidence for themselves.

1. The first argument against violent video game effects is that there is little evidence linking the playing of violent video games to very violent behaviours (such as school shootings). To better understand

this argument it is helpful to reflect on the difference between aggression and violence. In essence, violence is aggressive behaviour that has extreme harm as its goal (Anderson & Bushman, 2002). Thus, all violence is aggression but not all aggression is violence. With this in mind we make four points.

(a) Ethically it is not possible to use the most powerful methods – experimental manipulations – to test the causal link between violent video games and violence because we cannot rightfully incite people to cause extreme harm in a laboratory. There are, however, ways to test links with aggressive behaviour, which *can* be examined ethically in a laboratory. It is disingenuous to suggest that because there are no experimental studies that randomly assign children to years of playing violent or nonviolent video games and then measure which group commits the most violent crimes, that therefore there are no established negative or anti-social effects. This is like saying that because there are no experimental studies on humans showing that cigarette smoking causes lung cancer, smoking is not a causal risk factor. The causal links between violent video game playing and physical aggression are, in our opinion, well established.

(b) Cross-sectional (correlational) studies and longitudinal studies of violent video game effects have established significant links to violent behaviour. Several longitudinal studies in particular provide strong evidence that these are causal effects.

(c) Aggressive behaviour, which can include bullying, hurting other people physically, hurting other people's property or relationships and hurting people verbally, is a very important social phenomenon in its own right. Aggression does not have to escalate into violence to be harmful and destructive.

(d) No aggression researchers claim that media violence is the sole or even the most important source of violent behaviour. The most common approach, and the one taken by the authors, is the "risk factor" approach. According to this approach, people can have various risk factors for aggression or violent behaviour (see Figure 1). These might include coming from a violent home, having a violent peer group, high levels of trait aggression, exposure to violent media and a number of other factors. The more risk factors that

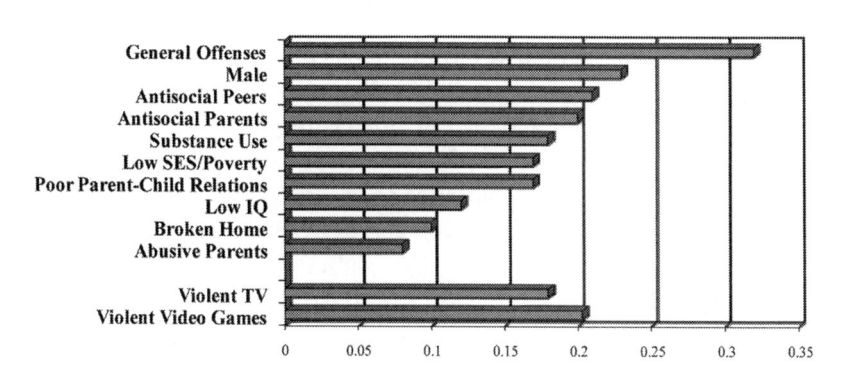

Figure 1: Some longitudinal factors for youth violence

Factor	Value
General Offenses	~0.33
Male	~0.22
Antisocial Peers	~0.22
Antisocial Parents	~0.20
Substance Use	~0.19
Low SES/Poverty	~0.18
Poor Parent-Child Relations	~0.18
Low IQ	~0.14
Broken Home	~0.12
Abusive Parents	~0.10
Violent TV	~0.19
Violent Video Games	~0.19

Adapted from US Department of Health and Human Services (2001), Bushman and Huesmann (2006) and Anderson et al (2010).

are present for a person, especially when they are present from a young age, the more likely that person is to be aggressive or violent. Strasburger (2009, p 203) notes that:

> The research on media violence and its relationship to real-life aggression is clear: young people learn their attitudes about violence at a very young age, and once learned, those attitudes are difficult to change (Anderson et al, 2003; Bushman & Huesmann, 2006). Conservative estimates are that media violence may be causing 10% of real-life violence – not the leading cause by any means, but an unhealthy chunk that we could do something about if we chose to (Strasburger et al, 2009; Comstock & Strasburger, 1990).

We believe that Victor Strasburger is right. Many risk factors for aggression and violence are very hard to deal with as parents, as educators, as professionals and as policy-makers. Media violence, though, is one risk factor that can be controlled and about which action can be taken from the level of the individual home through to the level of State and federal governments. This makes the research on media violence effects particularly important.

2. Detractors of the view that playing violent video games increases the likelihood of aggressive behaviour also criticise the methodology of video game studies and of meta-analyses of these studies. It is to this important scientific evidence that we now turn.

What is a meta-analysis and what evidence do the meta-analyses provide?

A meta-analysis is a statistical technique whereby scientific studies that test the same or a similar hypothesis (for example, that violent video game exposure compared to neutral video game exposure will result in increased aggression) and the same or a similar outcome (for example, aggressive behaviour) are combined to ascertain the strength ("effect size") of the average finding. To date there have been a number of meta-analyses of the effect of violent video games on aggressive thoughts, feelings and behaviours. In particular, studies by Distinguished Professor Craig Anderson and Dr Chris Ferguson have received a lot of publicity in recent years and it is valuable to compare them.

Dr Ferguson, a vocal critic of the research demonstrating a link between violent video game playing and aggression, along with video game industry representatives, claim that violent video game research is methodologically flawed and that mainstream media violence researchers selectively report biased findings. Dr Ferguson has also suggested that Professor Anderson's meta-analyses have a "publication bias" that undermines their results. Dr Ferguson cites his own three meta-analyses that examine the question of whether violent video game playing increases subsequent aggression. These examined 24, 17 and 14 published papers, encompassing 25, 21 and 15 separate tests of the same hypothesis respectively (Ferguson 2007a, 2007b; Ferguson & Kilburn, 2009). In total, 4205 and 3602 participants were tested in the first two meta-analyses (the number cannot be determined for the most recent study but is assumed to be lower). Dr Ferguson found a positive relationship between violent video game exposure and aggressive behaviour, with effect sizes of .29, .14 and .15 respectively. He then inappropriately (according to some meta-analysis experts, see Bushman, Rothstein, & Anderson, 2010) "corrected" for publication bias using a controversial statistical procedure called "trim and fill" that reduced these effect sizes. Such a procedure guesses what unpublished studies might be out there and adds these guesses to the averaging procedure. Based on the "corrected" figures, Dr Ferguson concluded there was no effect of violent video games on aggressive behaviour. These three meta-analyses, which use highly overlapping subsets of the same small sample of studies, are widely cited as the strongest evidence that violent video game playing does not increase the likelihood of aggressive behaviour.

Evidence that playing violent video games does increase the likelihood of aggression comes from many researchers. Professor Anderson and his colleagues have themselves conducted a large number of such studies and have also summarised the available studies in three comprehensive meta-analyses, the first in 2001 (Anderson & Bushman, 2001), the second in 2004 (Anderson et al, 2004) and the most recent in 2010 (Anderson et al, 2010). The latter paper was co-authored by Professor Hannah Rothstein, an expert in meta-analyses and publication bias. This paper detailed major shortcomings in the Ferguson meta-analyses (which failed to include numerous relevant studies) and included all relevant studies then known. Data from 136 articles, 381 separate tests of hypotheses, and across a massive sample of 130, 296 participants were analysed. In this large, all-inclusive meta-analysis, research methodology was also examined. Among the many findings was that studies with better research methods tended to find stronger effects of violent video game playing on aggressive behaviour.

We present a summary of the findings in Figure 2 (*over page*). We understand that the concept of effect size is a hard one to grasp without a detailed knowledge of statistical procedures, so we will provide some comparison data afterwards to help readers make sense of the results.

The middle bar shows the effect found, the bars on either side reflect how variable the findings were in the studies tested.

Figure 2 shows several meta-analyses. Each tests a different hypothesis. All hypotheses are tested as outcomes of exposure to violent video games, and these outcomes include aggressive behaviour, aggressive thoughts (cognitions), aggressive feelings (affects), physiological arousal, desensitisation to violence/low empathy and pro-social behaviour. As can be seen, the average effect across these many studies was one whereby exposure to violent video games led to an increase in aggressive behaviours, aggressive thoughts, aggressive feelings and physiological arousal (which is linked to aggressive behaviour), to desensitisation to violence and decreased empathy, and to a reduction in pro-social behaviours.

It is important to note that these findings come from a range of study types – experimental studies in which all participants have

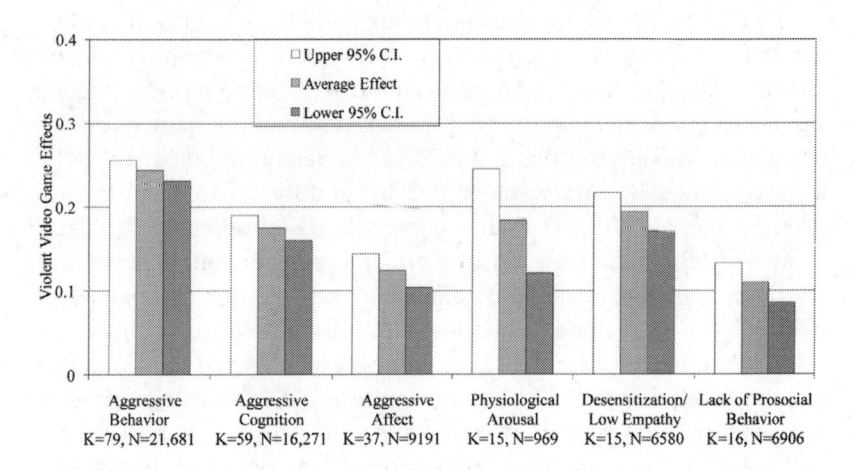

Figure 2: Results of the meta-analysis by Anderson et al 2010

	Aggressive Behavior K=79, N=21,681	Aggressive Cognition K=59, N=16,271	Aggressive Affect K=37, N=9191	Physiological Arousal K=15, N=969	Desensitization/ Low Empathy K=15, N=6580	Lack of Prosocial Behavior K=16, N=6906

K = number of separate tests of the same hypothesis included in the analysis
N = number of participants across studies
CI = Confidence Interval, a measure of how variable the data was.

exactly the same experience other than the media type they experience, correlational studies of the links between levels of violent video game playing and various types of aggressive behaviours in real life, and longitudinal studies that follow video game playing patterns and behavioural patterns in the same people over time.

Each study type makes a unique contribution to what we know. Experiments can be used to infer that one thing causes another, but it is harder to generalise these findings to "real life". Correlational studies involve "real life" behaviours and can test alternative hypotheses, but it is difficult to determine the causal direction of relationships found (that is, whether playing violent games causes aggression or whether aggressive people choose violent games). Longitudinal studies are real world studies and can be used to find whether one thing causes another over time in a person's life. Some media violence studies have followed the same people for over 40 years (eg, Huesmann et al, 2003) and have very detailed data. Because links between violent video game playing

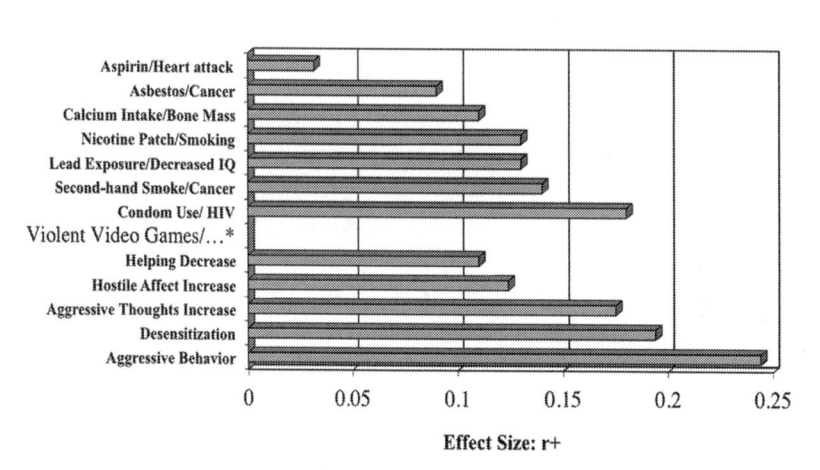

Figure 3: The comparative effect sizes of violent video game effects and other well known phenomena

Phenomenon	Effect Size: r+
Aspirin/Heart attack	~0.02
Asbestos/Cancer	~0.05
Calcium Intake/Bone Mass	~0.08
Nicotine Patch/Smoking	~0.09
Lead Exposure/Decreased IQ	~0.12
Second-hand Smoke/Cancer	~0.14
Condom Use/ HIV	~0.18
Violent Video Games/...*	
Helping Decrease	~0.13
Hostile Affect Increase	~0.14
Aggressive Thoughts Increase	~0.17
Desensitization	~0.19
Aggressive Behavior	~0.24

* From Best Practices studies, Anderson et al, Psychological Bulletin, 2010.

and aggression are found consistently across all three study types, the evidence converges to suggest both a causal link and an effect that is found in the real world.

The Anderson et al (2010) meta-analysis also found that when proper statistical methods are used, there was no evidence of systematic publication bias in the studies. The rather weak evidence of publication bias produced by Dr Ferguson was likely the result of several factors, including failure to use all of the relevant studies and the combining of cross-sectional and experimental studies in the publication bias analysis.

To understand how strong the obtained violent video game effect on aggression is, it can be helpful to get a sense of what the "effect size" numbers actually mean. It is easy to understand that a higher number means a stronger effect, but it is much harder to know how a big a number needs to be before it is considered important. Figure 3 shows some effect sizes for well known phenomena that can be used as points for comparison.

As can be seen from Figure 3, violent video game effects are larger than the effect of eating calcium on bone mass, of asbestos inhalation on related cancers, of condom use on reducing HIV infection numbers, of taking aspirin on reducing heart attacks and a range of other very important phenomena. Clearly, the size of violent video game effects is large enough to be considered socially important.

A final finding from the Anderson et al (2010) meta-analyses is that the violent video game effects occurred for both males and females, and across low-violence collectivistic Eastern countries (for example, Japan) and high-violence individualistic Western countries (for example, Australia and the United States). This is not a surprising finding, as other reviews have found that violent video games affect people regardless of age, gender, socio-economic status, game genre and game system (Barlett et al, 2009). In fact, to the knowledge of the authors, no group has yet been identified that are immune to the effects of exposure to violent media such as video games (see Anderson et al, 2003).

Perhaps the best brief summary of the evidence presented here is articulated in a statement produced by 13 researchers into violent video game effects (including the authors of this chapter), prepared for an *amicus curiae* (friend of the court) brief for the *Schwarzenegger and Brown v Video Software Dealers Association and Entertainment Software Association* case in the Supreme Court of the United States (Docket # 08-1448). This statement was supported as being accurate by a further 102 well-respected researchers in this area.

Statement on Video Game Violence

Both the American Psychological Association (APA, 2005) and the American Academy of Pediatrics (AAP, 2009) have issued formal statements stating that scientific research on violent video games clearly shows that such games are causally related to later aggressive behavior in children and adolescents. Extensive research has been conducted over many years using all three major types of research designs (experimental, cross-sectional, and longitudinal). Numerous original empirical research studies have been conducted on children and adolescents. Overall, the research data conclude that exposure to violent video games causes an increase in the likelihood of aggressive behavior. The effects are both immediate and long term. Violent video games have measurable and statistically significant effects on both males and females. Theoretically important effects of violent video games have been confirmed by many empirical studies. The effects have been replicated by researchers in different settings and in numerous countries. The psychological processes underlying such effects are well understood and include: imitation, observational learning, priming of cognitive, emotional and behavioral scripts, physiological arousal, and emotional desensitization. These are general processes that underlie all types of social behavior, not just aggression and violence; they have been confirmed by countless studies outside of the media violence domain. In addition to causing an increase in the likelihood of aggressive behavior, violent video games have also been found to increase aggressive thinking, aggressive feelings, physiological desensitization to violence, and to decrease pro-social behavior.

Importantly, this statement alludes to the psychological processes that are known to underlie the effect of exposure to violent video games on children. These are worth examining in more detail because they also provide some insight as to why the effects of violent video games, compared to other violent media, may be stronger.

The psychology of violent video game effects on children

Most of the explanations related to violent video game effects involve different types of learning. Because of certain features of violent video game playing – interactivity, repetition and the actual playing of the role of aggressor – the effects may be stronger and patterns of behaviour better learned.

Imitation

Humans seem to be hard-wired from birth to imitate others. Recently discovered "mirror neurons" in humans and primates represent one mechanism in the brain that may facilitate this (Caggiano et al, 2009; Gallese et al, 1996; Rizzolati et al, 1996; Umilta et al, 2001). Imitation has benefits, including the fast learning of important behaviours, and plays a role in human bonding. However, imitation of unhelpful and anti-social behaviours can have clear negative effects for the individual and for society. We know that children will imitate aggressive behaviours, even if the behaviours are totally new to the child and are not seen to be rewarded in any way (Bandura, 1965; 1973; Bandura et al, 1961; 1963a, 1963b).

We also know that children imitate characters from the media they see, with some characters more likely to be imitated than others – those that are attractive, heroic, rewarded for their behaviour or liked, or that have high social status. In violent video games the central characters often meet several of these criteria. Does this mean, though, that people will copy the behaviours of the characters in very violent games such as *GTA* and others? It is possible. For example, an 18-year-old youth in Thailand stabbed a taxi driver to death trying to "find out if it was as easy in real life to rob a taxi as it was in the game" (Reed, 2008). As a result, *GTA IV* was banned in Thailand. In 2003 William Buckner, 16, and his step-brother Joshua, 14, killed a man and seriously wounded a woman shooting at cars in Tennessee (Calvert, 2003). The boys claimed they were acting out the game Grand Theft Auto III. Also in 2003, Devin Moore, an 18-year-old from Alabama, killed three police officers following his arrest for a carjacking. On being re-arrested he is reported to have told police that "Life is like a video game. Everybody's got to die sometime" (Leung, 2005). Again, the killer told police he was copying behaviour he had learned playing *GTA III*. We are not suggesting that violent video game playing alone was causal in these crimes. As noted earlier, numerous risk factors influence the likelihood of aggressive and violent behaviour, and the most severe forms of violence virtually always require the convergence of many risk factors. Furthermore, it is difficult (perhaps impossible) to identify which risk factors were crucial to any particular aggressive or violent act. Nonetheless, imitation of media violence seems to have played some role in these cases.

There are numerous other stories of aggressive behaviours that seemingly imitate violent video games. These are easily accessed on the internet with a simple search. Clearly, for some violent video game players, simple imitation may play a causal role in some acts of aggression. However there are a number of other factors, also linked with imitation and learned aggression, that may also be important.

Identification

Although media effects can occur without the person identifying with any of the characters they have seen, identifying with an aggressor has been shown to increase the likelihood of adopting aggressive behaviours and attitudes (Cantor, 1994; Huesmann & Eron, 1986; Huesmann et al, 2003). People are more likely to identify with a character who is perceived as similar, heroic and attractive (Hearold, 1986; Heath et al, 1989), and are more likely to identify with and believe realistic portrayals because they are easier to relate to personal experiences (Berkowitz

& Alioto, 1973; Feshback, 1972; Geen, 1975). In violent video games, the player strongly identifies with (and usually takes the role of) the aggressor. The aggressive central character is usually glorified and portrayed as heroic and, in recent years, the portrayal of aggressive characters in video games has become increasingly realistic (Gentile et al, 2007). For these reasons, identification with violent/aggressive characters may be a key way that video games impact on children.

Repetition

It is well established that repetition of behaviours establishes them in memory, increases skill and automates them as learned responses (eg, Gentile & Gentile, 2008). Further, repeating an entire behavioural sequence commits it to memory better than repeating only part of a sequence (Gentile et al, 2007). Violent video games are much more repetitive than other forms of violent media and more often involve the repetition of complete behavioural sequences (Gentile et al, 2007). Players repeat the same behaviours and receive similar rewards throughout the game, experience similar thoughts and feelings during those actions and are exposed to the attitudes espoused in the game implicitly and explicitly (for example, sleeping with prostitutes and then murdering them to retrieve one's money in *GTA* implies misogyny, the acceptance of violence to get what one wants and that human life has little value). Simply put, the repetitive nature of violent video games is ideal for learning aggressive attitudes and scripts for behaviour.

Interactivity

Active participation assists learning as it requires attention, and closely attending to a task assists people to memorise the relevant behaviours and knowledge (Gentile et al, 2007; Gentile & Gentile, 2008). Violent video games are highly interactive, and the recent development of home consoles that allow players to use realistic weapons such as replica guns and swords further increases the level of interactivity and decreases the gap between game playing behaviours and "real world" behaviours. The combination of interactivity and frequent rehearsal is a potent one for learning. In essence, this is a key reason that video games are such powerful tools for teaching pilots, astronauts and soldiers their core skills. These factors give video games tremendous potential for pro-social pursuits and as learning tools, but have less welcome implications regarding the interactive rehearsal of anti-social and aggressive behaviours.

Lack of negative consequences

Another basic tenet of learning theory, demonstrated across thousands of studies, is that people are more likely to behave in ways that are rewarded and less likely to behave in ways that are punished. In terms of imitation, children imitate aggression they perceive as being rewarded more often than aggression they perceive as resulting in punishment. Interestingly, children will imitate unpunished aggression as often as rewarded aggression (eg, see Bandura, 1973).

With these facts in mind, it is relevant that most acts of violence in video games:

(a) go unpunished;
(b) are rewarded (for example, by points, money, status and elevation to higher game levels);
(c) have unrealistic consequences for the victim.

With relation to the final point, it is important for parents and professionals to note that seeing victims suffer realistic and negative consequences as a result of media violence should *reduce* the likelihood of subsequent aggression because pain cues usually inhibit aggressive behaviour (Baron, 1971a, 1971b, 1979). Also note, however, that in some circumstances pain and suffering cues can increase aggressive behaviour (see Berkowitz, 1993, p 174).

Associative learning

As noted in Chapter 1, the brain is a neural network in which concepts, ideas, feelings and memories are stored and interconnected. The way this network "wires up" depends on what people experience, with paired experiences (such as the smell of fresh coffee, pleasure and a craving for a hot beverage) becoming more strongly wired together the more they are experienced together. This means that people learn to associate one thing with another.

In media generally, and in violent video games especially, many things are frequently paired and thus become "wired" together. For example, guns are rarely used for any purpose other than violent action. This is why there is a well demonstrated "weapons effect", whereby the simple sight of a weapon increases the likelihood of aggression if the person has mentally paired a weapon such as a gun with killing or hurting people rather than with a non-aggressive use such as sports shooting (Bartholow et al, 2005; Berkowitz & LePage, 1967; Carlson et al, 1990). This suggests that children who often play video games where there is frequent weapon use for the purpose of killing and hurting others are more likely to be aggressive immediately after playing the game and are more likely to be aggressive when exposed to a weapon of a similar type in real life.

Associative learning also explains why whole sequences of behaviour are learned during video game play and why the acquisition of aggression-related knowledge structures is so important.

Acquisition of aggressive knowledge structures, attitudes and scripts for behaviour

Clearly, violent video games are powerful teachers, but what is the outcome of such learning for the individual child? In essence, the child (and adult for that matter) internalises clusters of associated knowledge about aggressive behaviour (knowledge structures or "schemas"), as well as attitudes about aggressive behaviour and "scripts" for how to behave in certain circumstances.

Schemas and scripts contain knowledge about an aspect of living, mental links to related attitudes, feelings and memories, and a repertoire of associated behaviours. Scripts additionally contain information about how commonly experienced situations "play out" (such as visiting a supermarket) and the typical sequence of behaviours in that situation (entrance at the left of the store, grab a trolley, milk at the back, bread in the second aisle, line up and pay). Schemas and scripts are activated by a trigger (for example, the supermarket logo) and, once active, help to direct our behaviour, often without our being aware of it. Children start to develop schemas about the world as toddlers (and perhaps earlier) and these can sometimes be aggressive in nature.

In relation to the development of aggressive knowledge structures and attitudes, there is considerable evidence that exposure to violent media (including violent video games):

(a) increases attitudes approving of aggressive behaviour as a "normal" social response (Huesmann, 1998);
(b) increases mental access to scripts for resolving conflict that involve aggressive behaviour and reduces access to conflict-solving scripts that are non-aggressive (Bushman & Anderson, 2002; Huesmann, 1998);
(c) underpins the attitude that aggression is (1) exciting and (2) increases one's social status (Groebel, 1998);
(d) increases the belief that the world is a frightening place (Cantor, 2003; Donnerstein et al, 1994);
(e) increases a hostile attributional bias whereby ambiguous but innocent behaviours by others are interpreted as deliberately hurtful (Anderson et al, 2010; Möller & Krahé, 2009); and
(f) increases the likelihood of aggressive behaviour (Anderson et al, 2010).

Regrettably, children are exposed to a lot of violent media. As noted in Chapter 1, by the age of 18, most US children will have seen many tens of thousands of murders and acts of violence on television alone. Heavy playing of violent video games that involve frequently killing of other people or creatures would add greatly to those figures, especially for murders. This means that for a lot of children, violent media influences may result in higher levels of aggressive schemas, fear about the wider world, hostile and anti-social attitudes, and scripts for behaving aggressively, than might otherwise occur without those influences.

Fictitious violence versus real violence

Recent brain imaging studies, in which children's brain activation patterns are "photographed" by fMRI machines whilst they are experiencing violent media, have shown that even when children know the violence they are watching is fictitious or fantasy violence, their brains respond to the violence as if there was a real threat (Murray et al, 2006; see also Weber et al, 2006). In addition, long-term memory systems were activated, suggesting that this effect could endure beyond the initial exposure. This research suggests that fantasy media violence seems to have a similar impact on children as exposure to realistic media violence.

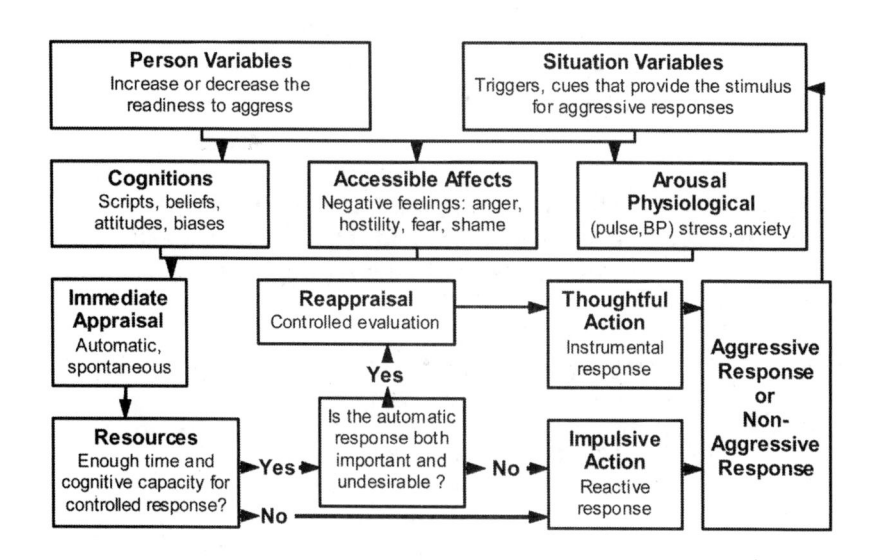

Figure 4: The General Aggression Model

Person Variables Increase or decrease the readiness to aggress		Situation Variables Triggers, cues that provide the stimulus for aggressive responses
Cognitions Scripts, beliefs, attitudes, biases	**Accessible Affects** Negative feelings: anger, hostility, fear, shame	**Arousal** Physiological (pulse, BP) stress, anxiety

Immediate Appraisal (Automatic, spontaneous) → Resources (Enough time and cognitive capacity for controlled response?) → Yes: Reappraisal (Controlled evaluation) — Is the automatic response both important and undesirable? Yes → Thoughtful Action (Instrumental response); No → Impulsive Action (Reactive response) → Aggressive Response or Non-Aggressive Response

The General Aggression Model

The General Aggression Model (GAM: Anderson & Bushman 2002; DeWall, Anderson & Bushman, in press) provides a theoretically sound and helpful way of understanding how exposure to violent media can increase a person's likelihood of being aggressive in both the short and long term (see Figures 4 and 5).

The GAM is a model of what is happening psychologically during an episode of aggression. In essence the person brings their own readiness to aggress, through their gender, beliefs and attitudes about aggression, personality and other stable factors. Each situation has cues and triggers for aggression, such as the presence of a weapon or an insult. When a person encounters an aggression-triggering situation, various relevant cognitions (memories, beliefs, attitudes, scripts for behaviour) are activated, along with feelings (such as fear and anger) and a level of physiological arousal. Higher levels of arousal make a dominant tendency to act more likely.

As a result of these activated cognitions and feelings, and of the level of arousal, the person has an immediate response. If they are very aroused or if the situation requires immediate action, this will probably be the ultimate response. If the person has the time and cognitive capacity for a more considered response they will evaluate their options and

Figure 5: Ways in which long term exposure to violent video games can increase aggressive cognitions and action tendencies and then feed into episodes of situational aggression

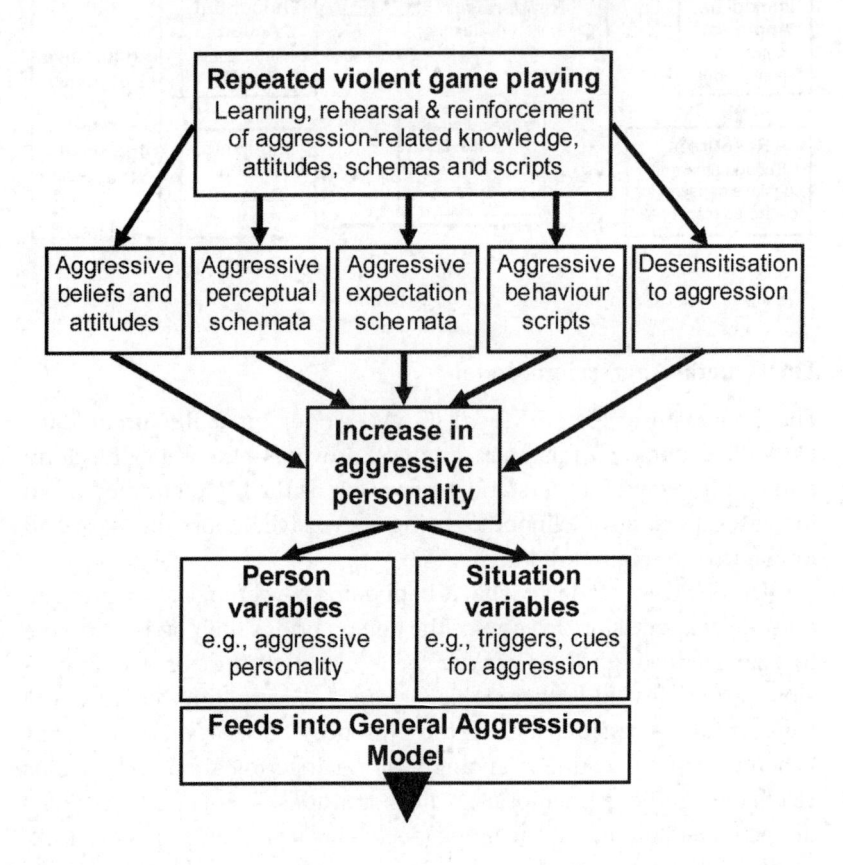

```
          Repeated violent game playing
          Learning, rehearsal & reinforcement
          of aggression-related knowledge,
            attitudes, schemas and scripts

  Aggressive   Aggressive   Aggressive   Aggressive   Desensitisation
  beliefs and  perceptual   expectation  behaviour    to aggression
  attitudes    schemata     schemata     scripts

                    Increase in
                    aggressive
                    personality

          Person              Situation
         variables            variables
       e.g., aggressive    e.g., triggers, cues
         personality         for aggression

         Feeds into General Aggression
                    Model
```

are more likely to make a thought-through response. Either way, the eventual response, which may be aggressive, is enacted, elicits a social response and the episode is encoded into memory. Once in memory, it becomes part of the "person" and can then affect their responses to future situations.

Although "person" characteristics are very important in determining how an individual reacts in a specific situation, the research presented in this chapter reveals that most people, regardless of personal characteristics, are influenced by violent video games. It also reveals that violent video games provide many cues for aggressive behaviour, activate aggressive cognitions and feelings, and can increase levels of arousal. These internal processes can explain why there is also a robust link between violent video game playing and aggressive behaviour.

Over the long term, exposure to the attitudes, ideas and scripts for behaviour in violent video games leads to stable knowledge structures, attitudes, biases in thinking, scripts for conflict resolution and action tendencies that include aggressive behaviour (see Figure 5). In turn, these increase the base level of aggressiveness in that person's personality and bring the person to an aggression-triggering type of situation with a higher predisposition to aggress.

Between the two models, it is easy to see how playing a video game can lead to aggression in the short term, and how repeated playing can lead to higher levels of aggression in the long term.

Conclusions and advice for parents and professionals working with children

In this chapter we have detailed the evidence that video games can be used for a wide array of helpful purposes, but that there can be many negative consequences for playing violent games, especially when played excessively. This raises an important question: "How do we help children to benefit from video games but escape their negative impacts?"

In Chapter 1 it was noted that the "you are what you eat" principle applies to the way media exposure affects the way the human neural network "wires up" as well as to food consumption. Using the food metaphor can be helpful for parents and professionals when it comes to advising children on how to use media in a beneficial way. Through school education many children are interested in healthy eating and this can be extended to maintaining a healthy media diet. For example, children could be told that, as with food, there are media that are good to consume regularly (in moderation), media that are for infrequent consumption and media that children should avoid. Helping a child to self-regulate what they watch and hear in the media can be very important to a child's development in this media saturated world. This may involve:

- educating children about media effects generally and about video game effects specifically, so that children can learn to make informed choices;
- helping children to limit their time playing video games;
- encouraging children to play pro-social and educational video games in preference to violent games;
- keeping video game consoles in public areas and out of children's bedrooms; and
- playing video games with your children so that you are aware of their content and can knowledgeably discuss the implications of playing certain types of games and screen out potentially harmful ones.

It is desirable for children to be able use video games for a range of educational and developmental objectives, but to have less exposure to the more harmful impacts. We hope that this chapter has helped to dispel some popular myths about the impact of violent video games on children and adolescents and has clarified for readers how positive outcomes might be achieved.

A Tragic Postscript

I see MW2 more as a part of my training-simulation than anything else ... You can more or less completely simulate actual operations

These were the chilling words with which Anders Behring Breivik referred to the computer game Modern Warfare 2 in a 1500-page manifesto disseminated just hours before he was responsible for the deaths of 76 of his fellow Norwegians (Moses, 2011; Shah, 2011; Townsend & Tisdall, 2011). The 32-year-old male behind the now infamous bombing of government buildings in Oslo and subsequent shooting massacre on Utoya island on 22 July 2011 made no secret of the fact that playing the violent video games Modern Warfare 2 and World of Warcraft aided him in preparing and executing his attacks. Breivik identified Modern Warfare 2 as helping him with "target practice" (Shah, 2011) and involvement with World of Warcraft as providing sufficient cover for his preparatory activities (Moses, 2011). As a result of the attacks, one of Norway's biggest retailers, Coop Norway, issued a ban of indefinite duration on these and other violent video games that, at the time of publication, has yet to be lifted (Narcisse, 2011; Navarro, 2011). When considering the impact of violent video games, particularly in light of the Norway atrocities, it should also be noted that video games in which acts of violence are executed in first-person, immersive environments have long been recognised and used by the US military forces as effective in both the training and recruitment of their members (Holguin, 2009; Robson, 2008).

References

AAP (American Academy of Pediatrics) (2009). Policy Statement—Media Violence. *Pediatrics, 124,* 1495-1503.

Abrams, A (1986). *Effectiveness of interactive video in teaching basic photography skills.* Paper presented at the Annual convention of the Association for Educational Communication and Technology. Las Vegas, NV, January

ACMA (Australian Communications and Media Authority) (2007). *Media and communications in Australian families, 2007.* Canberra: Australian Communications and Media Authority. Accessed 14 April 2001, <http://www.acma.gov.au/webwr/_assets/main/lib101058/media_and_society_report_2007.pdf>.

Anderson, CA, Berkowitz, L, Donnerstein, E, Huesmann, LR, Johnson, J, Linz, D, Malamuth, N, & Wartella, E (2003). The influence of media violence on youth. *Psychological Science in the Public Interest, 4,* 81–110.

Anderson, CA, & Bushman, BJ (2001). Effects of violent video games on aggressive behavior, aggressive cognition, aggressive affect, physiological arousal, and prosocial behavior: A meta-analytic review of the scientific literature. *Psychological Science, 12,* 353–359.

Anderson, CA, & Bushman, BJ (2002). Human aggression. *Annual Review of Psychology, 53,* 27–51.

Anderson, CA, Carnagey, NL, Flanagan, M, Benjamin, AJ, Eubanks, J, & Valentine, JC (2004). Violent video games: Specific effects of violent content on aggressive thoughts and behavior. *Advances in Experimental Social Psychology, 36,* 199–249.

Anderson, CA, & Gentile, DA (2008). Media violence, aggression, and public policy. In E Borgida & S Fiske (eds), *Beyond common sense: Psychological science in the courtroom* (pp 281–300). Malden, MA: Blackwell.

Anderson, CA, Gentile, DA, & Buckley, KE (2007a). *Violent video game effects on children and adolescents: Theory, research, and public policy*. Oxford: Oxford University Press.

Anderson, CA, Gentile, DA, & Dill, KE (in press). Prosocial, antisocial, and other effects of recreational video games. In DG Singer, & JL Singer (eds), *Handbook of Children and the Media* (2nd ed). Thousand Oaks, CA: Sage.

Anderson, CA, Shibuya, A, Ihori, N, Swing, EL, Bushman, B, Sakamoto, A, Rothstein, HR, & Saleem, M (2010). Violent video game effects on aggression, empathy, and prosocial behavior in Eastern and Western countries. *Psychological Bulletin, 136,* 151–173.

APA (American Psychological Association) (2005). *APA calls for reduction of violence in interactive media used by children and adolescents*. Washington DC: American Psychological Association.

Bailey, K, West, R, & Anderson, CA (2010). A negative association between video game experience and proactive cognitive control. *Psychophysiology, 47,* 34–42.

Bandura, A (1965). Influence of models' reinforcement contingencies on the acquisition of imitative responses. *Journal of Personality and Social Psychology, 1,* 589–595.

Bandura, A (1973). *Aggression: A social learning analysis*. Englewood Cliffs, NJ: Prentice Hall.

Bandura, A, Ross, D, & Ross, SA (1961). Transmission of aggression through imitation of aggressive models. *Journal of Abnormal and Social Psychology, 63,* 575–582.

Bandura, A, Ross, D, & Ross, SA (1963a). A comparative test of the status envy, social power, and secondary reinforcement theories of identificatory learning. *Journal of Abnormal and Social Psychology, 67,* 527–534.

Bandura, A, Ross, D, & Ross, SA (1963b). Imitation of aggression through imitation of film-mediated aggressive models. *Journal of Abnormal and Social Psychology, 66,* 3–11.

Barlett, CP, Anderson, CA, & Swing, EL (2009). Video game effects confirmed, suspected and speculative: A review of the evidence. *Simulation and Gaming, 40,* 377–403.

Baron, RA (1971a). Aggression as a function of magnitude of victim's pain cues, level of prior anger arousal, and aggressor-victim similarity. *Journal of Personality and Social Psychology, 18,* 48–54.

Baron, RA (1971b). Magnitude of victim's pain cues and level of prior anger arousal as determinants of adult aggressive behavior. *Journal of Personality and Social Psychology, 17,* 236–243.

Baron, RA (1979). Effects of victim's pain cues, victim's race, and level of prior *instigation* upon physical aggression. *Journal of Applied Social Psychology, 9,* 103–114.

Bartholow, BD, Anderson, CA, Carnagey, NL, & Benjamin, AJ (2005). Interactive effects of life experience and situational cues on aggression: The weapons priming effect in hunters and nonhunters. *Journal of Experimental Social Psychology, 41,* 48–60.

Berkowitz, L (1993). *Aggression: Its causes, consequences, and control*. New York: McGraw-Hill.

Berkowitz, L, & Alioto, JT (1973). The meaning of an observed event as a determinant of its aggressive consequences. *Journal of Personality and Social Psychology, 28,* 206–217.

Berkowitz, L, & LePage, A (1967). Weapons as aggression-eliciting stimuli. *Journal of Personality and Social Psychology, 7,* 202–207.

Bushman, BJ, & Anderson, CA (2002). Violent video games and hostile expectations: A test of the general aggression model. *Personality and Social Psychology Bulletin, 28,* 1679–1686.

Bushman, BJ, & Huesmann, LR (2006). Short-term and long-term effects of violent media on aggression in children and adults. *Archives of Pediatrics and Adolescent Medicine, 160,* 348–352.

Bushman, BJ, Rothstein, HR, & Anderson, CA (2010). Much ado about something: Violent video game effects and a school of red herring: Reply to Ferguson and Kilburn. *Psychological Bulletin, 136,* 182–187.

Caggiano, V, Fogassi, L, Rizzolatti, G, Their, P, & Casile, A (2009). Mirror neurons differentially encode the peripersonal and extrapersonal space of monkeys. *Science, 324,* 403–406.

Calvert, J (2003, October 23). *Families sue over GTA III-inspired shooting.* ZDNet News. Accessed 14 April 2011, <http://www.zdnet.com.au/families-sue-over-gta-iii-inspired-shooting-120280063.htm>.

Cantor, J (1994). Fright reactions to mass media. In J Bryant & D Zillmann (eds), *Media effects: Advances in theory and research* (pp 213–245). Hillsdale, NJ: Erlbaum.

Cantor, J (2003). Media and fear in children and adolescents. In DA Gentile (ed), *Media Violence and Children* (pp 185–203). Westport, Connecticut: Praeger.

Carlson, M, Marcus-Newhall, A, & Miller, N (1990). Effects of situational aggression cues: A quantitative review. *Journal of Personality and Social Psychology, 58,* 622–633.

Chan, PA, & Rabinowitz, T (2006). A cross-sectional analysis of video games and attention deficit hyperactivity disorder symptoms in adolescents. *Annals of General Psychiatry, 5,* 16–27.

Chiu, S-I, Lee, J-Z, & Huang, D-H (2004). Video game addiction in children and teenagers in Taiwan. *CyberPsychology and Behavior, 7,* 571–581.

Choo, H, Gentile, DA, Sim, T, Li, D, Khoo, A, Liau, AK (2010). Pathological video gaming among Singaporean youth. *Annals of the Academy of Medicine Singapore, 39,* 822–829.

Comstock G, & Strasburger, VC (1990). Deceptive appearances, television violence and aggressive behaviour – An introduction. *Journal of Adolescent Health Care, 11,* 31–44.

Corbett, AT, Koedinger, KR, & Hadley, W (2001). Cognitive tutors: From the research classroom to all classrooms. In PS Goodman (ed), *Technology enhanced learning* (pp 235–263). Mahwah, NJ: Lawrence Erlbaum.

Cordes, C, & Miller, E (2000). *Fool's gold: A critical look at computers in childhood.* College Park, MD: Alliance for Childhood.

Cummings, HMM, & Vandewater, EAP (2007). Relation of adolescent video game play to time spent in other activities. *Archives of Pediatric and Adolescent Medicine, 161(7),* 684–689.

DeWall, CN, Anderson, CA, & Bushman, BJ (2011). The general aggression model: Theoretical extensions to violence. *Psychology of Violence, 1,* 245–258.

Dill, KE (2009). *How fantasy becomes reality: Seeing through media influence.* New York: Oxford University Press.

Dill, KE, Gentile, DA, Richter, WA, & Dill, JC (2005). Violence, sex, age and race in popular video games: A content analysis. In E Cole & J Henderson-Daniel (eds), *Featuring Females: Feminist Analyses of Media* (pp 115–130). Washington, DC: American Psychological Association.

Donnerstein, E, Slaby, RG, & Eron, LD (1994). The mass media and youth aggression. In LD Eron, JH Gentry, & P Schlegel (eds), *Reason to hope: A psychosocial perspective on violence and youth* (pp 219–250). Washington DC: American Psychological Association.

Ferguson, CJ, & Kilburn, J (2009). The public health risks of media violence: A meta-analytic review. *Journal of Pediatrics, 154,* 759–763.

Feshbach, S (1972). Reality and fantasy in filmed violence. In GA Comstock & EA Rubinstein (eds), *Television and social behavior: A technical report to the Surgeon General's Scientific Advisory Committee on Television and Social Behavior: Vol. 3. Television and adolescent aggressiveness* (DHEW Publication No HSM 72-9058, pp 318–345). Washington, DC: US Government Printing Office.

Gallese, V, Fadiga, L, Fogassi, L, & Rizzolatti, G (1996). Action recognition in the premotor cortex. *Brain, 119,* 593–609.

Geen, RG (1975). The meaning of observed violence: Real vs. fictional violence and consequent effects on aggression and emotional arousal. *Journal of Research in Personality, 9,* 270–281.

Gentile, DA (2009). Pathological video-game use among youth ages 8 to 18: A national study. *Psychological Science, 20,* 594–602.

Gentile, DA, Anderson, CA, Yukawa, S, Ihori, N, Saleem, M, Ming, LK, Shibuya, A, Liau, AK, Khoo, A, & Sakamoto, A (2009). The effects of prosocial video games on prosocial behaviors: International evidence from correlational, experimental, and longitudinal studies. *Personality and Social Psychology Bulletin, 35,* 752–763.

Gentile, DA, & Gentile, JR (2008). Violent video games as exemplary teachers: A conceptual analysis. *Journal of Youth and Adolescence, 9,* 127–141.

Gentile, DA, Oberg, C, Sherwood, NE, Story, M, Walsh, DA, & Hogan, M (2004). Well-child exams in the video age: Pediatricians and the AAP guidelines for children's media use. *Pediatrics, 114,* 1235–1241.

Gentile, DA, Saleem, M, & Anderson, CA (2007). Public policy and the effects of media violence on children. *Social Issues and Policy Review, 1,* 15–61.

Gopher, D, Weil, M, & Bareket, T (1994). Transfer of skill from a computer game trainer to flight. *Human Factors, 36,* 387–405.

Green, CS, & Bavelier, D (2006). Effect of action video games on the spatial distribution of visuospatial attention. *Journal of Experimental Psychology: Human Perception and Performance, 32,* 1465–1478.

Greitemeyer, T, & Osswald, S (2009). Prosocial video games reduce aggressive cognitions. *Journal of Experimental Social Psychology, 45,* 896–900.

Groebel, J (1998). *The UNESCO Global Study on Media Violence: A joint project of UNESCO, the World Organization of the Scout Movement and Utrecht University, The Netherlands.* Report presented to the Director General of UNESCO, UNESCO, Paris.

Grüsser, SM, Thalemann, R, & Griffiths, MD (2007). Excessive computer game playing: Evidence for addiction and aggression? *CyberPsychology and Behavior, 10,* 290–292.

Hearold, S (1986). A synthesis of 1043 effects of television on social behavior. In G Comstock (ed), *Public communication and behavior* (Vol 1, pp 65–133). New York: Academic Press.

Heath, L, Bresolin, LB, & Rinaldi, RC (1989). Effects of media violence on children. *Archives of General Psychiatry, 46,* 376–379.

Holguin, J (2009). Uncle sam wants video gamers. *CBS News,* 11 February. Accessed 27 August 2011, <http://www.cbsnews.com/stories/2005/02/08/eveningnews/main672455.shtml>.

Huesmann, LR (1986). Psychological processes promoting the relation between exposure to media violence and aggressive behavior by the viewer. *Journal of Social Issues, 42,* 125–140.

Huesmann, LR (1998). The role of social information processing and cognitive schema in the acquisition and maintenance of habitual aggressive behavior. In RG Geen & E Donnerstein (eds), *Human aggression: Theories, research and implications for social policy* (pp 73–109). San Diego CA: Academic Press.

Huesmann, LR (2010). Nailing the coffin shut on doubts that violent video games stimulate aggression: Comment on Anderson et al (2010). *Psychological Bulletin, 136,* 179–181.

Huesmann, LR, & Eron, LD (eds) (1986). *Television and the aggressive child: A cross-national comparison.* Hillsdale NJ: Lawrence Erlbaum and Associates.

Huesmann, LR, Moise-Titus, J, Podolski, C, & Eron, L (2003). Longitudinal relations between children's exposure to TV violence and their aggressive and violent behavior on young adulthood. *Developmental Psychology, 39,* 201–221.

Huston, AC, Donnerstein, E, Fairchild, H, Feshbach, ND, Katz, PA, Murray, JP, Rubinstein, EA, Wilcox, BL, & Zuckernan, D (1992). *Big world. small screen: The role of television in American Society.* Lincoln: University of Nebraska Press.

Johansson, A, & Götestam, KG (2004). Problems with computer games without monetary reward: Similarity to pathological gambling. *Psychological Reports, 95,* 641–650.

Kahn, K (1999). *A computer game to teach programming.* Paper presented at the National Educational Computing Conference, Atlantic City, NJ, June.

Kirsch, SJ (2010). *Media and youth: A developmental perspective.* Malden MA: Wiley Blackwell.

Krahé, B, & Möller, I (2004). Playing violent electronic games, hostile attributional style, and aggression-related norms in German adolescents. *Journal of Adolescence, 27,* 53–69.

Lenhart, A, Kahne, J, Middaugh, E, Macgill, ER, Evans, C, & Vitak, J (2008). *Teens, video games, and civics.* Washington, DC: Pew Internet and American Life Project.

Leung, R (2005). Can a video game lead to murder? Did 'Grand Theft Auto' cause one teenager to kill? CBS News, 17 June. Accessed 14 April 2011, <http://www.cbsnews.com/stories/2005/06/17/60minutes/main702599.shtml>.

Lieberman, DA (2001). Management of chronic pediatric diseases with interactive health games: Theory and research findings. *Journal of Ambulatory Care Management, 24,* 26–38.

Lieberman, DA (2006). What can we learn from playing video games? In P Vorderer and J Bryant (eds), *Playing video games: Motives, responses, and consequences* (pp 379–397). Mahwah: NJ: Lawrence Erlbaum.

Möller, I, & Krahé, B (2009). Exposure to violent video games and aggression in German adolescents: A Longitudinal analysis. *Aggressive Behavior, 35,* 75–89.

Moses, A (2011). *From fantasy to lethal reality: Breivik trained on Modern Warfare game* Sydney Morning Herald Online, 25 July. Accessed 27 August 2011, <http://www.smh.com.au/digital-life/games/from-fantasy-to-lethal-reality-breivik-trained-on-modern-warfare-game-20110725-1hw41.html>.

Murphy, RF, Penuel, WR, Means, B, Korbak, C, Whaley, A, & Allen, JE (2002). *A review of recent evidence on the effectiveness of discrete educational software.* Washington, DC: Planning and Evaluation Service, US Department of Education.

Narcisse, E (2011). *Norway retail chain pulling violent video games in wake of Breivik killings.* Time – Techland, 1 August. Accessed 27 August 2011, <http://techland.time.com/2011/08/01/norway-retail-chain-pulling-violent-video-games-in-wake-of-breivik-killings>.

Navarro, A (2011). *Norwegian retailer indefinitely bans 'violent video games' even though no one asked.* Giant Bomb, 29 July. Accessed 27 August 2011, <http://www.giantbomb.com/news/norwegian-retailer-indefinitely-bans-violent-video-games-even-though-no-one-asked/3536/>.

Okagaki, L, & Frensch, PA (1994). Effects of interactive entertainment technologies on development. *Journal of Applied Developmental Psychology, 15,* 33–58.

Ortutay, B (2010). *'Call of Duty: Black Ops' sets earnings record for its 1st day.* TDT News, 12 November. Accessed 8 April 2011, <http://www.tdtnews.com/story/2010/11/12/70137>.

Peng, LH, & Li, X (2009). A survey of Chinese college students addicted to video games. *China Education Innovation Herald, 28*, 111–112.

Reed, J (2008). *Thailand bans Grand Theft Auto IV*. BBC News Online, 4 August. Accessed 14 April 2011, <http://news.bbc.co.uk/newsbeat/hi/technology/newsid_7540000/7540623.stm>.

Rhodes, RE, Warburton, DER, & Bredin, SSD (2009). Predicting the effect of interactive video bikes on exercise adherence: An efficacy trial. *Psychology, Health and Medicine, 14(6)*, 631–640.

Rideout, VJ, Foehr, UG, & Roberts, DF (2010). *Generation M2: Media in the lives of 8-18 year olds*. Merlo Park CA: Henry J Kaiser Foundation.

Rizzolati, G, Fadiga, L, Gallese, V, & Fogassi, L (1996). Premotor cortex and the recognition of motor actions. *Cognitive Brain Research, 3*, 131–141.

Robson, S (2008). *Not playing around: Army to invest $50m in combat training games*. Stars and Stripes, 23 November. Accessed 27 August 2011, <http://www.stripes.com/news/not-playing-around-army-to-invest-50m-in-combat-training-games-1.85595>.

Sell, K, Lillie, T, & Taylor, J (2008). Energy expenditure during physically interactive video game playing in male college students with different playing experience. *Journal of American College Health, 56*, 505–511.

Shah, K (2011). *Oslo killer played video games to 'train'* Tech 2, 28 July. Accessed 27 August 2011, <http://tech2.in.com/news/general/oslo-killer-played-video-games-to-train/232812>.

Sharif, I, & Sargent, JD (2006). Association between television, movie, and video game exposure and school performance. *Pediatrics, 118(4)*, e1061–1070.

Strasburger VC (2009). Why do adolescent health researchers ignore the impact of the media? *Journal of Adolescent Health, 44*, 203–205.

Strasburger, VC, Wilson, BJ, & Jordan, AB (2009). *Children, adolescents, and the media* (2nd ed). Thousand Oaks, CA: Sage.

Swing, EL, & Anderson, CA (2008). How and what do video games teach? In T Willoughby & E Wood (eds), *Children's learning in a digital world* (pp 64–84). Oxford, UK: Blackwell.

Swing, EL, Gentile, DA, Anderson, CA, & Walsh, DA (2010). Television and video game exposure and the development of attention problems. *Pediatrics, 126*, 214–221.

Townsend, M & Tisdall, S (2011). *Defiant from the dock, Breivik boasts more will die*. The Guardian Online, 25 July. Accessed 27 August 2011, <http://www.guardian.co.uk/world/2011/jul/25/anders-behring-breivik-terror-cells>.

Umilta, MA, Kohler, E, Gallese, V, Fogassi, L, Fadiga, L, Keysers, C, & Rizzolatti, G (2001). I know what you are doing. *Neuron, 31*, 155–165.

US Department of Health and Human Services (2001). *Youth violence: A report of the Surgeon General*. Rockville, MD: US Department of Health and Human Services, Centers for Disease Control and Prevention, National Center for Injury Prevention and Control; Substance Abuse and Mental Health Services Administration, Center for Mental Health Services; and National Institutes of Health, National Institute of Mental Health.

Weber, R, Ritterfeld, U, & Mathiak, K (2006). Does playing violent video games induce aggression? Empirical evidence of a functional magnetic resonance imaging study. *Media Psychology, 8*, 39–60.

Ybarrondo, BA (1984). *A study of the effectiveness of computer-assisted instruction in the high school biology classroom*. Idaho (ERIC Document Reproduction Service No Ed265015).

Chapter 4

How does listening to Eminem do me any harm? What the research says about music and anti-social behaviour

Wayne Warburton

My children love music. They hum and sing as they play, dance to music they hear or create, and still like to be sung to sleep when they are upset. As with most children, music plays an integral role in their emotional and social lives, and provides an important soundtrack that accompanies their developmental experiences. Music can have many positive impacts for children of all ages, particularly if it induces a positive mood, encourages pro-social behaviour, or enhances play or other social activities. However, exposure to music with violent and/or anti-social themes has also been linked with a number of detrimental effects, including aggressive and anti-social behaviour, substance use, premature sexual activity and suicide.

Because music, like other media, can both enhance and detract from children's healthy development, this chapter will focus on research findings that can help readers to make informed decisions about what constitutes healthy music use for children and adolescents. To this end, we begin by briefly examining the important role that music plays in the lives of children and adolescents, and provide statistics about the average amount of music that children and adolescents listen to. The following sections examine the positive effects of music on children and youth, the negative effects, and specific effects on aggressive and anti-social behaviour. The chapter concludes with advice for parents and professionals who work with children.

Music in the lives of children and teenagers

The importance of music

Music is of crucial importance in the lives of children and adolescents. Indeed, auditory learning seems to occur even before birth. The famous "Cat in the Hat" study (DeCaspar & Spence, 1986) has shown that reading to babies in the womb changes their behaviour at birth, and other studies show that music presented prenatally predicts music preferences up to a year after childbirth (Hepper, 1991; Lamont, 2001). At birth and during infancy, music is a fundamental medium by which parents communicate with their babies, often through "Infant Directed Singing", whereby parents sing songs to their babies that have a high pitch, slow tempo and are quite expressive (Trehub et al, 1997). Research also demonstrates that infants are fairly sophisticated listeners and have certain innate abilities to process music (eg, Trehub & Trainor, 1993). By 8-9 months babies can discriminate happy from sad music (Flom, Gentile & Pick, 2008), and during infancy and then into childhood music preferences become more differentiated (Roe, 1996) and music features more and more in games, play and social activities.

From childhood into adolescence music contributes increasingly to the consolidation of both personal and group identity, and helps children and youth to assert their personality, learn about new and forbidden things and develop social relationships through shared musical taste (eg, see Roe, 1996). In particular, popular music conveys themes that often resonate with the adolescent experience, such as defiance toward authority, the celebrating of love found and the bemoaning of love lost (Zillman & Gan, 1997). Because of this resonance, music can be used to carve out personal and group identities that are distinctly different, and at times resistant, to those of parents and other sources of authority in adolescent lives (Roe, 1996). In addition, the musicians themselves, by voicing such themes, can become highly admired role models, with considerable potential to influence the behaviour of children and adolescents (Strasburger et al, 2009). Thus, music and the people who make it are an important part of the life experience of children and youth, providing a musical and cultural soundtrack that plays throughout development.

How much?

Children enjoy music from early in life and the amount they listen to grows steadily with age. By primary school, listening to music is almost ubiquitous, with 98 per cent of US fourth to sixth graders listening to popular music and 72 per cent doing so on a daily basis (Christenson, 1992). In the largest recent US study, Rideout and colleagues (2010) found that 8-18-year-olds listened to two hours and 31 minutes of music per day on average, a substantial increase from the one hour and 48 minutes per day found for the same demographic in 1999. Rideout and colleagues also found differences in daily music listening according to gender, race and age. Females spent slightly more time listening to music per day on average than males, and black and Hispanic youth spent significantly more time listening to music than white youth (see Table 1, *over page*). Most notable was the almost linear increase with age, with average music exposure for 8-10-year-olds (one hour and eight minutes per day) increasing to three hours and 21 minutes for 15-18-year-olds. Other studies have also found evidence for consumption of music increasing through adolescence, with 14-16-year-olds reported to listen to music anywhere from 2.5 hours per day (North et al, 2000; Roberts, et al, 2005) to an average of 40 hours per week (American Academy of Pediatrics, 1996).

In Australia, the Australian Communications and Media Authority (ACMA, 2007) study of 8-17-year-olds found that they listened to less music per day than their United States counterparts (an average of 35 minutes per day; ACMA, 2007). This figure seems somewhat low given that by adulthood Australians listen to an average of one hour and 56 minutes per day according to a more recent Neilsen Australian Internet and Technology Report (Neilsen Company, 2010). Since the ACMA data collection in 2006, there has been an explosion in the use of i-pods, i-phones, netbooks, i-pads and laptop computers, all of which can be used to play music and music videos. It thus seems likely that a new poll would find significantly higher music use figures for Australian 8-17-year-olds.

Table 1: Music use in the United States and breakdown by demographics

Breakdown of the US figures – hours spent with music			
Age	8–10	11–14	15–18
Hours per day	1.08	2.36	3.21
Ethnicity	White	Black	Hispanic
Hours per day	1.56	3.00	3.08
Gender	Male	Female	
Hours per day	2.16	2.45	

Source: Rideout et al, 2010

Positive effects of listening to music

Given the prevalence and importance of music in the lives of children and adolescents, it is worthwhile examining the effects that music may have on the listener, beginning with research on the positive impacts.

Positive mood and pro-social behaviours

Bruner (1990) reviewed the effects of music on mood and found that specific types of musical structures could influence tranquillity/peacefulness, excitement, happiness, sadness and "seriousness". This means that music can be used to amplify a desired mood or state, or to counteract an undesired one. Indeed, Roberts and colleagues (2003) note that "for most young people, music use is driven primarily by the motivation to control mood and enhance emotional states" (p 156). Male children and adolescents will often use music to increase their energy level and levels of stimulation, and females to lift their spirits or dwell on a particular mood (Roberts et al, 2003). For infants and toddlers, lullabies are a traditional way to encourage sleep that is found across all cultures (Gregory, 1997).

Apart from simply helping children to feel good, research also suggests that music which induces a good mood in the listener can have a positive effect on their behaviour. Fried and Berkowitz (1979) found that playing soothing and stimulating music invoked positive moods in subjects whilst also increasing the likelihood of subsequent helpful behaviour. Similarly, when North and colleagues (2004) exposed 646 gymnasium users to either uplifting or annoying music during their workout, those who were played uplifting music were significantly more likely to offer their help to others on a costly, hypothetical task. Finally, Krahé and Bieneck (2012) have found that pleasant music reduced levels of anger, aggressive cognitions and aggressive behaviour following a provocation.

There is also evidence to suggest that exposure to music with pro-social lyrics is associated with pro-social behaviour in its listeners. Greitemeyer (2009; 2011) demonstrated that exposure to music with pro-social (compared to neutral) lyrics decreased aggressive thoughts, feelings and behaviours in university students, whilst also increasing the accessibility of pro-social thoughts and producing higher levels of interpersonal empathy and helping behaviours.

Music and musicians with pro-social messages have also been used to educate youth on important social issues. For example, rap music has been used to convey both anti-drug and safe sex messages (Pareles, 1990; Perry, 1995). The Kaiser Foundation, in their "Know HIV AIDS" campaign, used rap and hip hop artists to convey safe sex messages aimed at young African Americans. This campaign had great success, with 94 per cent of surveyed 18–24-year-olds found to be aware of the campaign and an impressive 83 per cent of these reporting they were more likely to take sexual relationships seriously as a result of the campaign (Kaiser Family Foundation, 2003).

Overall, the research findings suggest that if music invokes a good mood or conveys a positive message, it carries the potential to have various positive effects on the attitudes and behaviour of children and youth.

The clinical benefits of music

Music has been used throughout recorded history to soothe, heal and alleviate stress and distress. It is also currently used therapeutically and in clinical practice (see Bunt, 1997). It is beyond the scope of this chapter to go into detail, but music therapy and music in therapy are used to treat both children and adults who have a range of physical and mental health needs, and have been very successful. Music therapy has been used within psycho-analytic, cognitive behavioural and humanistic treatment paradigms, and has assisted many children to develop a healthier sense of self and to reduce aggressive, hyperactive or maladaptive behaviours (eg, Jorgenson, 1974). Music therapy has also assisted many children with attention, numeracy and reading (eg, Roskam, 1979). Interestingly, many genres of music, including rap music, can be used therapeutically with children and youth (eg, Tyson, 2002; 2006).

There are a growing number of music therapists who use the Rogerian "client-centred" approach, whereby music is used in the crucial process of developing empathic and connected client-therapist relations, and in working with clients (including children) towards personal growth, "self-actualisation" and healthy relationships.

Alleviating and dealing with pain

There have been many studies demonstrating the efficacy of music in alleviating pain and anxiety (eg, see Brown et al, 1989; Savarimuthu, 2004). Standley's (1995) review notes that there are least 125 applications in medical and dental practice described in the literature. These include children's respiratory problems, child anxiety, labour during childbirth, neonatal distress/crying and pain during a wide range of other medical/dental procedures and conditions. Standley notes that the benefits of music for pain are stronger for children than adults or infants, stronger for women than for men, stronger where the music is played "live" and changes with the needs of the patient (for example, by a trained music therapist), and are most effective for chronic pain, dental pain, respiratory problems and reducing the need for analgesic pain medication.

Identity formation and relations with peers

Roe (1996) notes that "music plays a central role in the process of identity construction of young people. This process includes not only elements of personal identity but also important aspects of national, regional, cultural, ethnic, and gender identity" (p 85). In terms of children's personal identity formation, changes in music preferences over time are interesting. Roe notes the following chronology that has been demonstrated in the research. Children generally enjoy "children's music" until the age of six or so, but by age four, up to 60 per cent of children are already interested in pop music and by age seven, 40 per cent of children have posters of musicians on their walls. By the age of eight, children begin to be influenced by the musical tastes of their peers and by nine children are increasingly distinguishing their tastes from those of their parents. Roe notes that "by the age of twelve rock and pop dominate completely, distinctions of genre begin to be more finely drawn, and preferences are forcibly articulated". The critical age where music starts to make an impact on child identity formation seems to be around eight, at about the same time as children's ability with abstract concepts makes a quantum leap in their cognitive development. However there is a clear gender effect, whereby girls differentiate their musical tastes earlier than do boys.

This convergence in musical preference as children age is also linked to the increasing influence of peers and the decrease of parental influence. For example, children are loathe to confess to musical tastes that differ from their peers (Finnäs, 1989) and the identity of many peer groups revolves around a preference for a particular musical style such as rap or heavy metal (Hansen & Hansen, 1991; Larson, 1995). Roe's own work in Sweden compared children with a demonstrated preference for rock music by the age of 11, with children who developed this preference later. In subsequent years, those with an early rock preference were significantly more influenced by peers than by parents in their decision-making processes (Roe, 1984), suggesting a clear influence on identity formation processes.

Solitary listening to music may also play an important role in children exploring and integrating their personal identity (Larson, 1995) and musical preferences can be an important facet of the "self" that is prized by individuals (eg, Dittmar, 1992).

Interestingly, national identities are often built around a flag and national anthem, with singing along to the national anthem being a strong symbol of national identity that begins early in schooling (Gregory, 1997). In Australia it is noteworthy that music is crucial to the identity of many Northern Territory Aborigines, with links to geographical location and ancestry expressed through art, music and dance (Magowen, 1994).

Children's games

Children's games are universal across cultures and often involve music and songs (Gregory, 1997). This music often enters new cultures as children move countries. Music enriches play, can be used as a mnemonic for learning key knowledge (such as the alphabet) and is an important social tool that can be shared by multiple children at once.

Courting, dancing, ceremonies and festivals

Music is a significant and positive contributor to many facets of social life, including ceremonies, festivals, dances, sporting events, parties, rallies and commemorative ceremonies (among others). As such, music is central to a number of core human activities that children observe or engage in, such as courting, celebrating, mourning, worshipping and connecting with others (see Crozier, 1997; Gregory, 1997 for reviews).

Educational effects

Much has been made of the so-called "Mozart effect" (Rauscher et al, 1993), which refers to claims that people perform better on tests of spatial abilities after listening to music composed by Mozart (Thompson et al, 2001). This has spurred a lucrative industry in music-based materials advertised as able to make kids "smarter", with titles such as *"Baby Genius"* and *"Baby Einstein Baby Mozart"*. It should be noted that the Mozart effect, when found, has been short-lived (10–15 minutes) rather than enduring, and may be due to changes to arousal and mood rather than the qualities of the music itself (eg, Thompson et al, 2001). In fact, preschoolers do better on tests of cognitive ability after listening to *any* type of music they like – even if it is pop music (and indeed, even after listening to stories they like: Nantais & Schellenberg, 1999; Schellenberg & Hallam, 2005). There have been very few studies on children under 12 and Kirsch (2010) concludes there is little or no scientific evidence for a Mozart effect in infant, child or adolescent samples (see also Črnčec et al, 2006).

In terms of the benefits of music in educational settings, nearly 60 years of research has revealed no benefit to academic performance by having background music playing in regular classrooms. However, there is some evidence that soothing background music can help special needs students with concentration and with maths tasks (Črnčec et al, 2006).

Negative effects of listening to music

The body of research into violent or anti-social visual media effects is huge and, in comparison, research about violent/anti-social music seems relatively neglected (Fischer & Greitmeyer, 2006; Strasburger et al, 2009; Warburton, Gilmour and Laczkowski, 2008). Nevertheless, over the last three decades there has been a steady stream of research findings about the possible negative effects of exposure to music with violent and/or anti-social themes. This research suggests links with aggression, anti-social behaviour, substance use, premature sexual behaviours, misogynistic attitudes and suicide. Before examining these effects in detail, there is some value in looking more closely at two genres of music that are more likely than others to contain these types of themes: rap and heavy metal (for reviews see American Academy of Pediatrics, 1996; 2009). Readers are warned that the following section contains lyrics and titles that they may find offensive and/or upsetting.

Rap music and heavy/death metal music

Music genres with extremely violent and/or anti-social themes such as suicide, mass murder and extreme sexual violence have had a low profile in the past but are becoming increasingly available to a wider audience over the internet (Whelan, 2010).

Rap music frequently features lyrics with angry, violent and anti-social themes that seem to reflect the lifestyles led by many high-profile artists within the genre. Police arrests, drug use, incarceration and murder have been a heavily publicised part of the lives of famous rap artists including Snoop Dogg, Tupac Shakur, Dr Dre, Lil Wayne and Biggie Smalls. As Samuels et al (2000) succinctly surmise, "hard core rap music [is] now driven almost exclusively by sex, violence and materialism", a conclusion also shared by some rap artists such as Mos Def. The highly misogynistic and anti-social themes prominent in many rap songs are exemplified in the music of the hugely successful rap artist Eminem. Take, for example, the song "Kill You", from *The Marshall Mathers LP*, which has sold in excess of 19 million copies:

> They said I can't rap about bein broke no more They say I can't rap about coke no more (AHHH!) Slut, you think I won't choke no whore til the vocal cords don't work in her throat no more?! (AHHH!) These motherfuckers are thinkin I'm playin Thinkin I'm sayin the shit cause I'm thinkin it just to be sayin it (AHHH!) Put your hands down bitch, I ain't gon' shoot you I'ma pull +YOU+ to this bullet, and put it through you (AHHH!) Shut up slut, you're causin too much chaos Just bend over and take it slut, okay Ma? "Oh, now he's raping his own mother, abusing a whore, snorting coke, and we gave him the Rolling Stone cover?" You god damn right BITCH, and now it's too late I'm triple platinum and tragedies happen in two states I invented violence, you vile venomous volatile bitches vain Vicadin, vrinnn Vrinnn, VRINNN! {*chainsaw revs up*} Texas Chainsaw, left his brains all danglin from his neck, while his head barely hangs on Blood, guts, guns, cuts Knives, lives, wives, nuns, sluts
> © Marshall Mathers III 2000 Aftermath Entertainment/Interscope Records

A number of violent themes are clearly manifest in this one small excerpt – in particular choking a "whore", shooting a "bitch", "raping his own mother" and "abusing a whore". There are also various cues for aggression, with the graphic description of a beheading with a chainsaw (accompanied by the sound of a chainsaw revving), as well as lines with numerous aggressive keywords (for example, "Blood, guts, guns, cuts, knives, lives, wives, nuns, sluts"). Like many rap songs the lyrics to "Kill You" also have an extreme misogyny, with women referred to as "sluts", "whores" and "vile venomous volatile bitches" just in this verse. The word "bitch", for example, is used 10 times in the song.

Heavy metal music and its sub-genre death metal (referred to from now on as heavy/death metal) are characterised by violent themes, including a frequent focus on death, murder, suicide, explicit sexual violence, anti-social behaviour and misogyny. A preference for such music has been linked to higher levels of "machismo" in its listeners. In addition, those with a preference for heavy/death metal are more likely to believe that the number of people who hold antisocial attitudes, use drugs and practice the occult is greater than the number of people who do so in reality (Strasburger et al, 2009). Although many lyrics in heavy/death metal are hard to understand, devotees of the genres are more likely than fans of other genres to listen closely to and know the lyrics to the songs, to feel that the music is an important part of their lives and to identify with performers (Arnett, 1991; 1998; Greenfield et al, 1987; Roberts et al, 2003; 2005).

There are many thousands of death metal bands, as a visit to <www.darklyrics.com> will reveal. One band that has two decades of albums, and is well-known to the point of having devotees in most courses I teach on, is Cannibal Corpse.

I remember clearly the first time I watched a Cannibal Corpse video clip. Their lead singer, George "Corpsegrinder" Fisher dedicated the song to "all the women out there tonight" and proceeded to sing "F - - k with a knife", a song about raping and dismembering a female victim. The lyrics were almost impossible to understand, but it was clear they were well known to many of the fans, male and female, who shouted the lyrics as they danced. One female fan with outstretched hands was carried away from the stage by bouncers. After the song concluded and the next song – "Stripped, raped and strangled" – was introduced with further reference to the women in the crowd, I closed the link to ponder the appeal of what I had seen.

Readers may wonder whether this is just a very extreme example. It does not seem so. The titles of Cannibal Corpse albums and songs are brutally unambiguous and consistently reveal anti-social themes:

Albums:

- *Butchered at Birth* (1991)
- *Hammer Smashed Face* (1993)
- *Gallery of Suicide* (1998)
- *Kill* (2006)
- *Evisceration Plague* (2009)

Songs:

- *Meat hook sodomy*
- *Entrails ripped from a virgin's c – – t*
- *She was asking for it*
- *Necropedophile*
- *Relentless beating*
- *Murder worship*
- *Five nails through the neck*
- *Submerged in boiling flesh*
- *Dismembered and molested*
- *Frantic disembowelment*
- *Hacksaw decapitation*

Clearly, the rap and heavy/death metal genres have a disproportionate number of songs devoted to, or describing, violent or anti-social behaviours. In this section, we look at research about the specific influences of such music on thoughts, feelings and behaviours in a number of key domains relevant to child and adolescent development.

Substance use

References to substance use are prevalent in popular music. In Markert's (2001) analysis of popular songs from 1960–1998, 800 explicitly described drug use. Primack et al (2008) found that, of the most popular songs in 2005, 42 per cent referenced cigarette, alcohol or drug use. Importantly, the frequency of references to substance use differed markedly by genre. Ninety per cent of the most popular rap songs contained references to substance use compared to 41 per cent of country songs, 27 per cent of R&B/HipHop songs and 23 per cent of rock songs. Of the songs that contained references to substance use, 68 per cent suggested positive substance-use outcomes, most commonly in the context of parties and sexual activity, and only 16 per cent suggested negative outcomes. Overall, the data of Primack and colleagues shows that "the average [US] adolescent is exposed to approximately 84 references to explicit substance use daily in popular songs" (p 169). Other studies have also found that rap lyrics contain a disproportionate amount of substance use references. Roberts et al (2005) found that 53 per cent of the rap songs they examined contained references to both alcohol and marijuana and 37 per cent of these songs referenced other illicit drugs. Gruber et al (2005) examined 359 music videos and found that 50 per cent of rap videos showed alcohol use and 31 per cent showed illicit drug use, whilst the figures for pop, rock and R&B videos were 26–27 per cent for alcohol use and 0–9 per cent for illicit drug use.

Clearly much popular music describes substance use, but does this actually lead to more substance use in children and youth? The results of a number of studies suggest there may be a relationship. Teenagers who watched multiple hours of music videos were found to be 239 per cent more likely to use alcohol when going out (Van den Buck et al, 2006) and listening to rap music has been associated with more alcohol use, drug use and aggression than listening to other genres (Chen et al, 2006). Listening to rap music has also been found to increase the odds of drinking alcohol by 150 per cent in females and exposure to high amounts of rap videos was found to be associated with higher levels of illicit drug use, even when relevant variables such as faith and parental control were held constant (Wingood et al, 2003). Primack and colleagues (2009) reported a correlation between exposure to cannabis references in popular music and early cannabis use amongst urban American adolescents.

Studies have also shown that among teenagers hospitalised for psychiatric illness, those with addictions were nearly four times as likely to prefer heavy metal music (King 1988; Weidiger & Demi, 1991). A large study in a normal population of US 14–16-year-olds also found a link between heavy metal preference and the use of various substances (Klein et al, 1993).

As with all correlational data, these results cannot be interpreted as proving causation. However, there are good theoretical grounds for suggesting a causal relationship between pro-substance song lyrics, substance use in the lifestyles of admired artists and substance use in children and adolescents. Research on advertising (see Chapters 1 and 6), research on imitation, learned behaviours and identification with role models (see Chapters 1 and 3), and research on the effects of parents' substance use on children's substance use, all suggest that the modelling and affirmation of substance use by important role models (either through their behaviour or through their music) can have a powerful effect on children's behaviour.

Anti-social behaviour

Links have also been found between listening to music genres with a high prevalence of violent/anti-social themes and anti-social behaviour. For example, in a study of 235 American adolescents, Arnett (1992) found that those reporting a preference for hard rock or heavy metal music reported higher levels of reckless behaviour such as speeding, unsafe sex, substance use, vandalism, shoplifting and driving whilst intoxicated. In another study of 2700 American teenagers aged 14–16, white males who reported five or more anti-social behaviours such as cigarette smoking, alcohol use, cheating at school, sexual promiscuity, wagging school, stealing and illegal drug use were the group most likely to report a preference for listening to heavy metal music (Klein et al, 1993). A further study that followed 522 African American adolescent females for a year found that those who watched 20 or more hours of rap videos per week were three times as likely to have hit a teacher, 2.5 times as likely to have been arrested and 1.5 to 2 times more likely to have had multiple sex partners, acquired a sexually transmitted disease, or used illegal drugs or alcohol (Peterson et al, 2007; Wingood et al, 2003).

Allen and colleagues (2007) reviewed and analysed 23 studies (with over 7000 participants) that had examined the link between popular music exposure and various anti-social attitudes, including toward violence, aggression, illegal drug use, vandalism, delinquency, racism and date rape. They found, on average, a robust positive relationship (r=.23) that was stronger for experimental than for correlational studies. This provides some basis for the assertion of Hansen and Hansen (1990) that even brief exposure to music videos with anti-social content can lead to greater acceptance of anti-social behaviours.

Sexual Behaviour

In terms of mass media with sexual themes, music is a medium that is especially influential for teenagers (Pardun et al, 2005). Sexual content in music is very appealing to young people (Hansen & Hansen, 1990; 2000). The addition of sexual images via music videos makes music more exciting again for adolescents (Zillmann & Mundorf, 1987) and may amplify the effect on youth (Greenfield & Beagles-Roos, 1988; Strasburger & Hendren, 1995). As noted in the previous section, music with anti-social lyrical content has been shown in a number of studies to have an impact on sexual behaviour in adolescent populations (Arnett, 1992; Klein et al, 1993; Peterson et al, 2007). Two further studies have examined sexual content explicitly. Martino and colleagues (2006) studied 1500 adolescents aged 12-17 and found that those who listened to music with lyrics that focused on casual sex, or which framed women as sex objects, were more likely than peers listening to other music to be having intercourse and to be advanced in sexual activities, even after statistically controlling for 18 other variables linked to early intercourse. They also concluded that music is a key medium by which teenagers learn about sex. Brown et al (2006) studied more than 1000 early adolescents (12-14) in North Carolina and found that exposure to sexual content in music accelerated teen sexual activity, as well as doubled the likelihood of early intercourse.

Misogynistic attitudes

In their analysis of 40 MTV music videos, Sommers-Flanagan and colleagues (1993) found an implicit misogyny, whereby men were portrayed as engaging in significantly more aggressive and dominant behaviour, whilst women were portrayed as engaging in more implicitly sexual and subservient behaviour, and were more frequently the object of sexual advances. Misogyny in music has become less subtle and more prevalent in recent years (Fischer & Greitemeyer, 2006), particularly in the rap and heavy/death metal genres, where the lyrics can be brutally misogynistic. There is now a fairly strong base of research suggesting that exposure to such music increases misogynistic attitudes in listeners in both the short- and long-term. For example, adolescent males with a high amount of music video exposure have been found to be more accepting of rape (Kaestle et al, 2007) and more likely to endorse violent behaviour in hypothetical conflicts (Johnson et al, 1995). Other studies have found that exposing males to violent music increased their adversarial sexual beliefs (Peterson & Pfost, 1989) and that males who heard misogynous lyrics were significantly more aggressive than controls to a female (compared to male) confederate (Fischer & Greitemeyer, 2006). Kistler and Moon (2010) exposed participants in their study to hip hop music with highly sexualised or minimally sexualised content and found, like Kaestle and colleagues, that males who watched the highly sexualised content were more likely to subsequently objectify women and be accepting of rape.

This type of effect is not just isolated to male misogyny. Adolescent women exposed to rap music with lyrics about female subordination were also found to be more accepting of date violence toward women than control subjects (Johnson, Jackson & Gatto, 1995).

Suicide

It is not uncommon for songs from the heavy metal/death metal genres to have themes about suicide. Indeed, there have been (unsuccessful) lawsuits against the band Judas Priest and against Ozzy Osbourne, by parents claiming their children's suicide was partially caused by the effect of their songs "Better by you, better than me" and "Suicide solution" respectively. The question is, does the research support such a link?

In an early study, Martin and colleagues (1993) found that thoughts of suicide and acts of deliberate self-harm were significantly associated with a preference for rock and heavy metal music. In another study carried out across 50 US States, Stack et al (1994) correlated subscriptions to heavy metal magazines and suicide rates. The higher the subscription rate, the higher the suicide rate, with subscription rates accounting for 51 per cent of the variance in youth suicide. In 1999, Scheel and Westefeld published a study which found that heavy metal fans from a US high school had more thoughts of suicide than non-listeners.

Although possibly indicative, these findings clearly cannot be used to infer the existence of a causal relationship between heavy metal music and youth suicide, or to infer that heavy metal music is a key contributor to many youth suicides. Personal and family circumstances are just two examples of major contributors to youth suicide that extend well beyond music preference. However, as Stack et al (1994) suggest, music with suicidal themes may nurture suicidal tendencies already present in members of the heavy metal subculture or, indeed, attract such members into the heavy metal subculture. Perhaps the safest approach, based on the research evidence, is to think of music with suicidal themes as one of many possible risk factors for adolescent suicide.

Violent and anti-social music

Music with violent and anti-social themes has been linked with acceptance of anti-social behaviour (Hansen & Hansen, 1990), acceptance of violence and date violence (Johnson et al, 1995; Johnson, Jackson & Gatto, 1995b), aggressive thoughts and feelings (Anderson et al, 2003; Warburton, Gilmour and Laczkowski, 2008), desensitisation to violence (Peterson & Pfost, 1989), hostility (Rubin et al, 2001) and risk taking (Arnett, 1992). More recent studies have also found links to aggressive behaviour (Brummert-Lennings & Warburton, 2011; Fischer & Greitemeyer, 2006; Warburton et al, 2008a).

Not all studies, however, have found such links. Ballard and Coates (1995) found no effect of violent song lyrics on levels of anger, Wanamaker and Reznikoff (1989) found no effects of violent lyrics on levels of hostility and St Lawrence and Joiner (1991) found no effect of sexually violent lyrics on males' acceptance of violence against women. Other studies, such as those of Wester et al (1997) have produced mixed results.

Given this inconsistency, it is fair to ask whether research in this area is able to provide any clear answers about violent music effects. In my view, it is.

After careful examination of the methods used in studies that failed to find an effect of violent music, Anderson and colleagues (2003) suggested that these "null-results" may have been due to "methodological problems involving confounds with arousal, or lyrics that were indecipherable" (p 961). More recent studies have tried to avoid previous methodological shortcomings by choosing songs for lyrical clarity, matching them for arousal and using multiple song stimuli. These studies have tended to find consistent effects of violent music on aggressive thoughts, feelings and behaviours (eg, Anderson et al, 2003; Brummert-Lennings & Warburton, 2011; Fischer & Greitemeyer, 2006).

One musical medium that seems to have substantial potential to influence levels of aggression and anti-social behaviour in children and youth is the music video.

Music videos

When considering the potentially negative effects of exposure to music videos with violent or anti-social songs and/or themes, it is important to distinguish between "performance" videos (simply comprising footage of the song being performed) and "concept" videos that include themed materials designed to complement the song they accompany. On television channels that play music videos (such as MTV), these tend to be split fairly evenly in programming (Strasburger et al, 2009). For this chapter, concept music videos are of greatest interest as they are likely to convey violent and/or anti-social themes more explicitly and with greater intensity than performance videos.

Content analyses of contemporary concept videos have confirmed the prevalence of themes that are antisocial or unhelpful for children's development. Escobar-Chaves and colleagues (2005) found that the most common themes in concept videos were sex, violence and crime. An early study by Davis (1985; as cited in Strasburger et al, 2009) found a high level of nihilistic themes such as destruction, death and aggression against authority. DuRant et al (2011) analysed 518 videos and found that 14.7 per cent contained overt violence, with over 90 per cent of violent videos portraying a man using violence and/or carrying a weapon. Violent episodes and weapon carrying were significantly more likely to be portrayed in rock and rap videos than in videos of other genres. This is borne out by a study of rap music videos by Jones (1997) which found that 36 per cent contained explicit violence and 59 per cent included frequent talk about guns. In addition, the content of MTV (a popular music video television channel with over 400 million subscribers in more than 60 countries), has been analysed by a number of media researchers. It has been reported that 57 per cent of concept videos shown on MTV contain violence and that in 90 per cent of these, the aggressor, typically a white male, is portrayed as both the protagonist and hero, with the outcomes of their aggression rarely shown (Ashby & Rich, 2005; Strasburger et al, 2009).

Given the preponderance of violent content on MTV, the findings of Waite et al (1992) are particularly interesting. They examined the effect of removing MTV from a maximum-security forensic hospital. They first measured the aggression levels of 222 patients for a period of 33 weeks. Then, MTV was removed and aggression levels were measured for a further 22 weeks. As can be seen in Table 2, the removal of MTV resulted in a large reduction in aggression across a number of dimensions.

Table 2: A summary of Waite et al's (1992) findings

Type of aggression	% Reduction
Verbal aggression	32.4
Against objects	51.7
Against others	47.5
Against self	5.5

In another study, Gentile and colleagues (2003) found that peers and teachers of third to fifth grade children who regularly watched MTV rated those children as being significantly more aggressive than children who did not watch MTV regularly. In addition, these children provided self-reports of higher engagement in physical fights than children who did not watch MTV regularly.

In their review of the research literature about the effect of music videos on adolescent attitudes, beliefs and behaviours, Ashby and Rich (2005) found links with adolescent aggression, acceptance of violence, alcohol consumption, risky sexual behaviour and body dissatisfaction. In one example cited, Hansen and Hansen (1990) examined the links between music videos and attitudes approving anti-social behaviour. They found that, compared to those who watched neutral videos, those who watched music videos with anti-social content were more likely to have a favourable impression of, and to like, a man they subsequently saw perform an antisocial act.

Given the strong link that past research has established between aggression and exposure to violent visual media, the potential for violent video clips to magnify the negative effects of auditory exposure to violent music has been noted by a number of researchers (eg, see Strasburger et al, 2009). Little research has tested this directly, however, and a series of consistent findings would be required to be confident about such an assertion.

Song lyrics and musical tone

Within literature examining the effects of exposure to violent music, much of the academic debate has been about whether they are more driven by violent song lyrics or by an aggressive musical "tone" in the songs. Researchers who have questioned the importance of lyrics have tended to do so either because they question the extent to which potentially damaging lyrics can be understood by those of a young age (or understood at all in some genres), or because they think that lyrics have less influence on behaviour than the "tone" and characteristics of the music itself. For example, Greenfield et al (1987) argue that lyrics can only have a negative effect if they are completely understood, and that comprehension is dependent on knowledge and life experience. In their study, 10 per cent of fourth graders in comparison to 95 per cent of college students were able to correctly interpret Madonna's "Like a Virgin". Not knowing what a virgin is, the authors suggest, reduces the potential for exposure to such lyrics to negatively affect a fourth grader. Prinsky and Rosenbaum (1987) made a similar argument, finding that teenagers' understanding of lyrics is influenced by their lack of experience and literary abilities, and is shaped more by what they desire the song to be about and less by what the song is actually about.

In terms of the effect of lyrics on hostility and aggression, some studies have already been noted as failing to find a lyrics effect (eg, Ballard & Coates, 1995; St Lawrence & Joiner, 1991; Wanamaker & Reznikoff, 1989), consistent with this line of argument. However, contrary to this approach, a number of well-designed recent studies have found a negative effect of violent or anti-social song lyrics. In the Fischer and Greitemeyer (2006) study, both males and females, after hearing misogynous or men-hating (compared to neutral) lyrics, were found to recall more negative attributes and report more feelings of vengeance towards members of the opposite sex. Males were also more likely to aggress against females after hearing misogynistic (compared to neutral) lyrics. Similarly, Anderson and colleagues (2003), across five methodologically careful experiments, found that exposure to violent (compared to non-violent) lyrics increased levels of hostility and aggressive thoughts in a sample of male and female college students. Importantly, these effects were replicated across a number of different songs and music genres and occurred regardless of participants' existing levels of trait hostility.

After reviewing the evidence to 2003 regarding the effects of music on children, Roberts et al (2003, p 166) concluded that negative effects resulting from listening to violent music are "more carried by the emotional sound of the music than by the lyrics" (see also Christenson & Roberts, 1998) and that any effect the lyrics may have should be weaker than the effect of the violent visual content in music concept videos. That is, they thought that the evidence supporting the notion that violent lyrics cause aggression or anti-social attitudes is weaker than the evidence suggesting an effect for the emotional tone of the music, and the addition of a violent visual video clip.

However, given the methodological concerns about early studies that found no lyrics effect, and the relatively consistent findings of lyrics effects in more recent and more carefully designed studies, the effect of lyrics may be more important than previously thought. Two studies conducted recently have compared the effects of violent music with and without accompanying video clips, and the effect of violent song lyrics compared to aggressive musical tone.

Warburton, Gilmour and Laczkowski (2008a) conducted questionnaire research examining the links between aggression and violent musical tone, violent lyrics and violent visual media. Measures included trait aggression, exposure to violent media, exposure to violent music and trait anger. Recent acts of aggression were also measured using the Warburton Aggression Index, which tallies the number of instances of physical, indirect and relational aggression over the previous two months, along with measures of hostile thoughts and angry feelings (see also Warburton et al, 2008b). The violent music exposure index contains a number of measures, including scores for exposure to violent lyrics, music with an angry feel and musicians with an angry attitude.

Violent lyrics and aggressive musical tone had a similar sized effect on aggressive behaviour. In terms of media mode, the type of aggression differed according to the type of media participants had been exposed to. Violent music exposure was associated more with recent instances of indirect and relational aggression whereas violent visual media exposure was associated with recent instances of physical aggression. This suggests that some of the variation in past research findings may have been due to the fact that different types of aggression were not measured. From these results, the authors suggest that violent music exposure may facilitate a more generalised aggressiveness in its listeners whilst violent visual media, by providing clearer scripts for aggressive behaviour, may facilitate action tendencies that involve physical aggression.

In a second study, Brummert-Lennings and Warburton (2011) randomly allocated 205 participants into one of five groups. In the four experimental groups half the participants heard a violent song with the lyrics intact and the other half heard the same song with the lyrics digitally removed. In addition, half the participants saw a video with violent images and the other half did not. A fifth baseline control group heard no music and saw no video. Participants heard one of three songs, one from rap, one from rock or one from heavy metal. After exposure to the music stimuli, aggressive behaviour was measured as the amount of very hot chilli sauce participants would make another participant eat, knowing that they strongly disliked hot foods and would have to eat all of the hot chilli sauce allocated to them (Lieberman et al, 1999; Warburton et al, 2006). In addition, changes to mood, arousal and hostility levels during the experiment were measured.

Although a combination of violent lyrics and violent video produced the strongest effect on aggressive responding in subjects, this difference was fairly small (see Figure 1). The clearest finding was that both groups who heard violent lyrics were substantially more aggressive than both groups who heard no lyrics (on average they gave 12 compared to 7 grams of hot sauce) and all groups who heard the songs were more aggressive than those who did not (4 grams). This effect was almost identical for the three different songs used (see Figure 1). The results of this study demonstrate a clear effect of exposure to violent lyrics on aggressive behaviour, regardless of the genre of song. Interestingly, the effect of violent lyrics on aggressive behaviour was equally strong when statistical methods were used to cancel out of the effect of gender, trait aggressiveness, past exposure to violent visual media, past exposure to violent music, hostility, militaristic thinking, violent occultism, personality variables and depression. That is, the effect occurred regardless of participants' personality characteristics or previous exposure to violent media. Violent lyrics, over and above musical tone and the presence of violent imagery, had the strongest effect on the aggression level of participants. According to these results, violent lyrics may account for much of the effect of violent music exposure on aggressive behaviour.

Figure 1: Hot chilli sauce allocation by group across the three music video stimuli (top and bottom left) and averaged across stimuli with baseline added (bottom right)

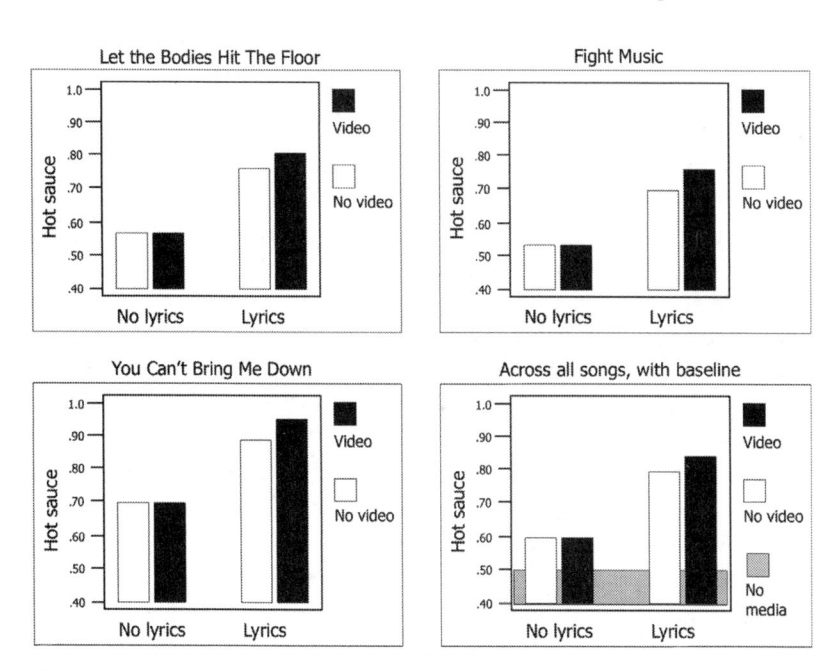

(From Brummert-Lennings and Warburton, 2011. Note that data has been transformed to reduce skewness.)

Conclusions and advice for parents and professionals working with children

Listening to music that invokes a pleasant mood, conveys pro-social messages, facilitates play or social engagement, or assists in psychological treatment can have various positive effects on children and adolescents. However, music with violent and/or anti-social themes can have a number of negative effects. Although some older studies have produced inconsistent findings, more carefully designed recent studies have consistently found that frequent exposure to violent or anti-social music is associated with aggressive or anti-social thoughts, feelings and behaviours. In addition, links have been found between relevant lyrical content and substance use, anti-social behaviour, sexual behaviour, misogynistic attitudes and suicide. Rap and heavy/death metal are examples of particular music genres that are more likely than others to convey such themes.

When taken together, these findings (both for positive and negative effects of listening to music), suggest that the "you are what you eat" principle introduced in Chapters 1 and 3 applies as much to music as it does to the other media sources discussed in this book. That is, as noted earlier, our brains wire up constantly in response to what we experience and listening to a great deal of violent or anti-social music will have an effect on the way children and youth (and adults) think, feel and behave. This happens via changes to the brain's neural network in response to these influences. Importantly, listening to music with positive influences should *positively* affect the way children and youth think, feel and behave.

Given the research findings, it would seem valuable for those parenting or working with children and adolescents to be aware of the type of music they listen to and to encourage positive musical choices. However, this is more easily said than done. By early adolescence a lot of identity is tied to musical preferences, peer-pressures related to musical preferences are strong, and children's own personal preferences for music are becoming well-established. Attempts by adults to listen to the same music are often not welcomed (and sometimes derided) and there is typically resistance when adults try to reduce access. Indeed, this might be seen as an attack on the child's emerging identity. In addition, the high portability of many devices which children and youth use to listen to music make it almost impossible to limit access.

So, what can be done in a practical sense?

In my view, education is very important. If children and youth are well educated about media effects generally and music effects specifically, they are better positioned to make healthy choices about the music they consume and to take control of the type of music they choose to identify with. Making a range of interesting music with benign or pro-social messages available to children and teenagers in *subtle* ways may also have an effect. Often, children will quietly sample and take on board the musical tastes of others if they find it interesting, unique and desirable to their developing identity. So, guidance that is neither intrusive nor critical of the child's existing preferences, but which empowers the child to make healthy musical choices of their own volition, may be a helpful strategy for parents and professionals who work with children.

Acknowledgements

I would like to thank Andrew Geeves for his generous assistance with this chapter. I would also like to thank Associate Professor Doug Gentile for his helpful and insightful comments on chapter drafts.

References

ACMA (Australian Communications and Media Authority (2007). *Media and communications in Australian families, 2007*. Canberra: Australian Communications and Media Authority. Accessed 14 April 2001, <http://www.acma.gov.au/webwr/_assets/main/lib101058/media_and_society_report_2007.pdf>.

Allen, M, Herrett-Skjellum, J, Jorgensen, J, Ryan, DJ, Kramer, MR, & Timmerman, L (2007). Effects of music. In RW Preiss, BM Gayle, N Burrell, M Allen & J Bryant (eds), *Mass media effects research: Advances through meta-analysis* (pp 263–279). Mahwah, NJ: Lawrence Erlbaum.

American Academy of Pediatrics (1996). Policy statement – Impact of music lyrics and music videos on children and youth. *Pediatrics, 98*, 1219–1221.

American Academy of Pediatrics (2009). Policy statement – Impact of music lyrics and music videos on children and youth. *Pediatrics, 124*, 1488–1494.

Anderson, CA, Carnagey, NL, & Eubanks, J (2003). Exposure to violent media: The effects of songs with violent lyrics on aggressive thoughts and feelings. *Journal of Personality and Social Psychology, 84*, 960–971.

Arnett, J (1991). Adolescents and heavy metal music: From the mouths of metal-heads. *Youth and Society, 23*, 76–98.

Arnett, J (1992), The soundtrack of recklessness: Musical preferences and reckless behavior among adolescents. *Journal of Adolescent Research, 7*, 313–331.

Arnett, JJ (1998). Learning to stand alone: The contemporary American transition to adulthood in cultural and historical context. *Human Development, 41*, 295–315.

Ashby, SL, & Rich, M (2005). Video killed the radio star: The effects of music videos on adolescent health, *Adolescent Medicine Clinics, 16*, 371–393.

Ballard, ME, & Coates, S (1995). The immediate effects of homicidal, suicidal, and nonviolent heavy metal and rap songs on the mood of college students. *Youth and Society, 27*, 148–169.

Barongen, C, & Hall, GCN (1995). The effect of misogynous rap music on sexual aggression against women. *Psychology of Women Quarterly, 19*, 195–207.

Brown, CJ, Chen, ACN, & Dworkin, SF (1989). Music in the control of human pain. *Music Therapy, 8*, 47–60.

Brown, JD, L'Engle, KL, Pardun, CJ, Guo, G, Kenneavy, K, & Jackson, C (2006). Sexy media matter: Exposure to sexual content in music, movies, television and magazines predicts Black and White adolescents' sexual behaviour. *Pediatrics, 117,* 1017–1027.

Brummert Lennings, HI, & Warburton, WA (2011). The effect of auditory versus visual violent media exposure on aggressive behaviour: The role of song lyrics, video clips and musical tone. *Journal of Experimental Social Psychology, 47,* 794–799.

Bruner, G (1990), Music, mood, and marketing. *Journal of Marketing, 54,* 94–105.

Bunt, L (1997). Clinical and therapeutic uses of music. In DJ Hargreaves & AC North (eds), *The social psychology of music* (pp 249–267). Oxford: Oxford University Press.

Chen, MJ, Miller, B, Grube, JW, & Waiters, ED (2006). Music, substance use, and aggression. *Journal of Studies on Alcohol, 67,* 373–381.

Christenson, P (1992). The effects of parental advisory labels on adolescent music preferences. *Journal of Communication, 42,* 106–113.

Christenson, PG, & Roberts, DF (1998). *It's not only rock & roll: Popular music in the lives of adolescents.* Cresskill, NJ: Hampton Press.

Črnčec, R, Wilson, SJ, & Prior, M (2006). The cognitive and academic benefits of music to children: Facts and fiction. *Educational Psychology, 26,* 579–594.

Crozier, WR (1997). Music and social influence. In DJ Hargreaves & AC North (eds), *The social psychology of music* (pp 67–83). New York: Oxford University Press.

DeCaspar, AJ, & Spence, MJ (1986). Prenatal maternal speech influences newborns' perception of speech sounds. *Infant Behaviour and Development, 9,* 133–150.

Dittmar, H (1992). *The social psychology of material possessions: To have is to be.* Hemel Hampstead: Harvester Wheatsheaf.

DuRant, RH, Rich, M, Emans, SJ, Rome, ES, Allred, E, & Woods, ER (2011). Violence and weapon carrying in music videos. *Archives of Pediatrics and Adolescent Medicine, 151,* 443–448.

Escobar-Chaves, SL, Tortoloero, SR, Markham, CM, Low, BJ, Eitel, P, & Thickstun, P (2005). Impact of the media on adolescent sexual attitudes and behaviours. *Pediatrics, 116,* 303–326.

Finnäs, L (1989). A comparison between young people's privately and publicly expressed musical preferences. *Psychology of Music, 17,* 132–145.

Fischer, P, & Greitemeyer, T (2006). Music and aggression: The impact of sexual-aggressive song lyrics on aggression-related thoughts, emotions, and behaviour toward the same and the opposite sex. *Personality and Social Psychology Bulletin, 32,* 1165–1176.

Fried, R, & Berkowitz, L (1979). Music that charms ... and can influence helpfulness. *Journal of Applied Social Psychology, 9,* 199–208.

Flom, R, Gentile, DA, & Pick, AD (2008). Infants' discrimination of happy and sad music. *Infant Behavior and Development, 31,* 716–728.

Gentile, DA, Linder, JR, & Walsh, DA (2003). *Looking through time: A longitudinal study of children's media violence consumption at home and aggressive behaviors at school.* Paper presented at the 2003 Society for Research in Child Development Biennial Conference, Tampa, FL, April.

Greenfield, PM, & Beagles-Roos, J (1988). Television versus radio: The cognitive impact on different socio-economic and ethnic groups. *Journal of Communication, 38,* 71–92.

Greenfield, PM, Bruzzone, L, Koyamatsu, K, Satuloff, W, Nixon, K, Brodie, M, & Kinsgsdale, D (1987). What is rock music doing to the minds of our youth? A first experimental look at the effects of rock music lyrics and music videos. *Journal of Early Adolescence, 7,* 315-329.

Gregory, AH (1997). The roles of music in society: The ethnomusicological perspective. In DJ Hargreaves & AC North (eds), *The social psychology of music* (pp 123-140). New York: Oxford University Press.

Greitemeyer, T (2009). Effects of songs with pro-social lyrics on pro-social thoughts, affect and behaviour. *Journal of Experimental Social Psychology, 45,* 186-190.

Greitemeyer, T (2011). Exposure to music with pro-social lyrics reduces aggression: First evidence and test of underlying mechanism. *Journal of Experimental Social Psychology, 47,* 28-36.

Gruber, EL, Thau, HM, Hill, DL, Fisher, DA, & Grube, JW (2005). Alcohol, tobacco and illicit substances in music videos: a content analysis of prevalence and genre. *Journal of Adolescent Health, 37,* 81-83.

Hansen, CH (1995). Predicting cognitive and behavioural effects of gangsta rap. *Basic and Applied Social Psychology, 16,* 43-52.

Hansen, CH, & Hansen, RD (1990). Rock music videos and antisocial behavior. *Basic and Applied Social Psychology, 11,* 357-369.

Hansen, CH, & Hansen, RD (1991). Schematic information processing of heavy metal lyrics. *Communication Research, 18,* 373-411.

Hansen, CH, & Hansen, RD (2000). Music and music videos. In D Zillmann & P Vorderer (eds), *Media entertainment: The psychology of its appeal* (pp 175-196). Mahwah NJ: Lawrence Erlbaum.

Hepper, PG (1991). An examination of fetal learning before and after birth. *Irish Journal of Psychology, 12,* 95-107.

Johnson, JD, Adams, MS, Ashburn, L, & Reed, W (1995a). Differential gender effects of exposure to rap music on African American adolescents' acceptance of teen dating violence. *Sex Roles, 33,* 597-605.

Johnson, JD, Jackson, LA, & Gatto, L (1995b). Violent attitudes and deferred academic aspirations: Deleterious effects of exposure to rap music. *Basic and Applied Social Psychology, 16,* 27-41.

Jones, K (1997). Are rap videos more violent? Style differences and the prevalence of sex and violence in the age of MTV. *Howard Journal of Communications, 8,* 343-356.

Jorgensen, H (1974). The contingent use of music activity to modify behaviours which interfere with learning. *Journal of Music Therapy, 11,* 41-46.

Kaestle, CE, Tucker-Halpern, C, & Brown, JD (2007). Music videos, pro wrestling, and acceptance of date rape among middle school males and females: An exploratory analysis. *Journal of Adolescent Health, 40,* 185-187.

Kaiser Family Foundation (2003). *Reaching the MTV Generation: Recent research on the impact of the Kaiser Family Foundation/MTV public education campaign on sexual health.* Accessed 9 August 2011, <http://www.kff.org/entmedia/upload/Reaching-the-MTV-Generation-Recent-Research-on-the-Impact-of-the-Kaiser-Family-Foundation-MTV-Public-Education-Campaign-on-Sexual-Health.pdf>.

King, P (1988). Heavy metal music and drug abuse in adolescents. *Postgraduate Medicine, 83,* 295-304.

Kirsch, SJ (2010). *Media and youth: A developmental perspective*. Malden MA: Wiley Blackwell.

Kistler, ME, & Moon, JL (2010). Does exposure to sexual hip-hop music videos influence the sexual attitudes of college students? *Mass Communication and Society, 13*, 67–86.

Klein, JD, Brown, JD, Childers, KW, Oliveri, J, Porter, C, & Dykers, C (1993). Adolescents' risky behavior and mass media use. *Pediatrics, 92*, 24–31.

Krahé, B, & Bieneck, S (2012). The effect of music-induced mood on aggressive affect, cognition and behavior. *Journal of Applied Social Psychology, 42*, 271–290.

Lamont, A (2001). *Infants' preferences for familiar and unfamiliar music: A socio-cultural study*. Paper presented at the Meeting of the Society for Music Perception and Cognition, Queens University, Kingston, Ontario, Canada, August.

Larsen, RJ (2000). Toward a science of mood regulation. *Psychological Inquiry, 11*, 129–141.

Larson, RW (1995). Secrets in the bedroom: Adolescents private use of media. *Journal of Youth and Adolescence, 24*, 535–550.

Lieberman, JD, Solomon, S, Greenberg, J, & McGregor, HA (1999). A hot new way to measure aggression: Hot sauce allocation. *Aggressive Behavior, 25*, 331–348.

Magowen, F (1994). The land is our märr (essence): It stays forever. The Yothu Yindi relationship in Australian Aboriginal traditional and popular musics. In M Stokes (ed), *Ethnicity, identity and music: The musical construction of place*. New York: Oxford.

Markert, J (2001). Sing a song of drug use-abuse: four decades of drug lyrics in popular music-from the sixties through the nineties. *Sociological Inquiry, 71*, 194–220.

Martin, G, Clarke, M, & Pearce, C (1993). Adolescent suicide: Music preference as an indicator of vulnerability. *Journal of the American Academy of Child and Adolescent Psychiatry, 32*, 530–535.

Martino, SC, Collins, PL, Elliott, MN, Strachman, A, Kamouse, DE, & Berry, SH (2006). Exposure to degrading versus non-degrading music lyrics and sexual behaviour among youth. *Pediatrics, 118*, e430–e441.

Nantais, KM, & Schellenberg, EG (1999). The Mozart effect: an artifact of preference. *Psychological Science, 10*, 370–373.

Neilsen Company (2010). *Neilsen Australian Internet and Technology Report*. Sydney.

North, AC, Hargreaves, DJ, & O'Neill, SA (2000). The importance of music to adolescents. *British Journal of Educational Psychology, 70*, 255–272.

North, AC, Tarrant, M, & Hargreaves, DJ (2004). The effects of music on helping behavior: A field study. *Environment and Behaviour, 36*, 266–275.

Pardun, CJ, L'Engle, KL, & Brown, JD (2005) Linking exposure to outcomes: early adolescents' consumption of sexual content in six media. *Mass Communication and Society, 8*, 75–91.

Pareles, J (1990). Rap: Slick, violent, nasty, and, maybe, hopeful. *New York Times*, 17 June, 19.

Perry, I (1995). It's my thang and I'll swing it the way that I feel! In JG Dines & JM Humes (eds), *Gender, race, and class in media: A test reader* (pp 524–530). Thousand Oaks CA: Sage.

Peterson, DL, & Pfost, KS (1989). Influence of rock videos on attitudes of violence against women. *Psychological Reports, 64*, 319–322.

Peterson, SH, Wingood, GM, DiClemente, RJ, Harrington, K, & Davies, S (2007). Images of sexual stereotypes in rap videos and the health of African American female adolescents. *Journal of Women's Health, 16*, 1157–1164.

Primack, BA, Dalton, MA, Carroll MV, Agarwal AA, & Fine MJ (2008). Content analysis of tobacco, alcohol, and other drugs in popular music. *Archives of Pediatrics and Adolescent Medicine, 162,* 169-175.

Primack, BA, Douglas, EL, & Kraemer, KL (2009). Exposure to cannabis in popular music and cannabis use among adolescents. *Addiction, 105,* 515-523.

Prinsky, LE, & Rosenbaum, JL (1987). "Lee-rics" or lyrics: Teenage impressions of rock 'n' roll. *Youth and Society, 18,* 384-397.

Rideout, VJ, Foehr, UG, & Roberts, DF (2010). *Generation M2: Media in the lives of 8-18 year olds.* Merlo Park CA: Henry J Kaiser Foundation.

Rauscher, FH, Shaw, GL, & Ky, KN (1993). Music and spatial task performance. *Nature, 365,* 611.

Roberts, DF, Christenson, PG, & Gentile, DA (2003). The effects of violent music on children and adolescents. In DA Gentile (ed), *Media violence and children: A complete guide for parents and professionals* (pp 153-170). Westport CT: Praeger.

Roberts, DF, Foehr, UG, & Rideout, V (2005). *Generation M: Media in the lives of 8-18 year-olds.* Washington, DC: Henry J Kaiser Family Foundation.

Roe, K (1984). *Youth and music in Sweden: Results from a longitudinal study of teenagers' media use* [Media Panel Reports, No 32]. Lund, Sweden: Sociologiska Institutionen.

Roe, K (1996). Music and identity among European youth: Music as communication. In P Rutten (ed), *Music in Europe* (pp 85-97). Brussels: European Music Office. Accessed 4 August 2011, <http://www.icce.rug.nl/~soundscapes/DATABASES/MIE/Part2_chapter03.shtml>.

Roskam, K (1979). Music therapy as an aid for improving auditory awareness and improving reading skill. *Journal of Music Therapy, 16,* 31-42.

Rubin, AM, West, DV, & Mitchell, WS (2001). Differences in aggression, attitudes towards women, and distrust as reflected in popular music preferences. *Media Psychology, 3,* 25-42.

Rustad, RA, Small, JE, Jobes, DA, Safer, MA, & Peterson, RJ (2003). The impact of rock videos and music with suicidal content on thoughts and attitudes about suicide. *Suicide and Life-Threatening Behavior, 33,* 120-131.

Samuels, A, Croal, N, & Gates, D (2000). Battle for the soul of hip hop. *Newsweek,* 9 October, 58-65. Accessed 4 August 2011, <http://bechollashon.org/database/index.php?/article/990>.

Savarimuthu, D (2004). When music heals. In JP Morgan (ed), *Focus on aggression research* (pp 175-187). New York: Nova Science Publishers.

Scheel, K, & Westefield, J (1999). Heavy metal music and adolescent suicidality: An empirical investigation. *Adolescence, 34,* 253-73.

Schellenberg, EG, & Hallam, S (2005). Music listening and cognitive abilities in 10 and 11 year olds: The Blur effect. *Annals of the New York Academy of Sciences, 1060,* 202-209.

Sommers-Flanagan, R, Sommers-Flanagan, J, & Davis, B (1993). What's happening on music television? A gender-role content analysis, *Sex Roles, 28,* 745-753.

Stack, S, Gundlach, J, & Reeves, JL (1994), The heavy metal subculture and suicide. *Suicide and Life-Threatening Behaviour, 24,* 15-23.

Standley, J (1995). Music as a therapeutic intervention in medical and dental treatment: Research and clinical applications. In T Wigram, B Saperston, & R West (eds), *The art and science of music therapy: A handbook.* Langhorne US: Harwood Academic.

St Lawrence, JS, & Joyner, DJ (1991). The effects of sexually violent rock music on males' acceptance of violence against women. *Psychology of Women Quarterly, 15,* 49–63.

Strasburger, VC, & Hendren, RO (1995). Rock music and music videos. *Pediatric Annals, 24,* 97–103.

Strasburger, VC, Wilson, BJ, & Jordan, AB (2009). *Children, adolescents, and the media* (2nd ed). Thousand Oaks, CA: Sage.

Thompson, WF, Schellenberg, EG, & Husain, G (2001). Arousal, mood and the Mozart Effect. *Psychological Science, 12,* 248–251.

Trehub, SE, Hill, DS, & Kamenetsky, SB (1997). Parents' sung performances for infants. *Canadian Journal of Experimental Psychology, 51,* 385–396.

Trehub, SE, & Trainor, LJ (1993). Listening strategies in infancy: The roots of music and language development. In S McAdams & E Bigand (eds), *Thinking in sound: The cognitive psychology of human audition* (pp 278–320). Oxford: Clarendon Press.

Tyson, EH (2002). Hip hop therapy: An exploratory study of a rap music intervention with at-risk and delinquent youth. *Journal of Poetry Therapy, 15,* 131–144.

Tyson, EH (2006). Rap-music attitude and perception scale: A validation study. *Research on Social Work Practice, 16,* 211–223.

Van den Bulck, J, Beullens, K, & Mulder, J (2006). Television and music video exposure and adolescent 'alcopop' use. *International Journal of Adolescent Medicine and Health, 18,* 107–114.

Waite, BM, Hillbrand, M, & Foster, HG (1992). Reduction of aggressive behavior after removal of Music Television. *Hospital and Community Psychiatry, 43,* 173–175.

Wanamaker, CE, & Reznikoff, M (1989). Effects of aggressive and nonaggressive rock songs on projective and structured tests. *The Journal of Psychology, 123,* 561–570.

Warburton, WA, Edwards, P, Hossieny, T, Pieper, L, & Yip, T (2008b). Factors that mediate the narcissism-aggression link. In S Boag (ed), *Personality down under: Perspectives from Australia* (pp 185–202). New York: Nova Science Publishers.

Warburton, WA, Gilmour, L, & Laczkowski, P (2008a). Eminem v Rambo: A comparison of media violence effects for auditory versus visual modalities. In S Boag (ed), *Personality down under: Perspectives from Australia* (pp 253–271). New York: Nova Science Publishers.

Warburton, WA, Williams, KD, & Cairns, DR (2006). Ostracism and aggression: The moderating effects of control deprivation. *Journal of Experimental Social Psychology, 42,* 213–220.

Weidinger, DK, & Demi, AS (1991). Music listening preferences and pre-admission dysfunctional psychosocial behaviours of adolescents hospitalised on an in-patient psychiatric unit. *Journal of Child and Adolescent Psychiatric Mental Health Nursing, 4,* 3–8.

Wester, SR, Crown, CL, Quatman, GL, & Heesacker, M (1997). The influence of sexually violent rap music on attitudes of men with little prior exposure. *Psychology of Women Quarterly, 21,* 497–508.

Whelan, AM (2010). *Free music and trash culture: The reconfiguration of musical value online.* In K Zemke & SD Brunt (eds), 2009 IASPM Australia-New Zealand Conference: What's it worth?: 'value' and popular music (pp 67–71). Dunedin, New Zealand: IASPM-ANZ.

Wingood, GM, DiClemente, RJ, Bernhardt, JM, Harrington, K, Davies, SL, Robillard, A, & Hook, EW (2003) A prospective study of exposure to rap music videos and African American female adolescents' health. *American Journal of Public Health, 98,* 437–439.

Zillmann, D, & Gan, S (1997). Musical taste in adolescence. In DJ Hargreaves & A North (eds), *The social psychology of music* (pp 161–187). Oxford: Oxford University Press.

Zillmann, D, & Mundorf, N (1987). Image effects in the appreciation of video rock. *Communication Research, 14*, 316–334.

Chapter 5

The internet as "fast and furious" content

Ed Donnerstein

The chapters in this book examine a substantial range of negative influences on children from media exposure. These include television/film violence, video game violence, advertising, sexual content and music with aggressive content. Newer technologies, such as the internet and mobile devices have drastically changed the availability, and consequently the influences, of potentially harmful media on children and adolescents. Unlike traditional media such as television and film, there are relatively fewer studies on the impact of exposure to harmful materials on the internet. In a recent chapter on sexual media, Wright, Malamuth and Donnerstein (2011) note the recent commentary of researchers about the potential and far-reaching influences of this "newer" technology on sexual socialisation, one of the themes of this book:

> Mass media play an important role in the sexual socialization of American youth and given its expanding nature and accessibility, the internet may be at the forefront of this education. (Braun-Courville & Rojas, 2009, p 156)

> Teens have access to a variety of adult-oriented Web sites on the internet. Chat rooms, pornography sites, adult-video sites, and romance/dating services are but a few of the many and easily accessible "adult-oriented" materials to be found. (Escobar-Chaves et al, 2005, p 319)

> Adolescents' increasing access to, and use of, sexually explicit internet material – material that is not meant for minors – has led to concerns about whether youth are able to make sense of the reality depicted in that material. (Peter & Valkenburg, 2008, p 584)

The potential influences go beyond just sexual content. As Donnerstein (2011) has noted, the internet has become the medium in which traditional media like television, film and video games can be downloaded, viewed and processed. The most recent survey of children and adolescent media use by Rideout et al (2010) in the United States indicated that the amount of time viewing television content had increased over the last decade, but this increase is accounted for primarily by the viewing of such programming over the internet and mobile devices. Adolescents now spend over 10 hours a day with some form of media (United States data).

Unlike traditional media such as television, the internet and these new technologies (for example, mobile devices) give children and adolescents access to just about any form of content they can find (eg, Livingstone & Haddon, 2009). Often with little effort they are able to view almost any form of violence, advertising, or sexual behaviour, which have the potential of producing negative effects (Donnerstein, 2011; Strasburger et al 2010). Furthermore, this can be done in the privacy of their own room with little supervision from their parents.

Is there any reason to expect that the internet or any of these newer technologies will have different effects than traditional media? Malamuth, Linz and Yao (2005) have provided a perspective on internet violence, but their theoretical perspective applies just as equally to all forms of harmful materials. According to these authors, the internet provides motivational, disinhibitory and opportunity aspects that make it somewhat different than traditional media in terms of its potential impact.

With regard to motivation, the internet is "ubiquitous", in that it is always on and can easily be accessed, thus leading to high levels of exposure. In the world of new technology there is no "family-viewing hour". Online content can be interactive and more engaging, which has the ability for increased learning and certainly exposure time. From a disinhibitory aspect the content is unregulated. Studies suggest that extreme forms of violent or sexual content are more prevalent on the internet than in other popular media (eg, Strasburger et al, 2010). Participation is private and anonymous, which allows for the searching of materials that a child or adolescent would normally not seek out with traditional media. There is the suggestion that finding such materials could increase social support for these images and messages (for example, sites for bulimia and hate groups: Strasburger et al, 2010). Finally, online media exposure is much more difficult for parents to monitor than media exposure in traditional venues. Opportunity aspects play a more important role in the area of cyberbullying or child sexual exploitation. Potential victims are readily available and reachable, and the identity of the "aggressor" is often disguised (as is often the case with pedophiles).

Are Children and Adolescents Online?

The amount of usage of the internet and newer technologies by youth is substantial. Studies by the Pew Internet and American Life Project (2009) revealed that 93 per cent of youth aged 12–17 are online sometime during the day and 71 per cent have cell phones. Whether it is watching videos (57 per cent), using social networking sites (65 per cent), or playing video games (97 per cent), children and adolescents have incorporated new technology into their daily lives. These frequencies are also observed across 21 different countries within Europe. The EU Kids Online Project found that in 2005, on average 70 per cent of 6–17-year-olds used the internet. By 2008, it was at 75 per cent with the largest increase occurring among younger children (6–10) in which 60 per cent were now online (Livingstone & Haddon, 2009).

The data for Australia is very similar to that found in other countries. The amount of time spent on the internet exceeds the amount of time individuals spend with television, radio or other types of media. One of the factors that probably accounts for the high usage of the internet in Australia is the significant increase in broadband use over the last five years. Only five years ago about 30% of homes with children under the age of 15 had broadband use whereas today it is over 80 per cent. In the group of children aged 5–14 years, internet use over the last five years has increased from around 50 per cent to over 80 per cent.

In thinking about the internet and its influences on children and adolescents, there are a number of concerns that we would like to look at in this chapter. These are the issues of cyberbullying, sexual exploitation, online marketing and the viewing, inadvertent or otherwise, of sexually explicit materials.

Cyberbullying

One of the issues over the years that has become of paramount concern is the use of the internet in terms of aggressing or harassing others. As it is commonly called, cyberbullying involves behaviours such as:

1. Sending unsolicited and/or threatening e-mail;
2. Spreading rumours;
3. Making inflammatory comments in public discussion areas;
4. Impersonating the victim online by sending messages that cause others to respond negatively to this individual;
5. Harassing the victim during a live chat or leaving abusive messages on webpages about the victim.

Surveys in the United States, Europe and Australia have indicated that somewhere between 15 per cent and 35 per cent of teens report being bullied online. More interesting is the finding that between 10 per cent and 20 per cent actually admit to bullying others. In terms of gender differences there are few, as girls are just as likely to be involved in cyberbullying behaviours as males (eg, Donnerstein, 2011)

When we examine the effects of cyberbullying we find that victims of this behaviour may experience many of the same effects as children who are bullied in person, including such effects as a drop in grades, lower self-esteem or depression. Many researchers have considered cyberbullying to be perhaps more extreme, because of a number of factors. First, it occurs in the child's home. The place the child considered to be the most secure has now become a place where he or she can be a victim. Secondly, because of the anonymity of the aggressor and the inability to see the victims reactions, effects can be perceived as harsher. Thirdly, the effects can be "forever" in cyberspace, as online materials cannot be removed by victims. Finally, for some individuals it may seem totally inescapable since online is the place where many of these children and adolescents socialise. Therefore, it often becomes very difficult to get away from potential online bullying (National Crime Prevention Council, 2009).

One question that has been raised is why children and adolescents engage in cyberbullying compared to traditional forms of bullying? Tokunaga (2010) has offered a number of suggestions for this behaviour:

1. There is anonymity offered through electronic media;
2. It is an opportunistic offense, since the resulting harm can occur without any actual physical interaction;
3. There is for the most part a lack of supervision and electronic media can require little, if any, planning;
4. Due to the high anonymity the threat of being caught has been reduced;
5. There is accessibility. Victims can be reached through a number of electronic devices, such as cellular phones, e-mail and instant messaging at any time of the day.

Sexual Exploitation

We would be remiss in our discussion of the internet if we did not acknowledge the potential for the sexual exploitation of children and adolescents. The sending of sexual information over e-mail or postings on bulletin boards by those targeting children has been an ongoing research issue. There are a number of reasons why we can expect the internet to play a role in sexual exploitation. As researchers have noted (Mitchell et al, 2010) children are more accessible to offenders through social networking sites, e-mail and texting because it is anonymous behaviour and normally outside the supervision of parents. Children may also find the privacy and anonymity of this type of communication much more conducive to having discussions of intimate relationships than to meet face-to-face. For the potential offender there is certainly easier access to websites and other internet groups that encourage and legitimise these types of behaviour with children and adolescents.

Perhaps the most comprehensive series of studies on these issues has come from the Crimes Against Children Research Center at the University of New Hampshire. These studies (see Wolak et al, 2008) involved a random national sample of 1500 children aged 10-17 interviewed in 2000 and then an additional sample of 1500 interviewed in 2005. This procedure allowed the researchers to look at changes in youths' experiences with the internet. The major findings from this study can be summarised as follows:

1. There was a 9 per cent increase over the 5-year period (25 per cent to 34 per cent of respondents) in exposure to unwanted sexual materials. It is interesting to note that this increase occurred in spite of the fact that more families were using internet filtering software (over 50 per cent) during this period.
2. Fifteen per cent of all of the youth reported an unwanted sexual solicitation online in the previous year, with 4 per cent reporting an incident on a social networking site specifically. Perhaps more important, about 4 per cent of these were considered "aggressive" in that the solicitor attempted to contact the user offline. These are the episodes most likely to result in actual victimisations.
3. Additionally, 4 per cent of those surveyed were asked for nude or sexually explicit pictures of themselves.
4. Four per cent said they were upset or distressed as a result of these online solicitations.

We can look at these small percentages and say that broad claims of victimisation may not seem justified. The problem with this interpretation is that these are large scale national surveys, so even if the percentages are small the number of youth impacted is actually quite substantial.

Viewing of Sexual Materials

Also significant are findings that indicate substantial viewing of sexually explicit materials by youth on the internet. In one large-scale survey, Salazar, Fleischauer, Bernhardt and DiClemente (2009) gathered data suggesting that 17 per cent of websites visited by teens were X-rated (sexually explicit) and at least 6 per cent contained sexual violence. Other studies have shown unwanted and accidental exposure to between 50 per cent and 65 per cent of teens (Braun-Courville & Rojas, 2009; Wolak et al, 2007). Given these data there is ample reason to expect effects from internet exposure. There are few studies, however, on the impact of internet exposure to sexually explicit material, particularly in areas such as e-mail and instant messaging. The few studies that have examined this issue are strongly suggestive of an association between internet exposure and unhelpful sexual attitudes and behaviours. Two large-scale, longitudinal surveys of youth conducted in the Netherlands (Peter & Valkenburgh, 2008; 2009) found that more frequent intentional exposure to sexually explicit internet material was associated with greater sexual uncertainty and more positive attitudes toward uncommitted sexual exploration (that is, sexual relations with casual partners/ friends or with sexual partners in one-night stands). Additionally, adolescents' exposure to internet sex appeared to be both a cause and a consequence of their belief that women are sex objects. More frequent exposure predicted stronger beliefs that women are sex objects, while at the same time stronger beliefs that women are sex objects predicted more frequent exposure to such materials.

Braun-Courville and Rojas (2009) looked at the sexual behaviours of adolescents in a cross sectional study in New York. Over 50 per cent of the participants had visited sexually explicit web sites. Analyses revealed that adolescents exposed to these types of sites were more likely to (a) have multiple lifetime sexual partners, (b) have had more than one sexual partner in the last three months, (c) used alcohol or other substances at their last sexual encounter, and (d) to have engaged in anal sex. Furthermore, adolescents who visit these sites displayed higher sexual permissiveness scores compared with those who had never been exposed. It is difficult to disentangle causality in this study, but we can certainly assume that internet exposure is at a minimum reinforcing already existing attitudes and behaviours.

In a study with Taiwanese adolescents, Lo and Wei (2005) also found that internet exposure was associated with greater acceptance of sexual permissiveness and a greater likelihood of engaging in sexually permissive behaviour. Of interest was the finding in this study that exposure to internet pornography had a stronger impact on sexual attitudes than exposure to such content in traditional media.

The above studies, while somewhat limited in design and generalisability, do suggest that the internet can be an influence on adolescents' sexual attitudes and behaviours. Besides the fact that traditional media (which we have already acknowledged as an influence) can easily be obtained via the internet, more explicit and potentially riskier materials are readily available to youth online. As Brown and L'Engle (2009) note in their longitudinal study of adolescents, "[b]y the end of middle school many teens have seen sexually explicit content not only on the internet but in more traditional forms of media as well. Such exposure is related to early adolescents' developing sense of gender roles, sexual relationships, and sexual behaviour, including perpetration of sexual harassment" (p 148). As children and adolescents move further away from traditional media channels to newer technologies it will become increasingly important for researchers to explore the extent and nature of online sexual social influence.

Online marketing

Recently the Institute of Medicine of the National Academy of Science in United States published a series of studies looking at childhood obesity as a major health problem in many children today (see Kunkel & Castonguay, 2011). One of the issues they were concerned with was food marketing to children and the proliferation of advertisements that primarily market unhealthy food choices. If we take a look at traditional media, such as television, many countries have fairly strict regulations regarding both the amount of advertising and the type of advertising that can be directed to children. In other words, we have some type of regulation in place. The internet, however, completely bypasses any of these regulations.

The Kaiser Family Foundation (2006) recently found that over 85 per cent of companies that advertise to children on television are also providing the same children with similar forms of advertising on the internet. In fact the vast majority of these have websites specifically created for children. In a recent content analysis by Cai and Zhao (2010), it was found that:

- 87 per cent of the children's most popular websites included some form of advertising;
- 75 per cent of these websites offered children the ability to download logos, screensavers, or even wallpaper they could use for their computers; and
- 75 per cent of the sites had what are now called advergames in which companies product or brand characters are featured in an online game format.

Advergames are able to engage children in interesting activities while immersing them in a product-related environment. They also begin to blur the boundaries between commercial and noncommercial content, something that is regulated in traditional media venues. The figure opposite gives some idea of the types of advergames to which children are exposed online. It is interesting to note in Figure 1 that in order for the child to play the game online they need to purchase the actual product (a sugar cereal).

In their review of children and advertising, Kunkel and Castonguay (2011) made the following conclusions:

1. The type of food ads which are most heavily advertised on television are also strongly featured online;
2. The pattern of marketing of unhealthy foods to children that we have seen on television is now being replicated on the internet; and
3. It is much more difficult for a child to discriminate a commercial from other material on the internet, compared to advertising in traditional media, like television.

Conclusions and advice for parents and professionals working with children

There are a number of more recent issues that have become of concern regarding new technology and children. Sexting, driving while texting and sleep deprivation are only a few that are beginning to emerge as areas for research and discussion. In thinking about potential solutions to these issues, I, for one, do not believe that governmental regulation would be an answer, particularly in a media platform that is global in nature. Rating systems, if handled adequately might help somewhat, but such systems are rarely utilised by parents and have not been effective even with simple technology like television. I strongly believe that various forms of education and media literacy are a reasonable solution. This can include:

- Professionals like paediatricians and teachers taking a more active role in discussing the impact of new media;
- Educating and empowering parents in their roles as monitors of children's media viewing (including the internet);

THE INTERNET AS "FAST AND FURIOUS" CONTENT

Figure 1: Example of an Advergame on a food product Website

Kellogg's Froot Loops

Compare this picture with the back of your *Froot Loops*® cereal box. Circle all the differences you find. (Hint: there are 10 differences in all. See below for the answers.)

ANSWERS: 1. The items under "Seek and Find" are missing 2. The aroma walk in the upper left corner is gone 3. The word "Taste" is missing from "Toucans Love Fruity Tasty" 4. The Nephew™ in the middle is looking down instead of up 5. The *Froot Loops*® logo in the lower right corner is upside down. 6. The Nephew™ on the right has a green beak 7. The big flower under the foot of Toucan Sam™ is red instead of yellow 8. The Nephew™ on the left has different color feathers on his head 9. The palm trees next to the first "Did you nose?" box are missing 10. There is a big yellow flower just above the last "Did you nose?" box

125

- Media literacy and critical viewing skills, being taught as part of school curriculum, acting as a strong intervention toward mitigating the impact of many negative media depictions; and
- The mass media itself being part of the solution. For example, movies and web sites about violence, sex and drinking that are professionally produced and also entertaining have great potential for informing the public and influencing risk-related attitudes and behaviours.

Within Australia, there are a number of excellent government websites which can be helpful to parents and others in this area. Some of these are:

- <www.cybersmart.gov.au>
- <www.netalert.gov.au>
- <www.staysmartonline.gov.au>

In summary, this chapter has presented a brief overview of some of the concerns we have about new media platforms. In reflecting on this brief review, it would be safe to conclude that the mass media, in all its domains, is a contributor to a number of risk behaviours and health related problems in children and adolescents. We must keep in mind, however, that the mass media is but one of a multitude of factors that contribute and, in many cases, not always the most significant. Nevertheless, it is one of those factors in which proper interventions, such as those I have suggested above, can mitigate its impact and, further, one factor which can be controlled with reasonable insight (Strasburger et al, 2010).

I expect most scholars would note that considerably more research is needed with regard to the internet in its role as a technology for the learning, social and cognitive development of children and adolescents. There is no question that we need to enrich our understanding of these new technologies as more and more children come online and the technology itself changes and expands. When thinking about these newer technologies we should keep in mind what Huesmann (2007) notes about the decades of research and theory on traditional media – that this extensive research and theory development has provided us with significant insights into the role new technology will play in the development and mitigation of aggressive behaviour. As some have said "The technology conduit may be changing, but the influential processes (for example, priming, activation and desensitisation) may be the same" (Ferdon & Hertz, 2007, p S5).

References

Braun-Courville, D, & Rojas, M (2009). Exposure to sexually explicit web sites and adolescent sexual attitudes and behaviors. *Journal of Adolescent Health, 45*, 156–162.

Brown, JD & L'Engle, KL (2009). X-Rated: Sexual attitudes and behaviors associated with US early adolescents' exposure to sexually explicit media. *Communication Research, 36*, 129–135.

Cai, X, & Zhao, X (2010). Click here, kids! Online advertising practices on popular children's websites. *Journal of Children and Media, 4*, 134–154.

Donnerstein, E (2011). The media and aggression: From TV to the internet. In J Forgas, A Kruglanski & K Williams (eds), *The psychology of social conflict and aggression* (pp 267–284). New York: Psychology Press.

Escobar-Chaves, S, Tortolero, S, Markham, C, Low, B, Eitel, P, & Thickstun, P (2005). Impact of the media on adolescent sexual attitudes and behaviors. *Pediatrics, 116*, 303–326.

Ferdon, CD, & Hertz, MF (2007). Electronic media, violence, and adolescents: An emerging public health problem. *Journal of Adolescent Health, 41*, S1–S5.

Huesmann, LR (2007). The impact of electronic media violence: Scientific theory and research. *Journal of Adolescent Health, 41*, S6–S13.

Kaiser Family Foundation (2006). *The media family: Electronic media in the lives of infants, toddlers, preschoolers, and their parents*. Menlo Park, CA: Kaiser Family Foundation.

Kunkel, D, & Castonguay, J (2012). Children and television advertising: Content, comprehension, and consequences. In D Singer & J Singer (eds), *Handbook of children and the media* (pp 395–418). Thousand Oaks, CA: Sage.

Livingstone, S, & Haddon, L (2009). *EU Kids Online: Final report*. LSE, London: EU Kids Online.

Lo, V, & Wei, R (2005). Exposure to internet pornography and Taiwanese adolescents' sexual attitudes and behavior. *Journal of Broadcasting and Electronic Media, 49*, 221–237.

Malamuth, N, Linz, D, & Yao, MZ (2005). The internet and aggression: Motivation, disinhibitory and opportunity aspects. In Y Amichai-Hamburger (ed), *The social net: Human behavior in cyberspace* (pp 163–191). New York: Oxford University Press.

Mitchell, K, Finkelhor, D, Jones, L, & Wolak, J (2010). Use of social networking sites in online sex crimes against minors: An examination of national incidence and means of utilization. *Journal of Adolescent Health, 47*, 183–190.

National Crime Prevention Council (2009). Accessed 20 April 2011, <http://www.ncpc.org/>.

Peter, J, & Valkenburg, PM (2008). Adolescents' exposure to sexually explicit Internet material, sexual uncertainty, and attitudes toward uncommitted sexual exploration: Is there a link? *Communication Research, 35*, 579–602.

Peter, J, & Valkenburg, PM (2009). Adolescents' exposure to sexually explicit Internet material and notions of women as sex objects: Assessing causality and underlying processes. *Journal of Communication, 59*, 407–433.

Pew Foundation (2009). *The Pew Internet and American Life Project*. Philadelphia, PA: The Pew Charitable Trusts.

Rideout, VJ, Foehr, UG, & Roberts, DF (2010). *Generation M2: Media in the lives of 8-to-18 year olds*. Menlo Park, CA: Kaiser Family Foundation.

Salazar, L, Fleischauer, PJ, Bernhardt, JM, & DiClemente, R (2009). Sexually explicit content viewed by teens on the Internet. In A Jordan, D Kunkel, J Manganello, & M Fishbein (eds), *Media messages and public health: A decision approach to content analysis* (pp 116–136). New York: Routledge.

Strasburger, VC, Jordan, AB, & Donnerstein, E (2010). Health effects of media on children and adolescents. *Pediatrics, 125*, 756–767.

Tokunaga, R (2010). Following you home from school: A critical review and synthesis of research on cyberbullying victimization. *Computers in Human Behavior, 26*, 277–287.

Wolak, J, Finkelhor, D, Mitchell, KJ, & Ybarra, ML (2008). Online "predators" and their victims: Myths, realities, and implications for prevention and treatment. *American Psychologist, 63*, 111–128.

Wolak J, Mitchell KJ, & Finkelhor, D (2007). Unwanted and wanted exposure to online pornography in a national sample of youth internet. *Pediatrics, 119*, 247–257.

Wright, P, Malamuth, N & Donnerstein, E (2012). Research on sex in the media: What do we know about effects on children and adolescents? In D Singer & J Singer (eds), *Handbook of children and the media* (pp 273-302). Thousand Oaks, CA: Sage.

Chapter 6
Messages, minds and mental contamination

Cordelia Fine

In 1957, in a book called *The Hidden Persuaders*, journalist Vance Packard (1957, p 3) provided an account of contemporary advertising techniques that he described as aiming "to channel our unthinking habits, our purchasing decisions, and our thought processes ... Typically these efforts take place beneath our level of awareness". With its promise to expose the "revealing, often shocking, explanation of new techniques of research and methods of persuasion", the potential for this best-selling book to cause harm to public perception of advertising was clear (see Nelson, 2008). Publication of *The Hidden Persuaders* was described by the *Advertising Age* as one of the most important events in American advertising. According to Nelson (2008, p 116), the potentially damaging effect of the book on public attitudes caused consternation within the advertising profession, leading to the "reframing of advertising practice" as a technique designed "to inform, educate, and persuade". As one industry defender put it, "[t]here are no hidden persuaders. Advertising works openly, in the bare pitiless sunlight" (Reeves, 1961, p 70). With this reframing came a model of the consumer whose behaviour is based on conscious deliberation about products.

This chapter begins with an explanation of how this model of consumer behaviour has framed the debate about the ethics of advertising to children. This debate typically centres on the age at which children understand the persuasive intent of advertising messages and can critically evaluate them. Then it reviews data that, contrary to what we would expect from such a model, finds that older children are no less influenced by advertising messages than are younger children. This, it is argued, is because it is based on an account of consumer psychology that overlooks the role of automatic mental processes in our attitudes and behaviour, and is therefore inadequate for fully understanding how our minds process, and are influenced by, advertising messages. These sections of the chapter draw heavily on work co-authored with E-M Lyon Business School Professor of Marketing Agnes Nairn (Fine, 2007; Nairn & Fine, 2008a; 2008b). Finally, the chapter briefly explores the potential implications of these arguments and research for the debate regarding the effects of sexualised media on children.

The mind of the consumer

As a number of social psychologists have observed, academic consumer research has been dominated by models that present consumer preferences and choice as the result of conscious deliberation (eg, Bargh, 2002; Fitzsimons et al, 2002). Two of the most dominant models of attitude change or persuasion are the Elaboration-Likelihood Model (Petty & Wegener, 1999) and the Heuristic-Systematic Model (Chen & Chaiken, 1999). Certainly, these incorporate the idea that in some circumstances such conscious deliberation can be cursory. Thus we may use less effortful short-cuts or "heuristics" in evaluating persuasive messages: for example, we may trust without scrutiny the conclusions provided by sources we regard as especially reliable and trustworthy. However, these models are largely concerned with the conscious processing of information and consciously held attitudes.

Understandably, the debate about the ethics of marketing has therefore focused on the age at which children acquire what is known as "persuasion knowledge" (Moses & Baldwin, 2005; Wright et al, 2005); that is, the age at which children can recognise advertising, understand its selling and persuasive intent and use this understanding in their conscious evaluation of the advertised product or service. For example, the consumer in possession of persuasion knowledge, seeing the Lynx deodorant tagline "Even angels will fall", will recognise that this is an advertising message and understand that its purpose is to sell, and to make him think more favourably of, the product. His attitude towards the product will change in a way that reflects his cynicism regarding the possibility that a whiff of Lynx will have a devastatingly seductive effect on attractive young women of solid moral virtue.

Persuasion knowledge is regarded by researchers and policymakers as a "developmental milestone" (Moore, 2004, p 162). Roughly speaking, children begin to understand its selling intent ("I know that company A is trying to sell me the product") between seven and 11 years of age, with the more sophisticated understanding of persuasive intent ("I know that company A is trying to change my mind") following after (see Oates et al, 2001; Oates et al, 2003). Clearly, children should be especially vulnerable to advertising before the acquisition of persuasion knowledge. As a review by the American Psychological Association (Kunkel et al, 2004) summarised the reasoning: "If it is unfair and deceptive to seek to bypass the defenses that adults are presumed to have when they are aware that advertising is addressed to them, then it must likewise be considered unfair and deceptive to advertise to children in whom these defenses do not yet exist" (p 21).

In other words, advertising to children who lack persuasion knowledge is morally similar to "undercover marketing", whereby an individual provides positive information about a product without disclosing to the target that they are acting on behalf of the marketer. The target is therefore ignorant of the intent behind the information and will not be as sceptical in her evaluation of it as she might otherwise be.

Defenders of the practice of advertising to children do not tend to challenge the premise that persuasion knowledge is the appropriate ethical benchmark. Instead, they may argue that children are more sophisticated consumers of advertising messages than is generally assumed. For example, Lumby and Fine (2006) suggest that "[t]o claim that children are entirely helpless and absolutely open to manipulation in such a wholesale way is actually to strip them of agency and, in a sense, to divest them of a level of humanity" (p 161).

Lumby and Fine note that children can be cynical and distrustful of advertising from as young as eight years old and take this as evidence that these kids are not "innocent lambs being led to the marketing slaughter". Similarly, Sternheimer (2003, p 158) decries the "media fears [that] continue to insist that we view children's minds as blank slates that advertisers easily manipulate". Rather, she argues, there is evidence that children as young as six can be critical of advertisements – and certainly all children by the age of eight are sceptical. Sternheimer and Lumby and Fine also reassure that preschoolers tend not even to recall advertisements they have seen. The implication here appears to be that young children of this age cannot therefore be lastingly influenced by such advertising, again reflecting the assumption that advertising influences via conscious deliberations and beliefs.

Does persuasion knowledge make a difference?

However, as an increasing number of researchers have pointed out, there is surprisingly little evidence to support the assumption that older children with greater persuasion knowledge are less influenced by advertising messages than are younger, more naive children (Livingstone & Helsper, 2006; Nairn & Fine, 2008b; Rozendaal et al, 2009). Studies that have compared age groups under-12 have generally found little or no effect of age or persuasion knowledge on children's preferences for advertised products (Chernin, 2008; Christenson, 1982; Kunkel, 1988; Mallinckdrodt & Mizerski, 2007). For example, Mallinckrodt and Mizerski (2007) explored the effects of a Froot Loop advergame on school-children's preferences for Froot Loops over other cereals and food products. They found an increased preference for Froot Loops after playing the game in the older group of 7–8-year-olds, but not the younger group. Moreover, children varied in the extent to which they understood the persuasive intent behind this new form of marketing, yet there was no evidence that the food preferences of the more "marketing savvy" children were less influenced by the game.

Moreover, a number of recent studies involving participants aged 11 and above (roughly the age at which persuasion knowledge should be in place for at least a portion of children) have again found no evidence of reduced susceptibility to advertising. A review of 50 studies into the influence of television advertising on food choice which looked at three age ranges (2–6 years, 7–11 years and 12–16 years) found no evidence of decreasing influence with age (Livingstone & Helsper, 2006). Similarly, Auty and Lewis (2004) found that seeing a branded movie clip (with previous exposure to the film) increased the likelihood of choosing the brand soon after watching the film – and no less so in an older group of 11–12 years olds than in a younger 6–7-year-old group. Lastly, a study of the effects of celebrity endorsement on advertised toy preferences found that 11–14-year-old boys were no less influenced than 8–10-year-olds. The authors concluded that "[c]ontrary to the speculation of many researchers, understanding about advertising intent and techniques and cynicism about ads had almost no influence on product preference after viewing" (Ross et al, 1984, p 185).

Automatic influences on the consumer

Why does persuasion knowledge in children appear to have so little effect on their susceptibility to advertising? Anyone who is familiar with how products are advertised to children (and indeed often to adults) may wonder at the focus on the ability of the child to sceptically evaluate an advertisement's claims, since so little advertising targeted to children presents propositional information about a product that can be evaluated (see Nairn & Fine, 2008b). This is especially so for popular contemporary advertising formats such as product placement within computer games, films, television shows, games and social networking sites (Carter, 2007; Nelson, 2005), and sponsored "advergames" on children's websites (Dahl et al, 2006). Yet even in the more traditional format of the television advert, there is little in the way of information-based advertising. A recent content analysis of children's television food adverting in Australia found that fantasy, fun and humour were the most common promotional appeals made to children (Roberts & Pettigrew, 2007). Rather than providing information about the product, these formats take the form of what is known as evaluative conditioning; that is, "a change in the valence of a stimulus that results from pairing the stimulus with another stimulus" (De Houwer, 2007, p 230). In other words, by pairing the product (or brand) with rewarding stimuli, the product becomes more positively viewed by the consumer. Evaluative conditioning is a robust phenomenon (for recent meta-analysis see Hofmann et al, 2010). It should be noted, however, that evaluative conditioning effects have been found to be considerably smaller in children, although Hofmann et al note that this is a conclusion that requires caution because of the small number of studies involved.

The predominance of advertising formats that do not provide propositional information that the child can critically assess and evaluate in light of knowledge of the selling or persuasive intent of the message, further challenges the relevance of persuasion knowledge as the appropriate benchmark of fairness. So what might be more relevant? Answering this question requires examining theory and data relating to what are known as dual process models of cognition, and in particular dual process accounts of attitudes. Dual process models distinguish between "automatic" and "controlled" mental processes. (Other terminology used includes implicit versus explicit, or impulsive versus reflective.) While by most accounts this contrast is relative rather than absolute (Gawronski & Bodenhausen, 2006; Strack & Deutsch, 2004; but see Wilson et al, 2000), automatic processes are thought to be activated automatically and effortlessly, without intention or awareness and are difficult to control. Thus, stimuli and events automatically activate a pattern of associations that "fill in information, quickly and automatically, about the characteristics that previously have been observed or affective reactions that previously have been experienced, in situations that resemble the current one" (Smith & DeCoster, 2000, p 110). By contrast, controlled processes are relatively effortful, intended and consciously accessible.

Attitudes are an especially important construct in consumer psychology, and dual process models of attitudes contrast "controlled" and "automatic" attitudes. However, once again, the distinction should not be seen as a sharp one. No measurement of an attitude will index the product of either purely automatic or purely controlled processes (see, for example, Payne et al, 2005). Controlled attitudes are deliberated evaluations based on the fast learning of consciously accessible propositions ("Coke tastes nice"). They are what are assessed when an individual is asked questions like, "How much do you like Coke?" or "Do you prefer bottled water or tap water?" For example, Mary's controlled consumer attitude might quickly change when she learns that most people cannot distinguish between the taste of bottled water and tap water.

"Automatic" attitudes, by contrast, arise from "automatic affective reactions resulting from the particular associations that are activated automatically when one encounters a relevant stimulus" (Gawronski & Bodenhausen, 2006, p 693). These associations are thought to develop gradually through the preconscious and automatic strengthening of associations between concepts over the course of a number of experiences, in a way that "reflects correlations between aspects of the environment and cognitive, affective, or motor reactions" (Strack & Deutsch, 2004, p 223). Evaluative conditioning therefore represents the "prototypical" means of automatic attitude formation and change (Gawronski & Bodenhausen, 2006, p 697): the stimulus or concept is repeatedly paired with a stimulus that evokes a particular affective response. Typically, automatic attitudes are assessed using reaction time tasks that exploit the idea that the stronger the association is between two concepts, the more the processing of the first, through the spreading of activation, will speed processing of the second (eg, the Implicit Association Test, Greenwald et al, 1998; see Nosek et al, 2005 for a methodological and conceptual review of the use of this test).

From even this brief and simplified account of dual process models of attitudes, speculations can be made regarding how automatic and controlled attitudes might come to diverge. For example, a concern for thrift and the environment might cause us to hold a fairly negative controlled attitude towards bottled water. However, exposure to evaluative conditioning that pairs bottled water with images of stunning natural scenery may mean that the automatically evoked attitude to bottled water is positive, even though consciously reportable attitudes are left relatively unaffected. (It should be acknowledged, however, that there are many unanswered questions regarding differences and similarities in the formation and change of automatic and controlled attitudes, and the nature of the relationship between them, see, for example, Hofmann et al, 2010; Whitfield & Jordan, 2009).

Of course, if it is only our controlled consumer attitudes that predict consumer behaviour then the traditional model of the consciously deliberative consumer is still valid. However, a large body of literature shows that our automatic attitudes can play an important role in behaviour, including consumer behaviour. A central tenet of dual process models is that the role of the effortful controlled processes is a self-regulatory one, which is to "overcome inappropriate automatic influences" (Sherman et al, 2008, p 320), inasmuch as the effects of automatic influences may conflict with consciously held beliefs or goals. However, since these self-regulatory controlled processes are cognitively expensive, their deployment depends on the extent to which the individual is both motivated, and able, to engage in them (for a review of this literature, see Friese et al, 2008b). For example, automatic social attitudes (such as an automatic negative bias against a particular ethnic group) have been found to have a greater influence on behaviour when choices or judgments are made spontaneously (see, for example, Dovidio et al, 1997; Rydell & McConnell, 2006), under time pressure (Payne, 2001) or when self-regulatory resources are either temporarily (Govorun & Payne, 2006) or chronically (Payne, 2005) low.

Consumer research is consistent with a dual process account of attitudes. For example, it has been found that automatic attitudes towards products can change following exposure to advertising messages (or simulations), even in the absence of similar change in controlled (that is, self-reported) consumer attitudes (Czyzewska & Ginsburg, 2007; Forehand & Perkins, 2005; Gibson, 2008). For instance, using a sample of participants who had no conscious preference for Coke versus Pepsi, Gibson (2008) was able to bring about a change in automatic attitudes towards Coke and Pepsi by pairing Coke and Pepsi words and logos with either positive or negative stimuli. However, participants' self-reported attitudes remained unchanged. In other words, while the experience of the participant was that she had been left unaffected by the evaluative conditioning procedure, influence was nonetheless present at the less consciously accessible level of automatic attitudes, at least temporarily.

As already noted, reduced capacity to control one's responses increases the likelihood of automatic attitudes influencing behaviour, and research shows this to also be true for consumer behaviour. People are more likely to be influenced by their automatic consumer attitudes when distracted (eg, Friese et al 2008a; Gibson, 2008), under time pressure (Friese et al, 2006); when making spontaneous choices (Perugini, 2005; Strick et al, 2009); and when temporarily (Friese et al, 2008a; Hofmann et al, 2007) or chronically (Hofmann et al, 2008) low in self-regulatory resources (for review see Friese et al, 2008b). For example, Friese and colleagues (2006) contrasted people's self-reported preferences for branded versus generic products with their automatic preferences. While only a third of the sample explicitly reported preferring brands, automatic attitudes were more positive to brands than to generics in 85 per cent of the sample. The researchers then offered their participants a choice of two gift baskets, of equal monetary value. One was made up of branded products – the other, of equivalent generics. When given plenty of time to make their choice, most of the participants acted in line with their self-reported preferences. Yet given the same choice under time pressure, nearly two thirds of the consumers whose controlled and automatic preferences diverged chose in line with the latter rather than the former. In other words, under time pressure they chose what they did not consciously prefer.

Mental contamination

These findings change the complexion of our understanding of how advertising messages can influence consumer behaviour. The pairing of products with positive stimuli can change automatic attitudes, without necessarily bringing about a corresponding change in self-reported attitudes. In turn, in low-control situations this automatic consumer attitude can direct consumer behaviour, even when that choice conflicts with the individual's consciously endorsed attitude (Friese et al, 2006). It can readily be seen that, on its own, persuasion knowledge will be of little assistance here, since the effect of the advertising message on behaviour largely bypasses conscious, deliberative processes. This is an example of what Wilson and Brekke (1994, p 117) have termed "mental contamination", defined as "the process whereby a person has an unwanted judgment, emotion, or behavior because of mental processing that is unconscious or uncontrollable". What is potentially morally objectionable about actions that lead to mental contamination is that when external forces influence us to respond in ways that we would prefer not to respond, our autonomy is undermined (Moles, 2007).

What seems critical in order to avoid such effects is the ability to "correct" or overcome automatic consumer attitudes (Nairn & Fine, 2008b). As noted earlier, this depends upon having both the motivation and capacity to engage in effortful self-regulatory controlled processes (Friese et al, 2008b). Motivation is likely to require some kind of awareness that one's preferences might have been unduly influenced by irrelevant factors; this is not a simple concept. What level of self-regulatory capacity should be seen as sufficient is both an empirical and moral question. It is also unlikely that there will be a fixed age at which children, on average, attain this acceptable level as it will likely depend, amongst other factors, on the advertising format in question (Nairn & Fine, 2008b). However, what seems clear is that a capacity to overcome the effects of advertising-mediated automatic attitude change will depend upon self-regulatory processes, and these continue to develop throughout childhood, adolescence and early adulthood (Luna et al, 2004).

Importantly, if for many advertising formats it is capacity for self-regulatory control of automatic influences that is critical for being capable of resisting the influence of advertising, rather than persuasion knowledge, then it is not clear how much benefit to expect from programs designed to build and develop the latter. As noted in Nairn & Fine (2008b), while a number of such media literacy programs have been developed, there is little evidence of their effectiveness (Eagle, 2007) and, according to the data and arguments presented here, little reason to confidently anticipate that future research into media literacy will demonstrate beneficial effects.

Implications for thinking about children and sexualised media

The data and arguments presented here raise an issue that, to date, has not enjoyed much attention in the debate regarding the effects of sexualised media on children: the potential for mental contamination arising from the use of sexualised images in advertising messages. Moles (2007) has argued that a particularly serious form of mental contamination is that which involves our attitudes and behaviour towards a particular social group. In line with this possibility, research into social attitudes and behaviour has found that patterns experienced in the environment can influence the automatic associations that people make, both for individuals and social groups. For example, Dasgupta and Agari (2004) found that a college environment rich in female leaders led to increased strength of the association between women and leadership, while other research has found that evaluative conditioning can change automatic attitudes towards individuals (Rydell & McConnell, 2006; Whitfield & Jordan, 2009). External stimuli can also activate characteristics stereotypically associated with particular social groups, making those characteristics more accessible to consciousness and therefore more likely to influence social perception (Kunda & Spencer, 2003) and self-perception (Steele & Ambady, 2006). As noted earlier, overcoming unwanted automatic influences on social judgments and behaviour requires both motivation and self-regulatory control resources (Friese et al, 2008b).

Of interest, then, is what associations and stereotypes might be automatically developed and reinforced by the repeated exposure of children to images of sexually objectified females (typically). While to date most research in this area has looked at the psychological effects of the emphasis on the body in sexually objectified images (see Chapter 7, this volume), social psychologists have recently become interested in what is *de*-emphasised in sexual objectification. Following Nussbaum (1999), Heflick and Goldenberg (2009) have pointed out that:

> [P]ossible ways that objectification influences perceptions of objectified persons ... are directly related to minimizing their competence: denying self-determination, agentic qualities and uniqueness of talents (ie, they can easily be replaced). Others likely minimize the perception of the individual as fully human, such as denying that their feelings and experiences matter and having less concern when they are physically or emotionally harmed. (p 598)

Research of this nature has only begun, but so far the evidence is largely consistent with these hypotheses. A number of studies have now found that objectification (achieved either by asking participants to focus on a target's appearance, or presenting the target in a sexually objectified way) can lead to the target being perceived as less competent (Glick et al, 2005; Heflick & Goldenberg, 2009; Heflick et al, 2011; Loughnan et al, 2010). An earlier study also found that viewing sexualised images of women in adverts primed men to perceive a non-sexualised female job candidate as less competent (Rudman & Borgida, 1995). Sexual objectification has also been found to result in reduced perceptions of humanness, in the form of reduced ratings of warmth and morality (Heflick et al, 2011), of experience of thoughts, feelings and intentions, and of deservingness of moral concern (Loughnan et al, 2010). These latter findings are interesting to consider in light of findings that exposure to sexually objectifying images has been linked with increased tolerance for sexual aggression (eg, Dill et al, 2008).

At this point, it is only possible to make speculations concerning potential mentally contaminating effects from pervasive sexually objectifying imagery in children's lives. Our understanding of the complex interplay between automatic and controlled processes, their responsiveness to the social environment and their relative roles in real world behaviour is far from complete; our understanding of the interaction of sexually objectified stimuli with these processes even less so. However, the research to date suggests that it would probably be unwise to assume in advance that repeated exposure to such stimuli (including those not targeted to children and to which they may pay little attention) will affect neither the representations of females in associative memory that they carry into teenage and adult years, nor social perception and behaviour, especially in low-control situations. Also worth emphasising is that automatic processes appear to be less influenced by factual information than are our consciously reportable attitudes and beliefs (Rydell & McConnell, 2006; Whitfield & Jordan, 2009). This raises a question mark over the extent to which media literacy training, or education by parents, can effectively counteract the effects on automatic associations of repeated encounters with sexually objectifying media.

Many, if not most parents, would presumably prefer their children to develop into adults who perceive women as fully human, equally competent to men and equally deserving of moral consideration – not just in coolly deliberative moments, but also while distracted, under time pressure, intoxicated or in any other low control state. If society is to support parents in that endeavour, which is in the interests of any society that values gender equality, then we should not neglect to consider and research how the proliferation of sexually objectifying images of females in children's lives may potentially undermine that aim.

Acknowledgments

I thank Emma Rush for her helpful comments on an earlier version of this chapter.

References

Auty, S, & Lewis, C (2004). Exploring children's choice: The reminder effect of product placement. *Psychology and Marketing, 21*(9), 697–713.
Bargh, J (2002). Losing consciousness: Automatic influences on consumer judgment, behavior, and motivation. *Journal of Consumer Research, 29*, 280–285.
Carter, M (2007). Online drama proves a lucrative hit. *Guardian*, 12 December, Media Pages, p 7.
Chen, S, & Chaiken, S (1999). The heuristic-systematic model in its broader context. In S Chaiken & Y Trope (eds), *Dual-process theories in social psychology* (pp 73–96). New York: Guilford Press.
Chernin, A (2008). The effects of food marketing on children's preferences: Testing the moderating roles of age and gender. *The ANNALS of the American Academy of Political and Social Science, 615*, 102–118.

Christenson, P (1982). Children's perceptions of TV commercials and products: The effects of PSAs. *Communication Research, 9*(4), 491-524.

Czyzewska, M, & Ginsburg, H (2007). Explicit and implicit effects of anti-marijuana and anti-tobacco television advertisements. *Addictive Behaviors, 32*(1), 114-127.

Dahl, S, Eagle, L, & Baez, C (2006). Analysing advergames: Active diversions or actually deception. An exploratory study of online advergames content. *Young Consumers 10*(1), 46-59.

Dasgupta, N, & Asgari, S (2004). Seeing is believing: Exposure to counterstereotypic women leaders and its effect on the malleability of automatic gender stereotyping. *Journal of Experimental Social Psychology, 40*, 642-658.

De Houwer, J (2007). A conceptual and theoretical analysis of evaluative conditioning. *The Spanish Journal of Psychology, 10*(2), 230-241.

Dill, KE, Brown, BP, & Collins, MA (2008). Effects of exposure to sex-stereotyped video game characters on tolerance of sexual harassment. *Journal of Experimental Social Psychology, 44*(5), 1402-1408.

Dovidio, J, Kawakami, K, Johnson, C, Johnson, B, & Howard, A (1997). On the nature of prejudice: Automatic and controlled processes. *Journal of Experimental Social Psychology, 33*, 510-540.

Eagle, L (2007). Commercial media literacy: What does it do, to whom – and does it matter? *Journal of Advertising, 36*(2), 101-110.

Fine, C (2007). Vulnerable minds? The consumer unconscious and the ethics of marketing to children. *Res Publica, 16*(1), 14-18.

Fitzsimons, G, Hutchinson, J, & Williams, P (2002). Non-conscious influences on consumer choice. *Marketing Letters, 13*(3), 269-279.

Forehand, M, & Perkins, A (2005). Implicit assimilation and explicit contrast: A set/reset model of response to celebrity voice-overs. *Journal of Consumer Research, 32 (December)*, 435-441.

Friese, M, Hofmann, W, & Wänke, M (2008a). When impulses take over: Moderated predictive validity of explicit and implicit attitude measures in predicting food choice and consumption behaviour. *British Journal of Social Psychology, 47*, 397-419.

Friese, M, Hofmann, W, & Schmitt, M (2008b). When and why do implicit measures predict behaviour? Empirical evidence for the moderating role of opportunity, motivation, and process reliance. *European Review of Social Psychology, 19*, 285-338.

Friese, M, Wänke, M, & Plessner, H (2006). Implicit consumer preferences and their influence on product choice. *Psychology and Marketing, 23*(9), 727-740.

Gawronski, B, & Bodenhausen, G (2006). Associative and propositional processes in evaluation: An integrative review of implicit and explicit attitude change. *Psychological Bulletin, 132*(5), 692-731.

Gibson, B (2008). Can evaluative conditioning change attitudes toward mature brands? New evidence from the Implicit Association Test. *Journal of Consumer Research, 35 (June)*, 178-188.

Glick, P, Larsen, S, Johnson, C, & Branstiter, H (2005). Evaluations of sexy women in low and high status jobs. *Psychology of Women Quarterly, 29*, 389-395.

Govorun, O, & Payne, B (2006). Ego-depletion and prejudice: separating automatic and controlled components. *Social Cognition, 24*(2), 111-136.

Greenwald, A, McGhee, D, & Schwartz, J (1998). Measuring individual differences in implicit cognition: The implicit association test. *Journal of Personality and Social Psychology, 74*, 1464-1480.

Heflick, NA, & Goldenberg, JL (2009). Objectifying Sarah Palin: Evidence that objectification causes women to be perceived as less competent and less fully human. *Journal of Experimental Social Psychology, 45*(3), 598–601.

Heflick, NA, Goldenberg, JL, Cooper, DP, & Puvia, E (2011). From women to objects: Appearance focus, target gender, and perceptions of warmth, morality and competence. *Journal of Experimental Social Psychology, 47*(3), 572–581.

Hofmann, W, De Houwer, J, Perugini, M, Baeyens, F, & Crombez, G (2010). Evaluative conditioning in humans: A meta-analysis. *Psychological Bulletin, 136*(3), 390–421.

Hofmann, W, Gschwender, T, Friese, M, & Wiers, R (2008). Working memory capacity and self-regulatory behavior: Toward an individual differences perspective on behavior determination by automatic versus controlled processes. *Journal of Personality and Social Psychology, 95*(4), 962–977.

Hofmann, W, Rauch, W, & Gawronski, B (2007). And deplete us not into temptation: Automatic attitudes, dietary restraint, and self-regulatory resources as determinants of eating behavior. *Journal of Experimental Social Psychology, 43*(3), 497–504.

Kunda, Z, & Spencer, S (2003). When do stereotypes come to mind and when do they color judgment? A goal-based theoretical framework for stereotype activation and application. *Psychological Bulletin, 129*(4), 522–544.

Kunkel, D (1988). Children and host-selling television commercials. *Communication Research, 15*(1), 71–92.

Kunkel, D, Wilcox, B, Cantor, J, Palmer, E, Linn, S, & Dowrick, P (2004). *Report of the APA task force on advertising and children. Section: Psychological issues in the increasing commercialization of childhood.* Washington, DC: American Psychological Association (APA).

Livingstone, S, & Helsper, E (2006). Does advertising literacy mediate the effects of advertising on children? A critical examination of two linked research literatures in relation to obesity and food choices. *Journal of Communication, 56*(3), 560–584.

Loughnan, S, Haslam, N, Murnane, T, Vaes, J, Reynolds, C, & Suitner, C (2010). Objectification leads to depersonalization: The denial of mind and moral concern to objectified others. *European Journal of Social Psychology, 40,* 709–717.

Lumby, C, & Fine, D (2006). *Why TV is good for kids: Raising 21st century children.* Sydney: Pan Macmillan.

Luna, B, Garver, K, Urban, T, Lazar, N, & Sweeney, J (2004). Maturation of cognitive processes from late childhood to adulthood. *Child Development, 75*(5), 1357–1372.

Mallinckdrodt, V, & Mizerski, R (2007). The effects of playing an advergame on young children's perceptions, preferences, and requests. *Journal of Advertising, 36*(2), 87–100.

Moles, A (2007). Autonomy, free speech and automatic behaviour. *Res Publica, 13*(1), 53–75.

Moore, E (2004). Children and the changing world of advertising. *Journal of Business Ethics, 52*(2), 161–167.

Moses, L, & Baldwin, D (2005). What can the study of cognitive development reveal about children's ability to appreciate and copy with advertising? *Journal of Public Policy and Marketing, 24*(2), 186–201.

Nairn, A, & Fine, C (2008a). Not seeing the wood for the imaginary trees. Or, who's messing with our article? *International Journal of Advertising, 27*(5), 896–908.

Nairn, A, & Fine, C (2008b). Who's messing with my mind? The implications of dual-process models for the ethics of advertising to children. *International Journal of Advertising, 27*(3), 447–470.

Nelson, M (2005). Exploring consumer response to advergaming. In C Haugtvedt (ed), *Online consumer psychology: Understanding and influencing consumer behaviour in the virtual world* (pp 167-194). Mahwah, NJ: Lawrence Erlbaum Associates Inc.

Nelson, M (2008). The Hidden Persuaders: Then and now. *Journal of Advertising*, 37(1), 113-126.

Nosek, B, Greenwald, A, & Banaji, M (2005). The implicit association test at age 7: A methodological and conceptual review. In J Bargh (ed), *Automatic processes in social thinking and behavior* (pp 265-292). New York: Psychology Press.

Nussbaum, M (1999). *Sex and social justice*. New York: Oxford University Press.

Oates, C, Blades, M, & Gunter, B (2001). Children and television advertising: When do they understand persuasive intent? *Journal of Consumer Behaviour*, 1(3), 238-245.

Oates, C, Blades, M, Gunter, B, & Don, J (2003). Children's understanding of television advertising: A qualitative approach. *Journal of Marketing Communications*, 9(2), 59-77.

Packard, V (1957). *The hidden persuaders*. London: Longmans.

Payne, B (2001). Prejudice and perception: The role of automatic and controlled processes in misperceiving a weapon. *Journal of Personality and Social Psychology*, 81, 181-192.

Payne, B (2005). Conceptualizing control in social cognition: how executive functioning modulates the expression of automatic stereotyping. *Journal of Personality and Social Psychology*, 89, 488-503.

Payne, B, Jacoby, L, & Lambert, A (2005). Attitudes as accessibility bias: Dissociating automatic and controlled processes. In R Hassin, J Uleman & J Bargh (eds), *The new unconscious* (pp 393-420). Oxford: Oxford University Press.

Perugini, M (2005). Predictive models of implicit and explicit attitudes. *British Journal of Social Psychology*, 44(1), 29-45.

Petty, R, & Wegener, D (1999). The elaboration likelihood model: Current status and controversies. In S Chaiken & Y Trope (eds), *Dual process theories in social psychology* (pp 41-72). New York Guilford Press.

Reeves, R (1961). *Reality in advertising*. New York: Knopf.

Roberts, M, & Pettigrew, S (2007). A thematic content analysis of children's food advertising. *International Journal of Advertising*, 26(3), 357-367.

Ross, R, Campbell, T, Wright, J, Huston, A, Rice, M, & Turk, P (1984). When celebrities talk, children listen: An experimental analysis of children's responses to TV ads with celebrity endorsement. *Journal of Applied Developmental Psychology*, 5(3), 185-202.

Rozendaal, E, Buijzen, M, & Valkenburg, P (2009). Do children's cognitive advertising defenses reduce their desire for advertised products? *Communications*, 34, 287-303.

Rudman, L, & Borgida, E (1995). The afterglow of construct accessibility: The behavioral consequences of priming men to view women as sex objects. *Journal of Experimental Social Psychology*, 31, 493-517.

Rydell, R, & McConnell, A (2006). Understanding implicit and explicit attitude change: A systems of reasoning analysis. *Journal of Personality and Social Psychology*, 91(6), 995-1008.

Sherman, J, Gawronski, B, Gonsalkorale, K, Hugenberg, K, Allen, T, & Groom, C (2008). The self-regulation of automatic associations and behavioral impulses. *Psychological Review*, 115(2), 314-335.

Smith, E, & DeCoster, J (2000). Dual-process models in social and cognitive psychology: Conceptual integration and links to underlying memory systems. *Personality and Social Psychology Review*, 4, 108-131.

Steele, J, & Ambady, N (2006). "Math is hard!" The effect of gender priming on women's attitudes. *Journal of Experimental Social Psychology, 42*, 428--436.

Sternheimer, K (2003). *It's not the media: The truth about pop culture's influence on children.* Boulder, Colorado: Westview Press.

Strack, F, & Deutsch, R (2004). Reflective and impulsive determinants of social behavior. *Personality and Social Psychology Review, 8*(3), 220–247.

Strick, M, van Baaren, R, Holland, R, & van Knippenberg, A (2009). Humor in advertisements enhances product liking by mere association. *Journal of Experimental Psychology: Applied, 15*(1), 35–45.

Whitfield, M, & Jordan, C (2009). Mutual influence of implicit and explicit attitudes. *Journal of Experimental Social Psychology, 45*, 748–759.

Wilson, T, & Brekke, N (1994). Mental contamination and mental correction: Unwanted influences on judgments and evaluations. *Psychological Bulletin, 116*(1), 117–142.

Wilson, T, Lindsey, S, & Schooler, T (2000). A model of dual attitudes. *Psychological Review, 107*(1), 101–126.

Wright, P, Friestad, M, & Boush, D (2005). The development of marketplace persuasion knowledge in children, adolescents and young adults. *Journal of Public Policy and Marketing, 24*(2), 222-233.

Chapter 7

The impact of sexualisation – Knowing and seeing too much

Louise Newman

The debate about the exposure of children to adult-type sexual themes, in media and popular culture, is complex. In part this reflects very different views about the so-called "sexualisation" or "hyper-sexualisation" of popular culture through open discussion and representation of sexual themes and representations to which children are exposed. On the one hand is a view that frank discussion and representations of sexual themes are progressive and potentially valuable to children, whilst on the other are concerns about premature exposure of young children to themes which they are not emotionally able to understand. This debate is also one concerning what is a more direct involvement of children as participants in sexualised representations as occurs in fashion, art and culture. This has raised concerns about the premature sexualisation of children through exposure to developmentally inappropriate sexualised material ("sexualisation"), its impact on psychological and emotional development and possible links to child abuse and exploitation.

The debate is both emotive and at times overly simplistic in that it may be seen as a simple issue around censorship as opposed to openness. This has brought up issues of adults' rights to engage with sexual imagery and issues such as the right of the artist to explore sexuality in children and adolescents. Neither of these issues tend to acknowledge or focus on the more concerning area of the impact of sexualisation on children and young people and the possible effects on psychological and emotional well-being. The emphasis has been more on the need to support openness of expression and to avoid a censorship approach based on moral panic and opposition to sexual themes. Questions around "premature" exposure of children to adult sexual themes, child protection and child risk overall have usually been raised by disciplines such as psychology and child psychiatry rather than by artists or cultural theorists. This in turn has led to a resurgence of debate about the models of sexuality and gender found in theories of developmental psychology and in particular their assumptions and role in a socio-political sense as being regulatory and controlling of sexual expression. In other words, the debate around the conservative and controlling nature of psychology and its practice. It is in this context that some of the recent discussions around children and sexualisation have been formed.

As a starting point it should be acknowledged that children are "intrinsically" sexual and developing ideas about bodies, sex and relationships from birth. Although children are sexual beings from birth, theirs is not an adult sexuality. Based on developmental accounts from Freud's initial theorising in the "Three Essays on Sexuality", childhood sexuality has often been viewed in an ambivalent way by adults but nonetheless its regulation is seen as a core part of the parental function. The concerns about "over exposure" of children to adult sexual themes have largely been raised by parents who have stressed the undermining of their role and their right to teach their children about sex and gender according to their own values. The community understanding of the "innocence" of children may not be congruent with the psychoanalytic model of the sexual child, but it raises core questions about early development. What are the impacts of premature sexualisation on children and how do children adapt to this exposure? How much is too much?

The discussion below will review the available psychological evidence relating to the impact of sexualisation and discuss the implications for children's mental health.

Defining sexualisation

The concept of the "hyper-sexualisation" or "pornification" of popular culture (Paasonen et al, 2007) refers to the increasing emphasis on sexuality in many Western cultures, including a public shift to permissive sexual attitudes and sexual exploration. For young people, who are developing their ideas about sexual identity and expression, this creates a set of values about the centrality of the "desirable" and sexual self in which self-evaluation and self-esteem are linked to being "sexy". This is fundamentally a linking of socially determined ideals of desirability with self-worth, to the exclusion of other aspects of the self. Preoccupation with fashion, flirting, sexual exposure and imitation of marginal sexual practices such as bondage has become part of daily life and popular culture for many adolescents. Whilst it may be argued that sexual exploration has always occurred amongst young people, there are also concerns about the impact on younger children and the way in which a focus on the "sexual being" may not support broader development and identity. The impact on children and adolescents of internalising this model of the self are potentially very significant and are arguably related to ongoing impacts on psychological and emotional development. The focus on the external and appearance, along with the need to be seen only as desirable by others in a particular way, at the very least limits development of other attributes such as empathy and interpersonal understanding. Hypersexualisation then, as a social trend, may be related to changes in self-development and corresponding increases in difficulties of self-functioning seen in young people.

The American Psychological Association (APA) (2007) defines sexualisation as the process whereby a person's value is based on their appearance or behaviour to the exclusion of other characteristics (such as internal characteristics) and where "attractiveness" as a person is equated with being "sexy". This relates self-worth to sexual attractiveness as opposed to broader personal characteristics. Sexualisation also occurs when a person is sexually objectified and seen as an object for the sexual use of another, or when sexuality is inappropriately imposed upon a person. In the case of young children the imposition of adult sexual themes or behaviours may also involve threat, force or intimidation. The APA's view is that any one of these conditions is sufficient to indicate sexualisation (p 2) and that most evidence available relates to the third condition (sexual objectification). Inappropriate imposition of adult sexuality onto children does not include self-motivated sexual exploration between children even if this may be of concern to parents.

Sexualisation then, as defined above, is a broad term with some expressions having limited impact on children and others potentially related to serious abuse or exploitation. The impact of different types of sexualisation will also vary. As part of a response to popular culture children and adolescents will in a simple way internalise values and beliefs about appearance and desirability as they develop a sense of social identity. For some, being influenced by particular representations of female "beauty" and popularity and being preoccupied with unattainable ideals may have a major impact on self-esteem and confidence and influence choices in relationships and sexual behaviour.

The APA (2007) proposes that sexualisation occurs with three domains (p 3);

1. *Cultural Domain* – cultural norms, expectations and values which normalise certain representations and images. This will include broad representations of gender, sexuality and concepts of the roles of children, adults and generational boundaries;
2. *Interpersonal Domain* – family relationships, peers and interactions which promote sexualisation. This may include family and adult-child interactions which equate adult and child sexuality or which deny the difference between children and adults; and
3. *Self Domain* – internalised values and self-definition. This includes the psychological identification with sexualised images and values and the process of attempting to "become" the image despite other related negative impacts.

From a developmental and psychological perspective the impact on self and personality development is significant and raises questions about the changes that sexualisation may produce in the development of self-definition and gendered understanding. This impact may be most salient on significant points in development – early childhood when sense of self and gender are being established and in adolescence when the "sexual self" is being consolidated and relationships external to the family are explored.

Sexualisation of children also occurs within a specific economic context – the construction of the "Tween" market which targets children aged 6–12 years, a potential market of around 2–3 million in Australia. The child consumer has significant influence on family spending and this has produced a large market in terms of magazines, toys and fashion with associated large investment in advertising. The success of the Bratz dolls and magazines such as "Total Girl" generates ongoing marketing of certain "fashion looks" and a preoccupation with image and physical appearance. The contemporary "tween" is focused on themes previously reserved for "teens" and are increasingly aware of celebrity, glamour and success. Bouchard and Bouchard (2003), in an examination of tween magazines, found the typical "ideal" girl being defined by shopping and style and preoccupied with appearance and the body, with social acceptance and identity becoming fused with attaining the marketed image.

The Australia Institute (2006) report on sexualisation of children in Australia noted the recent development of direct sexualisation of children where children are presented in ways clearly modelled on "sexy" adults, particularly in advertising and media. Children in these images are dressed in adult type clothes and posed in ways designed to draw attention to adult sexual features that children do not yet have, which paradoxically reinforces the sexual theme. Girls magazines, aimed at the young market, contain around 50 per cent of sexualising content including beauty, fashion and "crushes" on boys. These publications provide celebrity gossip, fashion and interviews reinforcing values of appearance and attractiveness. Content encourages the development of crushes on teen and older men and to "grow up" as soon as possible.

The Australia Institute report points out that within advertising, the desirability of both consumption and sexualisation are linked with the marketing aimed at the "tween" group. There is little research available on children's media literacy and capacity to reflect on marketing functions and on particular products or brands. Whilst adolescents have greater understanding of the "persuasive" power and intent of advertising (Rush & La Nauze, 2006), younger children have much less capacity for "resistance" and understanding of media intent. Comprehensive information about media literacy education for primary school age children in Australia is not available.

The developmental impact of sexualisation

An increasing body of psychological and developmental research points to the potential harm of sexualisation of children, particularly those of primary school age.

Of particular concern is the way in which sexualisation impacts on self-development. Girls exposed to the image and values of sexual objectification are likely to incorporate these as part of self-identity. These preoccupying concerns may result in self-scrutiny, anxiety about appearance, self-consciousness and low-self esteem. The influence on gender roles and expectations of relationships is also concerning and likely to be shaped by their early exposures (Fredricksen & Roberts, 1997; Gabinski et al, 2003).

The APA Task Force Report on the sexualisation of girls (2007) outlines several possible mechanisms by which sexualisation may impact development:

1. Socialisation or the social conditioning of gender roles and models of "femininity";
2. Sociocultural context and the internalisation of values;
3. Cognitive models and beliefs regarding gender, objectification and sexualisation;
4. Psychodynamic accounts which stress impact on development of identity and role of traumatising sexual exposure.

All of these processes are likely to be involved in mediating the impact of sexualisation on development and particularly on the broad process of identity development. The development and consolidation of sexual identity and self-esteem in adolescence are also likely to be influenced by exposure earlier in childhood to unrealistic ideals of body and appearance. Problems with self-esteem may make girls particularly vulnerable to cultural messages linking a "sexy" look with popularity and social acceptance.

Mental health and sexualisation

There is ongoing concern about the relationship between media representations of body-ideal and girls' self-esteem and body-image. Media emphasis on a particular body image is largely viewed as an unattainable cultural image but one which can powerfully generate feelings of body shame and, in some cases, be related to the concept and perpetuation of disordered eating. Self-scrutiny and anxiety about appearance, largely studied in adolescent girls, has been found in those influenced by media representations and objectification. Data from the United States documents an increasing interest amongst teens in having cosmetic surgery procedures, ranging from botox injections to breast implants and liposuction (Olding & Zuckerman, 2004) with a threefold increase in under 18-year-olds having breast surgery between 2002 and 2003.

Whilst some of these may be classified as "necessary" procedures, this data suggests at least a greater social acceptance of the use of enhancing procedures.

Body image preoccupation and dissatisfaction is also seen in young children suggesting they too may be influenced in a significant way by medial representation. Australian and overseas research finds that children as young as six to seven years of age express the desire to have a thinner body and are aware of restricted eating as a way of losing weight, with some already engaging in eating disordered behaviour (Dohnt & Tiggeman, 2006). A study of 100 girls aged 9–12 years found that 49 per cent expressed the desire to be thinner and that media exposure to thin ideals was related to body dissatisfaction.

The literature regarding psychological harm and sexualisation largely focuses on the increasing rate of eating disorders in Western societies and depressive disorders. Increasing incidence of eating disorders such as anorexia nervosa are associated with changes in fashion and idealised body image. Several studies also report associations between exposure to thin ideal body images and disordered eating attitudes and symptoms (Field et al, 1999, Harrison, 2000).

Girls and adolescents are commonly found to experience lower self-esteem, negative mood and depressive symptoms when exposed to sexualised female ideals. Self-objectification and anxiety about the body have also been related to depressive symptoms and body shame (Harrison & Fredrickson, 2003). Whilst it is likely that there are individual differences in vulnerability to negative response to these images, there is a clear association between marketed ideal images and the sort of negative emotional response that may be associated with the development of clinical eating disorders.

Impact on sexual identity and relationships

The more complex and often subtle effects of sexualisation relate to children's emerging concepts of gender, gender role and sexuality. The representations of girls and women as sexual objects and boys and men as sexual predators are ubiquitous and particularly reinforced in some media and music sub-cultures. The influences of these types of messages may be to "normalise" gender stereotypes and behaviour in relationships and even the degrading treatment of, and violence towards, women.

Concerns have been raised about the use of images of sexualised children in clothing advertising and the use of poses that attribute sexual awareness (in an adult sense) to young children. It is feared that these may have the effect of normalising child-adult sexual interaction, or denying the limitation on children's understanding of adult sexuality and their capacity to "consent" to sexual behaviour. The development of the understanding of sexual relationships and behaviours is a complex developmental process across childhood and adolescence, with the impact of pubertal change and psychological development being essential to the establishment of sexual identity. Sexual experimentation is of course common and can occur in a healthy and positive way that leads to a sense of positive sexual expression. This process however can be disrupted by external coercion or exploitation, or by encouragement of experimentation in a premature way where it is eroticises children for adult purposes.

There is limited research regarding the effects of sexual content in media on the sexual attitudes and behaviours of adolescents. Most studies do, however, find an association between viewing of sexual contact and actual sexual activity, suggesting that media sex content normalises early onset sexual activity and makes it more likely that a young person will be involved in adult-type behaviour.

Children and young people's developing understanding and models of relationship and interpersonal functioning are also shaped by repeated exposure to gender-stereotypical ideas and images in media and popular culture. These frequently include themes of sexual harassment, violence towards women and models of relationship based on male control and dominance and sexual objectification of women. Models of femininity, masculinity and gendered behaviour are influenced by crude and limited values, with sexual behaviours and interactions also presented in ways reinforcing these values. Music videos, for example, often portray female performers as sexually available in multiple ways, accepting of sexual violence in an eroticised way and interacting with men in stereotyped ways (see Chapter 4, in this volume). Apart from sexualised music being linked with accelerated sexual activity and a doubled pregnancy risk in teens (Brown et al, 2006;

Pardun et al, 2005), it is likely that sexualised music video images have the effect of normalising aggressive sexual themes and again reinforce gender stereotypes.

Several studies of adolescents and young adults viewing music videos have found a relationship between video watching and adversarial sexual beliefs (Peterson & Pfost, 1989), as well as acceptance of sexual harassment (Strouse et al, 1994), date violence (Johnson et al, 1995) and rape (Kaestle et al, 2007). The study by Strouse and colleagues also identified a relationship between viewing sexualised images of girls and greater acceptance of young girls being suitable sexual partners and even tolerance of child sexual abuse (Strouse et al, 1994).

The impact of sexualisation on relationships and particularly on violence in relationships is a focus of the United Kingdom Sexualisation of Young People Review (Papadopoulos, 2010). Studies suggest that exposure to stereotypical images of women and images of men as dominant and aggressive are associated with greater tolerance of sexual harassment and attitudes blaming women for sexual assault (Dill et al, 2008).

The crucial question is whether these impacts on attitudes and beliefs translate into behaviour in relationships. A survey conducted by the NSPCC (Barter et al, 2009) reported a concerning level of partner violence and unwanted sexual acts (25 per cent and 33 per cent) experienced by 13–17-year-old girls in relationships. Seventy-five per cent of girls reported emotional abuse in relationships including controlling behaviours by partners and degrading treatment. Another concerning trend found in the NSPCC review is an increasing role of sexualised violence in schools, including sexual offending in 10–15-year-old children. Again, exposure to sexualised images and pornography appear to influence views about the acceptability of sexual aggression, risk taking and transient sexual encounters.

Children and young people assimilate and attempt to process the complex values and messages in these materials and it is likely that several factors will influence the degree to which they are influenced by them in behavioural enactments. For example, females caught up in gendered domestic violence, where this is the model of intimacy, may be more vulnerable to the "reinforcing effects of media representations". This again raises the issue of how best to support young people in reading and resisting media messages.

Figure 1: Sexualised images

Sexualisation and child protection

Child exploitation and abuse may be a consequence of, or associated with, child sexualisation. Whilst the majority of viewers of this material do not abuse children, there are specific issues raised for potential child abusers in viewing sexualised images and, in a broader sense, the consequences of normalising these images in popular culture. In a minor way, proliferation of "adultified" images of children blurs the boundaries between sexual maturity and immaturity and legitimates the notion that children can be sexual objects (Papadopoulos, 2010).

The sexualisation of children thus has a series of social consequences that can contribute to the risk of exploitation and abuse. The adult perpetrator (or potential perpetrator) of child sexual abuse receives conflicting cultural messages about children with the underlying theme promoting an adult-type "sexual child". This can potentially impact on the cognitive distortions and rationalisations common in paedophilia, where the child is seen as "sexual" and as able to consent to sexual involvement with adults.

Children as well are confused and unable to fully understand the implications of their own sexualisation. The linking of self-worth, self-esteem and identity with sexualised themes and values, reinforced by advertising and marketing, has created a specific "sexual child" where adultification and imposition of adult sexuality becomes the norm. The risk of the normalisation of child exploitation and child abuse is significant. Adult sexual motivation is attributed to children and along with this a distorted view that children, therefore have the same responsibilities for sexual behaviour as adults. The proliferation of sexualised content has the consequence of normalisation and serves to support a market in child sexualised images (Newman, 2009).

Conclusions

Today's children are exposed to multiple sexualised images. These images convey messages relating to the "desirable self", social and personal values, and shape emotional and psychological development. Girls and women are objectified and judged against sexualised ideals. The mental health and developmental consequences of this are significant with impacts on identity, self-esteem and body perception. There is evidence of an association between exposure to sexualised images and depression, anxiety and eating disordered behaviour. The risk for children inherent in this proliferation of sexualised images is one that is difficult to estimate but clearly relates to the normalisation of the representation of the "sexualised child" within popular culture. This cultural trend has potential implications for child and adolescent identity, family functioning and child protection.

Figure 2: Child sexualisation

References

APA (American Psychological Association (2007). *Taskforce on the Sexualisation of Girls*. Report accessed 30 May 2011, <http://www.apa.org/pi/women/programs/girls/report.aspx>.

Bagnall, D (1999). The Y factor. *The Bulletin* (ISSN 1440-7485), March, pp 14–19.

Barter, C, McCarry, M, Berridge, D, & Evans, K (2009). *Partner exploitation and violence in teenage intimate relationships*. Accessed 30 May 2011, <www.nspcc.org.uk/INFORM>.

Bouchard, P, & Bouchard, N (2003). "Miroir, miroir..." La précocité provoquée de l'adolescence et ses effets sur la vulnérabilité des filles. *Les cahiers de recherché du GREMF 87, Groupe de recherché multidisciplinaire féministe*. Québec: Université Laval.

Brown, JD, L'Engle, KL, Pardun, CJ, Guo, G, Kenneavy, K, & Jackson, C (2006). Sexy media matter: Exposure to sexual content in music, movies, television and magazines predicts Black and White adolescents sexual behaviour. *Pediatrics, 117*, 1017–1027.

Clark, L, & Tiggeman, M (2006). Appearance culture in 9 to 12 year old girls: media and peer influences on body dissatisfaction. *Social Development, 15*, 628–643.

Dill, K, Brown, B, & Collins, M (2008). Effects of exposure to sex-stereotyped video game characters on tolerance of sexual harassment. *Journal of Experimental Social Psychology, 44*, 1402–1408.

Dohnt, HK, & Tiggemann, M (2006). Body image concerns in young girls. *Journal of Youth and Adolescence, 35*, 141–151.

Field, AE, Camargo, CAJ, Taylor, CB, Berkey, CS, & Colditz, JA (1999). Relation of peer and media influences to the development of purging behaviours among preadolescent and adolescent girls. *Archives of Paediatrics and Adolescent Medicine, 153*, 1184–1189.

Fredericksen, BL, Roberts, TA (1997). Objectification theory: Toward understanding women's lived experience and mental health risks. *Psychology of Women Quarterly* 21, 173–206.

Freud, S (1905/1976). *Three essays on the theory of sexuality* (Standard Edition). London: Penguin.

Gabinski, K, Brownell, KD, & LaFrance, M (2003). Body objectification and 'fat talk': Effects on emotion, motivation, and cognitive performance. *Sex Roles, 48*, 377–388.

Harrison, K (2000). The body electric: Thin-ideal media and eating disorders in adolescents. *Journal of Communication, 53*, 216–232.

Harrison, K, & Fredrickson, BL (2003). Women's sports media, self-objectification and mental health in Black and White adolescent females. *Journal of Communication, 50*, 119–143.

Johnson, JD, Adams, MS, Ashburn, L, & Reed, W (1995). Differential gender effects of exposure to rap music on African American adolescents' acceptance of teen dating violence. *Sex Roles, 33*, 597–605.

Kaestle, CE, Tucker-Halpern, C, & Brown, JD (2007). Music videos, pro wrestling, and acceptance of date rape among middle school males and females: An exploratory analysis. *Journal of Adolescent Health, 40*, 185–187.

Newman, L (2009). The psychological and developmental impact of sexualisation on children. In M Tankard Reist (ed), *Getting Real* (pp 75–85). Melbourne: Spinifex Press.

Olding, MD, & Zuckerman, D (2004, October 26). Cosmetic surgery and teens. *Washington Post Health Feature*. Accessed 22 June 2011, <http://www.washingtonpost.com/wp-dyn/articles/A63931-2004Oct26.html>.

Paasonen, S, Nikumen, K, & Saarenmaa, L (eds) (2007). *Pornification: Sex and sexuality in media culture*. Oxford: Berg.

Papadopoulos, L (2010). *Sexualisation of Young People Review*. Retrieved from <http://webarchive.nationalarchives.gov.uk/20100418065544/http:/homeoffice.gov.uk/documents/Sexualisation-of-young-people.html>.

Pardun, CJ, L'Engle, KL, & Brown, JD (2005). Linking exposure to outcomes: Early adolescents' consumption of sexual content in six media. *Mass Communication and Society, 8,* 75–91.

Peterson, DL, & Pfost, KS (1989). Influence of rock videos on attitudes of violence against women. *Psychological Reports, 64,* 319–322.

Rush, E, & La Nauze, A (2006). *Australia Institute report: Corporate paedophilia: Sexualisation of children in Australia*. Discussion paper No 90. Canberra: The Australia Institute.

Strouse, JS, Goodwin, MP, & Roscoe, B (1994). Correlates of attitudes toward sexual harassment among early adolescents. *Sex Roles, 31,* 559–577.

Chapter 8

Children, media and ethics

Emma Rush

The public debate around children's interaction with violent and sexualised media content is hampered by some deep disagreement, not only about *how* to address such interaction but about *whether* such interaction even poses a problem. I demonstrate in this chapter that the debate can be advanced beyond its current status by using ethical perspectives to enable powerful analysis of particularly persistent points of disagreement. These ethical perspectives may also help readers to better understand their own values and decision-making processes with respect to children and media.

In the first part of the chapter, I briefly introduce the method and content of the academic discipline of ethics and explain in general terms how ethics is related to political philosophy and to the public debate around children's interaction with violent and sexualised media content. I then introduce four of the major perspectives available within ethics and close by noting that ethics has an institutional manifestation in codes of ethics and codes of practice. In the second part of the chapter, I apply these ethical perspectives to recurring issues in the public debate around children's interaction with violent and sexualised media content.

Introduction to ethics

The academic discipline of ethics is a sub-discipline within philosophy. While the *method* of ethics reflects the general philosophical preoccupation with "thinking about how we think", the *content* of ethics distinguishes it from other parts of philosophy. The content of ethics is framed by its central question: "How should we live?" This question encompasses two further questions: "What is a good life for human beings?" and "What is the (ethically) right thing for me (or us) to do in this situation?" Within ethics, any proposed answer to such questions will be evaluated using philosophical method, which involves identification of the fundamental beliefs underlying that answer and then analysis of the arguments that are based on these beliefs.

In the Western philosophical tradition, broadly secular ethical perspectives have been developed in answer to these questions over the last 2500 years at least. Each ethical perspective has a characteristic focus and offers an associated decision procedure. It is worth emphasising this point: within ethics, there is not just one ethical perspective on offer – a range of perspectives are available (Beauchamp, 2006). This means that the fear that ethics as an academic discipline might be just a "front" for a political position – either right-wing "moralism" or left-wing "political correctness" – is unjustified. In fact, the foundations for all political positions may be found within ethics and some experts even argue that political philosophy is simply a branch or application of ethics (Gewirth, 1965). There is no general agreement within the discipline of ethics as to which perspective provides the best understanding of ethical issues and I will not attempt to resolve that contentious issue here. In the absence of such general agreement, consideration of different perspectives is particularly valuable: first, the different perspectives highlight the complexity of ethical issues and the need for careful thought; and secondly, each perspective offers a distinct conceptual framework to help structure our thinking. Combined with philosophical method more generally, ethical perspectives offer insight into some of the recurring issues in the public debate over children and media content. The conflict around these issues is based either on *different applications* of the same ethical perspective or on *fundamentally different* ethical perspectives.

Below, I sketch an introduction to four broad ethical perspectives that appear in the public debate over children and media: consequence-based ethics, principle-based ethics, character-based ethics and ethical relativism. Since this book is motivated by concerns about children's engagement with media, I include the general answer that each perspective gives to the question: "What is the (ethically) right thing for me (or us) to do in this situation?" I also comment briefly on the typical strengths and weaknesses of each perspective. The introductions provided below aim to provide just enough detail for readers to follow the discussion in the next section.

Consequence-based ethics

This focuses on the consequences of an action when deciding what the right action is in a given situation. By far the most influential form of consequence-based ethics is utilitarianism, first articulated by Jeremy Bentham in the late eighteenth century and later refined by John Stuart Mill during the nineteenth century. Utilitarianism focused on maximising happiness ("the greatest happiness for the greatest number"), but in consequence-based ethics more generally, the (ethically) right action is the one that will have the best consequences overall. The great strength of consequence-based ethics is that it allows us to recognise the specific consequences of a given action – and almost everyone agrees that such consequences are relevant to ethical thinking. However, some persistent questions are also raised about consequence-based ethics, most notably: "How should we define 'best' consequences?" and "How successfully can we predict the consequences of our action?"

Principle-based ethics

This focuses on action-guiding principles or rules when deciding what the right action is in a given situation. Most religious ethics are principle-based (for example, the Ten Commandments of Judeo-Christianity, the Five Precepts of Buddhism and so on) but there are also secular systems of principle-based ethics, in particular, that which Immanuel Kant developed during the eighteenth century. In Kantianism, the key concepts are respect for persons, in the sense that a person must never be treated solely as a means to another person's end; and the universal nature of ethical rules (that is, ethical rules must be the same for everyone – not one rule for the behaviour of self towards others and another rule for the behaviour of others toward self). A modern version of principle-based ethics may be drawn, for example, from the United Nations Universal Declaration of Human Rights (1948). In principle-based ethics, the ethically right action is the action that follows the relevant principle. Principle-based ethics provides a guide for action even in cases where it is very difficult to predict the consequences of different actions. It also ensures consistency of action across similar situations. However, sometimes it is unclear which principle should apply to a situation and where principles conflict it may not be clear what should be done. What is more, following principles may lead to actions that do not produce the best consequences. To give a simple example, rigorously following the principle that one must tell the truth may cause distress to others.

Character-based ethics

This focuses on the development of good character in those who act, rather than on action in accordance with either predicted best consequences or a set of principles. This ethical perspective is usually traced back to Aristotle's work during the fourth century BCE and is commonly referred to as "virtue ethics", since the standard translation of the original Greek *aretê* is "virtue" or "excellence". From this perspective, the ethically right action is the action that would be taken by a person of good character. The advantage of character-based ethics is that natural language (as opposed to the technical language of academic ethics) is rich with character-based concepts. We describe character both positively – honest, caring, courageous – and negatively – greedy, nasty, irresponsible. Since we use such concepts in our ethical thinking, it seems reasonable to acknowledge them in our ethical theory. However, some philosophers argue that character-based ethics collapses into principle-based ethics, since every positive character trait can be redescribed as a principle. For example, the character trait of honesty can be redescribed as the principle, "Be honest". Therefore, this ethical perspective may not be genuinely distinct from principle-based ethics.

In many straightforward ethical situations, all three of the above perspectives agree on what the right thing to do is, although they arrive at this point by different routes. To give a very simple example, if a child is injured, all three perspectives would agree that the right thing to do is to provide care for the child. Consequence-based ethics would explain this decision in terms of the best consequences: "It is best that an injured child be cared for *to minimise their suffering and to promote their longer term health*". Principle-based ethics would explain this decision in terms of following a principle: "*One must provide appropriate care for children*". Character-based ethics would refer to character: "It would be *unkind* to deny the child care". In more complicated situations, the conclusions of the different perspectives may diverge. Where they diverge, good ethical thinking will provide a careful argument as to why the decision finally made is the right one.

Ethical relativism

Ethical relativism is based on the recognition that there is no neutral standpoint from which ethical assessment can be made. This is then taken to imply that there cannot be universally valid ethical standards. (The other ethical perspectives discussed above do claim to offer universally valid ethical standards.) Ethical relativism focuses on context, so it often appears as "cultural relativism" – the position that the ethically right action is relative to the culture the action occurs in. Although the idea of ethical relativism has been discussed in Western ethics since the time of Plato (who dismissed it), recent exponents tend to be influenced by existentialism (most prominently, the nineteenth-century thinker Friedrich Nietzsche). The advantage of ethical relativism is that it alerts us to a genuine risk in ethical discussion: the risk of uncritically assuming that ethical standards within our own culture are superior to the standards of other cultures. Ethical relativism's great disadvantage is that it leads to consequences that many find deeply objectionable. For example, the denial that there are any universally valid ethical standards requires that the idea of universal human rights be dismissed as a mistake.

Repeating the injured child example above, the answer that ethical relativism will give will depend on what is seen to be relevant in the context of the situation. For example, a relativist might agree that care should be provided for the child ("the cultural norm is to care for children"), or they might argue that the child should not be cared for ("the cultural norm is that female/black/ethnic minority/disabled/and so on children are not worthy of special care"). An ethical relativist would not agree that there was any universally ethically right action with respect to an injured child.

These four ethical perspectives will be broadly familiar to readers, since they operate throughout personal and public life – the above descriptions simply formalise and clarify them. Readers are also likely to be familiar with the institutional manifestation of ethics: codes of ethics and codes of practice that are specific to professions or industries. Such codes may include influences from all of consequence-based, principle-based and character-based perspectives, as well as from the relevant cultural context. They aim to guide the deliberations of professional practitioners about what is and is not ethically appropriate (see, for example, the codes of practice set by the various industry bodies overseen by the Australian Communications and Media Authority, at ACMA, 2010; see also AANA, 2009a; AANA, 2009b; IIA, 2005). However, the existence of a code of ethics (or practice) does not guarantee ethical outcomes: both the formulation and the application of such codes may be criticised (see for example Rush & La Nauze, 2006; Young Media Australia, 2007; ACCM, 2010). While codes of ethics (or practice) can be useful in guiding professional decision-making, I do not refer to these in the discussion below about recurring issues in the public debate around children and media. Specific professional codes generally do not address these "bigger picture" underlying issues.

Ethical analysis of recurring issues in the public debate around children and media

The four ethical perspectives introduced above will now be applied to recurring issues in the public debate around children's interaction with violent and sexualised media content. Each issue is expressed as a question which has provoked conflict among participants in the debate.

1. *How should the research evidence about the consequences of children's interaction with media be interpreted?*

Understandably, most of the debate about children's access to violent and sexualised media has been conducted in terms of the consequences of different courses of action. Indeed, evidence-based policy requires careful consideration of such consequences, since once policy principles have been set, the "right" policy will be the one with the best overall consequences – an example of the consequence-based ethical perspective in operation.

However, while those participating in the debate agree that consequences are important, there is profound disagreement over *which* evidence of consequences for children should count. This reflects a familiar problem within consequence-based ethics: relevant parties may not agree about what the consequences are. Commentators working in areas linked to child development (developmental psychology, neuropsychology, paediatric psychiatry) refer to evidence from (mostly) quantitative research on the effects of specific kinds of media content on children (see Chapters 2 to 6, this volume). On the other hand, at least some commentators working in media and cultural studies disparage the media effects research (Lumby & Albury, 2008) and argue that the evidence that should count is that provided by (mostly) qualitative research within their own disciplines. For example:

> When it comes to media material marketed to children, which is necessarily classified as suitable for them under the current regimes, we believe that any consideration of potential harm to them must be based on a consideration of what children themselves tell us about their media consumption habits and the influence popular media has on them. (Lumby & Albury, 2008, p 23)

While it is important to include what children have to say on these issues in an overall consideration of potential harm to them, the suggestion that their perspective is the only one that matters seems unjustifiably exclusive of other sources of information. Such a suggestion stands in stark contrast with the conclusion reached by Hargrave and Livingstone (2006) in their extensive interdisciplinary review of recent (mostly post-2000) research regarding harmful effects of media content. After noting different disciplinary methodologies and the consequently politically contested nature of the research area, they stressed "the value of integrating qualitative and quantitative research findings" (pp 8–9).

If such integration is to successfully reflect how children interact with media, it would seem that an appropriate model of how the human mind works must guide both inclusion of research evidence and interpretation of it. The dual-process model of human psychology, introduced in detail in Chapter 6, this volume, may be just such an appropriate model. This model suggests that mental processing occurs at both a controlled (conscious, self-reported) level and an automatic (without awareness) level. If this is correct, the controlled mental processing reflected in "what children themselves tell us about their media consumption habits and the influence popular media has on them" only accounts for part of the interaction between children and media. The dual-process model could thus contextualise the different kinds of research evidence, thereby showing that different research conclusions are not contradictory, although at face value they may previously have seemed so.

It is not possible here to explore more fully the question of how to interpret the research evidence about the consequences of children's interaction with media. Such questions commonly appear within consequence-based ethics. I have argued that the research evidence should be appropriately integrated and interpreted and I have given one example of what might count as an appropriate framework for such integration and interpretation. I have also noted the implausibility of the view that what children themselves say is the only relevant evidence.

2. Is it better to empower children through media literacy education or to protect them through media regulation?

This issue can be understood through character-based ethics: which character trait (empowering or protective) is preferable in this context?

Discussion in the previous section raises the question: Why do commentators in media and cultural studies place such a strong emphasis on the need to hear children's own voices in assessing the consequences of their media consumption? One possible explanation is their focus on individual empowerment as a solution to collective political problems: "We are concerned by moves to protect children that do not simultaneously strive to develop and enhance children's and young people's agency, resilience and capacity to engage with the world around them" (Lumby & Albury, 2010, footnote, p 151). Hence, when "moves to protect children" from harmful media effects by stronger media regulation are suggested, some commentators working in media and cultural studies instead advocate age-appropriate media literacy (or "critical social literacy") education as a way to improve children's agency (Lumby & Albury, 2008, p 5; Taylor, 2010, p 55). Building the capacity of others is understood to be the most relevant good character trait. This can be extended to a political philosophy in which the character of the ideal State is empowering as much as it is protective (compare this with the pejorative "Nanny State" sometimes used by right wing political commentators to imply a State of overly protective or controlling character).

While an empowerment approach of improving children's agency via media literacy education may appear entirely unobjectionable, it is a dubious solution to the problem of harmful media effects for two reasons. The first reason is that it may be relatively ineffective in meeting the goal of avoiding harm to children (the desired *consequence*): as I discuss below, there is little evidence that media literacy education is effective in this way and there are theoretical reasons why it is unlikely to be wholly effective. The second reason is that even if improving children's agency via media literacy education were effective in avoiding harmful media effects, it would contravene the *principle* of distributive justice. This principle states that benefits and burdens should be distributed fairly, which implies that the most vulnerable members of society (including children, as in this case) should not be allocated the burden of avoiding harmful effects when the benefits of such effects accrue to much more powerful members of society (the producers of often profit-driven media, in this case). This issue is discussed further in the next section.

Returning to the consequences of an empowerment (media literacy) approach, the extensive review conducted by Hargrave and Livingstone (2006, p 207) concluded that "[e]vidence is lacking ... for the claim that an increase in media literacy will reduce the potential for harm, although this is widely believed", and recommended that this "should be the subject of future research". Pending the conclusions of such research, however, there are theoretical reasons to believe that the capacity of media literacy education to reduce the potential for harm to children will be quite limited. The dual-process model of human psychology, discussed in detail in Chapter 6 of this volume, suggests that controlled attitudes – typically targeted by media literacy training – may be *undermined* by automatic attitudes, even in adults. People learn a great deal through "incidental learning" (processing information that they are not concentrating on) and, wherever children are concerned, the likelihood of controlled attitudes being undermined by automatic attitudes increases because children's capacity for cognitive self-regulatory control is lower than that of adults (see Fine, this volume). For example, when media content links violent or sexualised behaviours with positive stimuli (such as celebrity endorsement), this may affect child media consumers' automatic attitudes to these behaviours regardless of their controlled attitudes – and where this occurs, these automatic attitudes may be revealed by their own behaviour, depending on their capacity or motivation for self-regulation (see Fine, this volume). So although media-literate children might articulate controlled attitudes that are intelligent, thoughtful, critical or even cynical regarding violent or sexualised media (paraphrasing Gauntlett, 1998, as cited in Lumby & Albury, 2009, p 23), to focus only on such attitudes "is to overlook important implicit [automatic] effects that children may have difficulty overriding" (Nairn & Fine, 2008b, p 904).

One recommendation arising from consideration of the dual-process model is that "media literacy programmes should also educate about the non-conscious routes by which advertising can affect consumer preference and behaviour" (Nairn & Fine, 2008a, p 463). Although there is currently no evidence that such media literacy programs reduce automatic effects on adults, there are two possibilities for how understanding automatic effects might reduce their impact. First, the more that people are aware they could be automatically biased, the more likely they are to control for this bias. Secondly, if people are aware of automatic effects, they can choose, where possible, to avoid media environments that associate positive stimuli with phenomena they explicitly object to – for example, violence and sexualisation. However, both these strategies require the application of cognitive self-regulatory control, either to control for bias or to recognise and avoid certain media environments and, as noted above, children have lower cognitive self-regulatory control than adults.

In summary, consideration both of likely consequences (informed by research evidence and theoretical models) and relevant principles (distributive justice) suggests that a protective attitude rather than an empowering one is the preferable character trait when it comes to avoiding harmful media effects on children.

3. What is the best balance between the principles of media "freedom of expression" for adults and "protection from harm" for children?

Both "freedom of expression" and "protection of children from harm" are widely accepted ethical principles, so this issue belongs firmly within the domain of principle-based ethics. In debates around media harm to children, it is common to see these two principles represented as being in conflict with one another when it comes to public policy. This representation of the problem tends to produce the resolution that a reasonable "balance" between the two principles should be sought. For example, in their Report on the Inquiry into the Sexualisation of

Children by the Contemporary Media, the Australian Senate Committee wrote: "Systems of self- or co-regulation are not prescriptive of public tastes and community standards but instead seek to strike a responsible balance between the protection of children and the preservation of the individual's right to choose what they see and hear" (SCECA, 2008, pp 86–87). Determining the appropriate balance between "freedom" and "protection" is a deep and complex task that cannot be attempted here. What will be offered, however, are some considerations that are rarely recognised in public debate, but which provide useful context for such a task.

First, it can be argued that representing "freedom of expression" and "protection of children from harm" as opposed to one another is a distortion of liberal philosophy. Foundational liberal texts show that "liberalism itself justifies and, indeed, morally requires restrictions on the rights of adults, including the right of free speech, in relationships and situations involving children" (Dworetz, 1987, p 192). While those seeking regulation to promote healthy development for children are sometimes criticised as being politically illiberal, in fact, regulation to prevent harm is perfectly consistent with liberal philosophy.

Secondly, it is important to consider the ethical and political status of those who would benefit from protection relative to those whose freedom may be restricted. Hargrave and Livingstone (2006, p 198) identify the issue of "vulnerability" in their major review: while there is no "standard academic definition of 'vulnerability' ... research findings do suggest that vulnerable audiences/users may include children and young people, especially boys, together with a range of other groups among the adult population (including psychologically disturbed individuals, people who are depressed, sexual offenders, young offenders, etc)".

"Vulnerability" is a standard concern for both ethics and political philosophy. Within liberal democracies, the aim of a just government is to achieve the best outcome for the population overall, without harming the worst off among them. This is democracy – government for the majority – modified by the liberal principle of respect for the individual. (We can also see the ethical parallel: a consequence-based perspective – maximising good consequences overall – modified by a principle-based perspective that insists on respect for persons.)

Recognition of vulnerability is important because, if violent or sexualised media content does not affect many people but disproportionately affects those who are already relatively disempowered or at-risk, then a total cost-benefit analysis will be inadequate to deliver a just policy solution. It is a matter of social justice to pay particular attention to vulnerability: we should strive to avoid making the lot of those who are already disempowered or at-risk worse, even if this requires some restrictions on the rest of the population.

In short, when considering the appropriate balance between the principles of "freedom" and "protection" in media regulation regarding children's wellbeing, the importance of protection is emphasised by both a proper understanding of liberal political philosophy and an appreciation of the importance of attending to vulnerability considerations.

4. Understandings of childhood are relative to context – is the current concern about media justified?

Concern expressed about potentially harmful effects of media on children has sometimes been explicitly or implicitly dismissed by those working in media and cultural studies as moral panic (see for example Taylor, 2010, p 49). It is noted that understandings of childhood vary across cultures, across historical periods and between different social classes within the same period, and it is claimed that "[e]ver since the introduction of mass communication technologies, there has been apprehension about children's exposure to age-inappropriate content and agitation about parents' rights to gate-keep such content" (Taylor, 2010, p 49). The argument then holds that with hindsight, we can see that past anxieties about new forms of media were without rational basis (thus the "panic" in "moral panic"), with the implication that in the future, we will be able to see that our current concerns about "the loss of authentic childhood" are similarly irrational (Taylor, 2010, p 49, pp 52–53). This conclusion relies on the perspective of ethical relativism, because it implicitly holds that the various understandings of childhood are ethically equal, that is, that there is no valid basis for preferring one over another. There are at least two weaknesses in this kind of argument.

First, it is well-understood by all participating in the debate that understandings of childhood have been specific to historical periods, cultures, social classes and so on. The position of those working in child development, although it is rarely stated explicitly, appears to be that the recent Western middle-class understanding of childhood is ethically superior to many alternative understandings because: (1) it leads to the best consequences overall; (2) it follows the principle of respect for the child; and, (3) the good character traits of caring and kindness are promoted among adults who hold it. The recent Western middle-class understanding of childhood is importantly informed by insights from paediatrics and developmental psychology which acknowledge that children are in a formative stage of their lives, one which requires them to be treated with particular care. These insights – about the importance of adequate nutrition, health promotion practices, education, gender equality, and protection from practices of child marriage – are recognised to apply to children universally (UNICEF, 2010). Why? Because some biologically based physical and psychological potentialities are common to all human children by virtue of their species, regardless of their historical period, culture, social class, and so on. As such, an experience of childhood similar to the recent Western middle-class understanding of childhood which recognises these universal potentialities is more likely to promote healthy individual development both in childhood and throughout later life, than would many alternative understandings of childhood. This appears to be at least partly recognised by some in media and cultural studies: "Contemporary Australian ideas about childhood, which include a strong belief in the importance of educating all children and protecting them from participating in the adult worlds of work and sexuality, as well as ensuring that girls have equal opportunities, represent important human rights advances" (Lumby & Albury, 2008, p 3).

Secondly, even if past concerns about the impact of media on children have later been found to be unwarranted, it does not follow that current concerns are similarly unwarranted. Logically speaking, the assumption that what has occurred in the past will continue to occur in the future is not necessarily true. This is known as the problem of induction, sometimes taught to undergraduate philosophy students using the example of the Christmas turkey: the turkey thinks that because she's had a nice life in the past, her nice life will continue at the current time – but it's Christmas and out comes the axe! The research evidence about the negative effects of some media content that is presented in this volume suggests that current concerns have considerable theoretical and empirical support.

To summarise, a comparison of what the four ethical perspectives have to say about different understandings of childhood, along with consideration of the general impacts of these different understandings on children, suggests that not all understandings of childhood are equally ethically worthy. There are good ethical reasons to think that some current concerns about the negative effects of some media content are justified.

Conclusion

In this chapter, four ethical perspectives (consequence-based, principle-based, character-based and relativist) that appear in the debate over children and media content were introduced. These perspectives were identified as present in four recurrent issues in the debate, and the arguments around these recurrent issues were presented and analysed. My conclusions on the four issues are that:

- research evidence on children and media content needs to be interpreted in an appropriately integrated fashion;
- the effectiveness of media literacy education for protecting children is unproven, is unlikely to be found to be wholly effective and reliance on or preferencing of that approach over media regulation is unjust in any case;
- proper consideration of both liberal political philosophy and the ethical issue of vulnerability will emphasise protection for children over freedom of expression in regards to media content that is likely to negatively affect children; and
- the current cultural understanding of healthy childhood development is ethically preferable to many alternative understandings of childhood so, on the related evidence, current concerns about media content are well-justified.

It is hoped that readers finish the chapter with a better understanding of these recurrent issues and with some new ethical perspectives to use in their thinking about children and media content more generally.

Acknowledgments

I thank the following colleagues for their very helpful comments at various stages during the drafting of this chapter: Cordelia Fine, Martin Rush, Steve Douglas, Morgan Luck, Daniel Cohen, Wylie Breckenridge and Merrilyn Crichton.

References

AANA (Australian Association of National Advertisers) (2009a). *Code of Ethics*. Accessed 2 January 2011, <http://www.aana.com.au/advertiser_ethics_code.html>.

AANA (2009b). *Code for Advertising and Marketing Communications to Children*. Accessed 2 January 2011, <http://www.aana.com.au/childrens_code.html>.

ACCM (Australian Council on Children and the Media) (2010). *Submission on the AANA Code of Ethics Review 2010*. Accessed 2 January 2011, <http://www.youngmedia.org.au/publications/submissions.htm>.

ACMA (Australian Communications and Media Authority) (2010). *Broadcasting codes and schemes index*. Accessed 2 January 2011, <http://www.acma.gov.au/WEB/STANDARD/pc=IND_REG_CODES_BCAST>.

Beauchamp, T (2006). Applied Ethics. In DM Borchert (ed), *Encyclopedia of Philosophy* (2nd ed) (pp 235-240). Detroit: Thomson.

Dworetz, SM (1987). Before the age of reason: Liberalism and the media socialization of children. *Social Theory and Practice*, 13(2), 187-218.

Gewirth, A (1965). *Political Philosophy*. New York: MacMillan.

Hargrave, AM, & Livingstone, S (2006). *Harm and offence in media content: A review of the evidence*. Bristol: Intellect.

Internet Industry Association (IIA) (2005). *Internet Industry Codes of Practice*. Accessed 2 January 2011, <http://www.acma.gov.au/WEB/STANDARD/pc=PC_300106>.

Lumby, C, & Albury, K (2008). *Submission to The Senate Standing Committee on Environment, Communication and the Arts Inquiry into the sexualisation of children in the contemporary media environment*, April. Accessed 26 December 2010, <http://www.aph.gov.au/senate/committee/eca_ctte/sexualisation_of_children/submissions/sublist.htm>.

Lumby, C, & Albury, K (2010). Too much? Too young? The sexualisation of children debate in Australia. *Media International Australia (incorporating Culture and Policy)*, 135, 141-152.

Nairn, A, & Fine, C (2008a). Who's messing with my mind? The implications of dual-process models for the ethics of advertising to children. *International Journal of Advertising*, 27(3), 447-470.

Nairn, A, & Fine, C (2008b). Not seeing the wood for the imaginary trees. Or, who's messing with our article? A reply to Ambler (2008). *International Journal of Advertising*, 27(5), 896-908.

Rush, E, & La Nauze, A (2006). *Letting children be children: Stopping the sexualisation of children in Australia*. Canberra: The Australia Institute. Accessed 30 October 2010, <www.tai.org.au/index.php?q=node%2F19&pubid=433&act=display>.

SCECA (Senate Standing Committee on Environment, Communications and the Arts) (2008). *Sexualisation of children in the contemporary media.* Canberra: Standing Committee on Environment, Communications and the Arts, The Senate. Accessed 31 October 2010, <www.aph.gov.au/SENATE/committee/eca_ctte/sexualisation_of_children/index.htm>.

Taylor, A (2010). Troubling childhood innocence: Reframing the debate over the media sexualisation of children. *Australasian Journal of Early Childhood,* 35(1), 48–57.

UNICEF (United Nations Children's Fund) (2010). *Progress for Children: Achieving the MDGs with Equity.* Accessed 23 February 2012, <http://www.childinfo.org/files/PFC_No.9_En_090710.pdf>.

United Nations (1948). *The Universal Declaration of Human Rights.* Accessed 23 February 2012, <http://www.un.org/en/documents/udhr>.

Young Media Australia (2007). *Submission to the Review of the AANA Code for Advertising to Children,* November. Accessed 2 January 2010, <http://www.youngmedia.org.au/pdf/Submissions/yma_submission_aana_code_1207.pdf>.

Chapter 9

There oughta be a law: The (potential) role of law and regulation in slowing down and calming down

Elizabeth Handsley

This chapter discusses some of the challenges associated with the search for legal and regulatory means of reducing children's exposure to sexualising and violent media. It concludes that most of the existing legal frameworks that would normally come to mind in the contexts of sexualisation, such as broadcasting regulation and classification/ censorship law, have significant flaws and limitations. On the other hand, it recommends further consideration of a consumer law-based approach, to keep the focus on the power imbalance between the media publishers and the audience. In relation to violent media the chapter analyses the recent debate in Australia over the classification of video games and concludes that a broader review of the system is required.

Slowing down: defining and addressing sexualisation of children in the media

The problem(s):

The American Psychological Association (APA) defines sexualisation in the following way:

> [S]exualization occurs when:
> - a [child]'s value comes only from his or her sexual appeal or behavior, to the exclusion of other characteristics;
> - a [child] is held to a physical standard that equates physical attractiveness (narrowly defined) with being sexy;
> - a [child] is sexually objectified — that is, made into a thing for others' sexual use, rather than seen as a person with the capacity for independent action and decision making; and/or

- sexuality is inappropriately imposed on a [child]. (APA, 2010, p 1)

The APA (2010) has identified a number of likely negative consequences from these experiences. These include:

(1) the cognitive and emotional consequences of undermining a girl's confidence in and comfort with her own body, leading to emotional and self-image problems such as shame and anxiety (pp 22–23);
(2) mental and physical health consequences such as eating disorders, low self-esteem, depression/depressed mood (pp 23–24); and
(3) negative consequences on girls' ability to develop a healthy sexual self-image (pp 25–26).

Media and industry practices

There are two distinct kinds of media and industry practices that may be seen as contributing to the sexualisation of children. The first is exposure of children to aspects of adult sexuality they cannot understand, or do not need to understand. The most notorious examples of this in Australia are the Advanced Medical Institute billboards, promoting treatment of erectile dysfunction. However, there are numerous others. Society has generally become freer in discussing and representing sexual matters in public fora and this means that children in public places are frequently casually exposed to such discussions and representations.

A subset of this form of sexualisation is the use of children as vehicles for ribald adult humour. The most infamous example of this is the baby's T-shirt with the message "All Daddy wanted was a blow job". In my view these practices do not amount to sexualisation of the child being used in this way: while these practices raise serious questions about the attitudes of the parents concerned, the children concerned are too young to notice or be confused by the message, or to have their sense of self undermined. However, to the extent that these messages are exposed to the public, they will also be exposed to older children and in this sense they are no different from a billboard.

The second kind of practice occurs in the context of marketing to and for children. We are familiar with the expression "sex sells" – it sums up the use of sexuality to tap into consumers' insecurities and create demand for products that are seen as addressing those insecurities. Sexualisation of children is an extension of this same strategy to the child market. Examples include fostering children's insecurity as to their appearance and locating the proposed solutions to that insecurity in the trappings of adult sexuality; normalising the place of those trappings in children's lives; a strong focus on appearance and sexuality as a/the source of girls' power in society; and objectifying girls (including to themselves).

"Sexualisation" in this latter sense has little or nothing to do with sex or sexual activity. It is more to do with practices and artefacts that are culturally linked to sex. For example, there is nothing inherently sexual about the Playboy bunny. However, it symbolises a world in which women are put on display for the sexual stimulation of men. This explains why many people would consider it inappropriate for a child to wear clothing or jewellery bearing the symbol even if that clothing or jewellery were otherwise child-appropriate. The problem here is not "sex" but rather "sexiness" as broadly understood in our society. Therefore I want to refer to this second kind of practice as "sexification".

These kinds of practices are also seen as objectionable simply on the ground that any marketing to children at all is inappropriate and unethical. Many are concerned about the increasing commercialisation of childhood; this branch of sexualisation can be seen as a subset of that.

There are three main types of media practices that raise concerns relating to sexification. The first is in the way children are represented to themselves, especially through marketing campaigns for children's products. The instruction to a photographer shooting a children's clothing catalogue to make the models look "more adult and sexy" (Black, 2009) is a good example of this.

The second type of practice is the propagation of a boy-crazy, celebrity-obsessed, highly image-conscious view of the world in magazines that are marketed to young girls. (These often also include the first type of sexualisation, with explicit advice about sex and sexual practices.)

The third area of concern is the high level of sexualised content in video clips that are made to accompany popular music and are broadcast at times of day when many children watch television. These, too, sometimes come close to crossing the line to the first kind of sexualisation, but mostly they include lyrics, behaviours and so on that are highly suggestive of sexual themes, but are not actually sexual per se. At the same time they link those themes strongly with social success.

Legal and regulatory responses to sexualisation

In 2007, on the motion of Australian Democrat Senator Lynn Allison, the Senate Standing Committee on Environment, Communications and the Arts undertook an inquiry into the sexualisation of children in the contemporary media environment with terms of reference to:

- *examine the sources and beneficiaries* of premature sexualisation of children in the media;
- *review the evidence* on the short- and long-term effects of viewing or buying sexualising and objectifying images and products and their influence on cognitive functioning, physical and mental health, sexuality, attitudes and beliefs; and
- *examine strategies to prevent and/or reduce* the sexualisation of children in the media and the effectiveness of different approaches in ameliorating its effects, including the role of school-based sexuality and reproductive health education and change in media and advertising regulation such as the [industry Codes]. (SCECA, 2008, pp 1-2)

The Australian Association of National Advertisers (AANA), released a revised Code for Advertising and Marketing Communications to Children ("AANA Code") shortly before submissions closed on the Senate inquiry. Among other things, the revised AANA Code included a new provision purporting to deal with "sexualisation", section 2.4:

> *Sexualisation*
> Advertising or Marketing Communications to Children:
> (a) must not include sexual imagery in contravention of Prevailing Community Standards;

(b) must not state or imply that Children are sexual beings and that ownership or enjoyment of a Product will enhance their sexuality.
Advertising or Marketing Communications to Children are defined as:
Communications which having regard to the theme, visuals and language used, are directed *primarily* to Children *and* are for Product. [emphasis added]
"Product" is defined as:
goods, services and/or facilities which are targeted toward *and* have *principal* appeal to Children. [emphasis added]

This definition limits the application of the AANA Code generally to certain child-oriented products, but more specifically section 2.4 applies only to communications using sexual imagery to promote a *child-oriented product* (for example a toy) or that state or imply that such a product will enhance a child's sexuality.

In other words the AANA Code bans two kinds of advertising that have probably never existed. At the same time it fails to address the exposure of children to advertising for adult products, or advertising that links the trappings of adult sexuality with children's social success.

Outcome of Senate inquiry

The Senate Committee reported in August 2008 with a list of 13 recommendations. The first was more of a broad statement recognising the complexity of the task of defining this issue: "This is a community responsibility which demands action by society. In particular, the onus is on broadcasters, publishers, advertisers, retailers and manufacturers to take account of these community concerns" (SCECA, 2008, p 3).

The other recommendations were as follows:

2. Major longitudinal study into the effects of premature and inappropriate sexualisation of children;
3. Change to the Children's Television Standards (CTS) scheduling requirement so as to make appropriate children's content more accessible;
4. Broadcasters review classification of music videos specifically with an eye to sexualising imagery;

5. The establishment of dedicated children's channels;
6. That publishers consider providing reader advice on magazines;
7. That the Senate review effectiveness of the operation of the new AANA Code in 18 months;
8. That the advertising and television industries consider establishing a complaints clearing house;
9. That the Advertising Standards Board (ASB) produce half-yearly list of complaints regarding children;
10. That the ASB consider pre-vetting advertisements;
11. That the ASB formalise processes of community consultation;
12. That the ASB rigorously apply standards to outdoor ads; and
13. That the State and Territory governments introduce comprehensive sexual health and relationships education programs in schools.

Government response

The vast majority of the Committee's recommendations did not call on the government to do anything but rather left it in the lap of industry to take action. The statement in Recommendation 1 that "the onus is on broadcasters, publishers, advertisers, retailers and manufacturers" suggests that government is not counted as part of the "society" whose action is demanded. Therefore it is not surprising that when the Australian Government in July 2009 issued its response to the recommendations, this consisted for the most part of simply "noting" them.

Recommendation 4 on the matter of broadcasters' classification of music video clips is an exception. In the course of the Inquiry, Free TV Australia had submitted:

> There is no level of viewer concern expressed in relation to the contribution of free to air television to the sexualisation of children. ...
> Video clips have been identified through discussion of this issue as a contributing factor to the sexualisation of children. Network complaint figures do not support this view. (Free TV Australia, 2008, pp 8–9)

The Government's response also relied on complaints statistics, effectively to reject the Committee's recommendation, and echoed the wording of the statement about "no level of concern" (Australian Government, 2009, p 7). In this it appears to have overlooked the Committee's statements about the level of concern expressed in submissions to it (p 42). The response made it appear that the Government had relied directly on advice from the industry body.

The government also stated a strong view on Recommendation 13: "sex education should be implemented in consultation with the school community; be respectful of religious and philosophical views; and be age appropriate" (Australian Government, 2009, p 10). One can hardly disagree with all of these principles; indeed it would be useful to see them applied to advertising and other media practices.

From the foregoing it is possible to conclude that the media industry enjoys a privileged position in relation to the sexualisation of children. While the government might wish to seem concerned and responsible, its bias is very much in favour of self-regulation and on at least one issue it appears to have been "captured" by industry.

As to industry itself, Free TV Australia reviewed its Commercial Television Industry Code of Practice in 2009–2010 and did not change one word in the sections that might have addressed the video clip recommendation.

The Advertising Standards Board has taken certain steps to raise awareness of its complaint-handling activities and also undertaken research to inform its views of "community standards". For example, in June 2010 it released a report on Community Perceptions of Sex, Sexuality and Nudity in Advertising (ASB, 2010).

Case study: the AMI billboards

The billboards erected by the Advanced Medical Institute (AMI) consisted simply of the text, in large letters: "Want longer lasting sex?" and the details of how to contact AMI and access its erectile dysfunction treatments.

The difficulty with these billboards is not primarily the use of the word "sex" but rather the need to be aware of some intricate details of adult sexuality in order to understand their message. Young children have no need for information on such details and parents should not be expected to explain them.

Yet the AMI, when responding to the complaints that the ASB received about the billboards in early 2007, said "it is not just cause for advertisers to remove all advertising relating to sex because certain parents don't wish to answer questions raised by their young children" and claimed that the advertising "is really only an endeavour to invoke/embed a self-diagnostic question and in this sense is educative and helpful to a far greater proportion of the community" (ASB, 2007).

On 13 February 2007 the ASB issued a report, holding the billboards not to be in breach of section 2.3 of the AANA Code of Ethics. It said: "[T]he advertisement is for a sex-related product and … it was legitimate for such a product to mention sex. … [T]he billboard did not contain any graphic images and … the word 'sex' was itself not offensive".

The day after the release of the Senate Committee report, AMI announced a decision to "ramp up its coverage" (Lee, 2008). This prompted further complaints and the ASB considered the matter again, only 18 months after its initial exoneration of the advertiser. This time, the billboards were held to be in breach of section 2.3. The difference, according to the ASB, was that "there has been a shift in community standards and that the content of this billboard is no longer acceptable" (ASB, 2008).

Following the breach finding, AMI gave an undertaking to take down the billboards. It is not known whether any billboards were taken down, but it was observed in the ensuing months that many remained up, with the word "censored" pasted across them. More recently, billboards have been seen with the message "Making Love? Do it … Longer!"

These responses demonstrate a fundamental failure to understand what community concerns are about these billboards. The problem is not the word "sex" but rather children's exposure to information and issues relating to sexuality before they are ready. Changing the wording does not address this.

However, the disappointing outcome is not completely down to AMI. This case study also shows the limitations of the self-regulatory approach in general. AMI was quite free to take the approach it did, because the ASB as a self-regulatory body has absolutely no coercive power to enforce its decisions. From a corporate perspective, its actions were completely justified.

What government could do

(Changes to) State legislation

It would be possible for any State parliament to legislate against any of the practices outlined above. Unlike the Commonwealth Parliament, the State parliaments have no constitutional constraints as to the subjects on which they can pass legislation.

However, State legislation, to be valid, needs to avoid "inconsistency" with Commonwealth legislation: see section 109 of the Constitution. The existence of Commonwealth laws on broadcasting, content classification and other matters is more of a minefield than it sounds, because the High Court has interpreted "inconsistency" to include any legislation that exists in a "field" that the Commonwealth intended to "cover" (*Ex parte McLean* (1930) 43 CLR 472). So even if State legislation is trying to achieve the same aims as Commonwealth legislation, it may still be inconsistent in constitutional terms.

There are numerous examples in history of the States taking the lead in relation to social issues. Sex discrimination is a case in point. South Australia first legislated on this in 1975 and the Commonwealth did not do so until 1984. With their smaller size and the relative closeness of their governments to their populations, it seems that the States are in a position to experiment more boldly than the Commonwealth.

Therefore they should not necessarily be put off by the existence of Commonwealth regulations on things like the classification of publications and broadcast material.

Children's Television Standards

The Children's Television Standards (CTS) are developed by the Australian Communications and Media Authority (ACMA) under the authority of the *Broadcasting Services Act 1992* (Cth) and have the force of law. They meet two main aims: to require commercial free-to-air broadcasters to show a minimum amount of high-quality children's programming and to regulate the kinds of advertising that can be shown during that programming. At the moment they contain little of potential relevance to sexualisation or sexification.

The CTS could be a useful starting point for addressing sexualisation of children, because these standards are easier to change than legislation. However they are very limited in their application, not just to the narrow medium of free-to-air commercial television, but to the special programming they require. In addition, children's most watched time slots are outside of children's television programming zones (that is, from 6.00 pm to 9.00 pm; see Chapters 1 and 10).

Unless the scope of the CTS were to be increased – which probably would require legislation – they could not be used to address current concerns about sexualisation through television content (for example music videos).

Broadcasting Services Act 1992 (Cth) (BSA)

In addition to forming the basis for the CTS, the *BSA* imposes certain requirements on broadcasters via licence conditions. This extends to all forms of broadcasting (with the exception of the national broadcasters, ABC and SBS) – so radio, television, commercial, community, free-to-air and subscription services are all covered. Breach of a licence condition can result in cancellation of the licence (section 143 of the Act), or the issue of a remedial direction (section 141). Breach of a remedial direction can lead to a civil penalty (sections 141–142A).

Some examples where the *BSA* directly controls the activities of broadcasters are the fields of tobacco and political advertising. It would be legally possible for the Commonwealth to add provisions on sexual references or representation of children to that list.

However, the Act is still limited in that it applies only to electronic media. As we have seen, there are major concerns with other media such as magazines and outdoor advertising. Therefore changes to the *BSA* could only ever address part of the problem.

Moreover, even the strongest regulations are of limited effectiveness unless there is a strong watchdog to monitor practices and interpret the rules strictly. It is not clear that the ACMA, as currently constituted, meets this description. It has no resources for monitoring, relying instead on consumer complaints, and it has a record of construing rules in a way that favours the broadcaster. Therefore one cannot assume that simple changes to the *BSA* would, on their own, make much difference on the ground.

National Classification Code

Films, publications and computer games are subject to *National Classification Code* (May 2005) (Cth) ("*National Classification Code*") that is administered by the States under a cooperative federal scheme. The system has an indirect effect on television and the internet, as the same categories are used to classify material on those media. Therefore it has a broader reach than any of the legal structures considered thus far.

However I believe that the classification system is severely limited in its ability to deal with sexualisation of children. Having grown out of the ancient law of obscenity, its intellectual roots lie in prudery and moralism, not in child development and sex equality. Yet these are the real roots of community concerns about sexualisation. Even though the system now incorporates the concept of "harm" (clause 1(b) of the Code), and this can be interpreted to relate to child development (among other things), the dominant concept is offensiveness.

A good example of the tension between these two sets of concepts is provided by the AMI billboards: the company's response seemed to be based on the idea that there is something wrong with the word "sex". This would be well-founded if the community were simply offended by references to sex or sexuality. However, the community's concerns are based on the more subtle idea that children's developing sexuality and sexual self-image will be influenced by the representations they see and the observation that those representations are often stereotyped or exploitative. The problem is not with "sex", it is with "sex sells". It would require a root-and-branch reform of the whole classification system to express this.

However such reform is even harder to achieve than a change in Commonwealth legislation, because the consent of all States is needed in order to change any part of the Code. At the time of writing there are a number of reviews going on but it remains to be seen whether any of these will lead to any meaningful change.

The Commonwealth Competition and Consumer Act 2010

Until recently this piece of Commonwealth legislation was known as the *Trade Practices Act 1974*. It was originally passed in 1974 and it applies to commercial activity in general by trading, financial and foreign corporations in general.

Perhaps the best-known section is section 18 of the *Australian Consumer Law*, which replaces section 52 of the old Act. It reads: "A person must not, in trade or commerce, engage in conduct that is misleading or deceptive or is likely to mislead or deceive".

The conceptual underpinning of this legislation contrasts with that of the *National Classification Code*. As we have seen, the classification system has grown out of moralistic concerns about what might offend people's sensibilities. Under the consumer protection paradigm, by contrast, the fundamental aim is to protect consumers' interests against exploitation by unscrupulous corporations. In this it is more closely aligned to the community's concerns about sexualisation: as discussed above, the problem is not just with "sex" but with "sex sells". A consumer protection paradigm facilitates engagement with the "sells" part of the equation and also recognises the power imbalance between industry and consumer.

How might a consumer protection paradigm be used as a basis for legislative responses to sexualisation of children? Here are some adaptations of the wording of section 18 that could pick up the concerns and curb the practices identified in this chapter:

> A person must not, in trade or commerce, engage in conduct that is likely to expose children to inappropriate sexual content.
>
> A person must not, in trade or commerce, engage in conduct that places children in a position of appearing to be sexually alluring.
>
> A person must not, in trade or commerce, engage in conduct that links children's wellbeing to the trappings of adult sexuality.

It will be apparent that the concepts used here (for example "sexually alluring", "trappings of adult sexuality") are open to interpretation. There would be room for debate in many cases as to whether conduct fell foul of the provisions. However, this is not unusual in law. The application of the wording to real-life practices would have to be worked out over time, just as it has been in relation to section 52. In the meantime, however, the adoption of these or similar provisions could have the salutary effects of giving a name to the practices that are of concern to the community, raising awareness of them and sending a message to the corporate world that the named practices are unacceptable.

Calming down: the legal approach to media violence

The problem

There is cogent evidence that media violence can have an undesirable influence on the attitudes and behaviour of its consumers. This is well documented elsewhere in this volume (Chapters 1–5). There is also evidence that interactive violence has a greater influence than violence which is viewed passively (see Chapter 3). Yet violent interactive video games are some of the most popular entertainment products in history, especially among young people, and players often spend long hours playing, thereby enhancing the effect.

The classification of violence

Under the *Guidelines for the Classification of Films and Computer Games 2005* (Office of Film and Literature Classification), violence is defined as "Acts of violence; the threat or effects of violence" (p 21).

Material is classified against a hierarchy of impact, from "very mild" to "high". These brief descriptors are given more content in the guidelines (see Table 1 *over page*).

The criteria for RC (refused classification) material are different for films and publications on the one hand and for video games on the other. For films and publications they are:

> (a) depict, express or otherwise deal with matters of sex, drug misuse or addiction, crime, cruelty, violence or revolting or abhorrent phenomena in such a way that they offend against the standards of morality, decency and propriety generally accepted by reasonable adults to the extent that they should not be classified; or

Table 1: National Classification Code Guidelines

Classification	Impact level	Guidelines
G	Very mild	Violence should have only a low sense of threat or menace, and be justified by context
PG	Mild	Violence should be mild and infrequent, and be justified by context
M	Moderate	Moderate violence is permitted if justified by context
MA15+	Strong	Violence should be justified by context
R18+ (only for films)	High	Violence is permitted
X18+	N/A	No depiction of violence, sexual violence, sexualised violence or coercion is allowed
RC	Very high	Detailed instruction or promotion in matters of crime or violence OR Gratuitous, exploitative or offensive depictions of: (1) violence with a very high degree of impact or which are excessively frequent, prolonged or detailed; (2) cruelty or real violence which are very detailed or which have a high impact; (3) sexual violence.

(b) describe or depict in a way that is likely to cause offence to a reasonable adult, a person who is, or appears to be, a child under 18 (whether the person is engaged in sexual activity or not); or

(c) promote, incite or instruct in matters of crime or violence … (clauses 2 and 3 of the Code)

In the case of computer games, the RC criteria include all of the above, *plus*:

or (d) are unsuitable for a minor to see or play (clause 4).

There is no R18+ classification for games, because the criteria that would otherwise have described that classification have been subsumed into RC.

This variation on the criteria was introduced when games were first included in the classification system, in 1996. The policy justification for the different treatment of games was based on evidence that this form of media has a greater impact on attitudes and behaviour, due to its interactive nature. The judgment was made that material of high enough impact to warrant an R18+ classification should not be available at all on the Australian market.

The gaming lobby has campaigned against this approach for some years, but especially since 2009 there has been enormous pressure brought to bear on decision-makers to legalise R18+ games. In the remainder of this chapter I critique the arguments that have been put forward and explain the most recent developments.

However before I do so it will be useful to outline the structure of the Australian classification system.

As explained above, any changes to the descriptions of the classifications and guidelines must be approved by all States and Territories. In particular, the introduction of a legal R18+ classification for computer games can be resisted – vetoed, if you like – by a single State.

Such decisions are made by the Standing Committee of Attorneys-General (SCAG), although the relevant Commonwealth minister is the Minister for Home Affairs, and it is to be presumed that all ministers represent the views of their respective cabinets.

Each State and Territory has its own legislation laying down the legal consequences of different classifications; for example in South Australia, R18+ DVDs must appear in a plain wrapper in rental stores, but in other States they can have the same promotional covers as any other film. However, some consequences of classifications are nationwide: for example, throughout Australia R18+ means minors cannot legally access the material and RC means that nobody can legally access the material.

R18+ classification: A better protection for children?

The gaming lobby's campaign has been spearheaded by the industry body, the Interactive Games and Entertainment Association (IGEA). IGEA engaged a public relations firm, Espresso Communications, which developed an award-winning campaign to "educate and inform government policy makers as well as the broader community about issues associated with the lack of an adult games classification in Australia" (PRWire, 2011). While there is no publicly available information on exactly what the strategy's key messages were (or are), there is evidence that they included the idea that legalising R18+ material would protect children better.

If this is true, it appears that the strategy may have backfired on the industry body, by requiring the gaming lobby persistently to draw attention to the strong violence that is available in the MA15+ category. The assumption underlying this part of the argument appears to have been that such material is currently being misclassified and would somehow magically migrate to R18+ if only such a category were available.

The ministers were rightly sceptical of such an illogical and unfounded claim. Following a meeting in December 2010, their communiqué suggested they were taking the more rational approach to the problem of too much violence in MA15+, namely to reconsider the guidelines for MA15+ (SCAG, 2010, pp 1–2). The communiqué made it clear that the Ministers "do not support the dilution of the refused classification category" (p 2). Therefore the industry may end up with the worst of both worlds: no permission to sell any higher-level material and a restricted market for material that is currently legal.

Draft revised guidelines for MA15+ were released during 2011, but were then subject to discussion amongst the various Ministers and at the time this book went to press the current state of the draft was not publicly known. However, this has not prevented a Bill to introduce an R18+ classification, the *Classification (Publications, Films and Computer Games) Amendment (R18+ Computer Games) Bill 2012*, from being passed by the House of Representatives. At the time of going to press, that Bill was before the Senate, and the Senate Legal and Constitutional Affairs Legislation Committee had held hearings and tabled its report, recommending that the Senate pass the Bill. All of this had been done in ignorance of what the revised guidelines for MA15+ would say.

Not all of the gaming lobby's arguments stuck to the child-protection script. Much of the commentary touched on two further themes: civil liberties and the determination of older gamers to be (in their view) recognised as mature adults.

Civil liberties

In the absence of a constitutional guarantee of freedom of expression, civil liberties in relation to media are an important consideration, but one that needs to be weighed against other interests (see also Chapter 8). The *National Classification Code* follows this approach by naming adult civil liberties as a principle on the same level with the protection of minors from harmful or disturbing material, and "the need to take account of community concerns about ... depictions that condone or incite violence" (clause 1(d)).

This balancing exercise makes it necessary to identify the precise nature of the civil liberty interest. As the gaming lobby is fond of pointing out, high-impact games can be accessed online or by international mail order anyway. This means that the only civil liberty that is being interfered with, in relation to high-impact games, is that of purchasing material over the counter. In the balancing of gamers' interests against those of children and their communities, this is hardly a consideration to carry much weight.

Some games are modified for the Australian market. The most frequent modifications seem to be matters such as reducing the size of blood spatters and making corpses disappear rather than pile up after the protagonist has killed them. Such changes do not appear to interfere with the functionality of the game. Therefore the "civil liberty" in question here is the ability to see more realistic results of one's virtual violence. It is not surprising that the gaming lobby has not generally taken this argument far, in public at least.

Numbers of adult gamers

Another key plank to the gaming lobby's argument has been the proposition that the majority of gamers are adults, or alternatively that the average age among gamers is 30 and rising. The subtext seems to be that disallowing R18+ might have been justified when gaming was predominantly a children's activity, but now that the child gamers of the 1980s are in their 30s, and still playing, a further door needs to open.

Such arguments are perplexing and illogical. Disallowing R18+ material in no way denies the existence of adult gamers; indeed it presupposes that there would be somebody who would otherwise be willing and legally able to access the material. If anything, the more adult gamers there are, the more high-impact material one would expect to find in distribution outlets and in homes – and the greater the reason to place restrictions on it to avoid it falling into the hands of children.

The gaming lobby has rarely, if ever, addressed the reasons why one might want to say that in the case of games the cut-off for availability should be lower than it is for films.

The first reason is the evidence that interactivity increases the impact of violent material found in games. The best anybody has been able to do with that is to declare the evidence inconclusive. This is surely not the end of the story on matters of public policy, but rather one needs to consider whether the evidence is *sufficient* to justify a *precautionary* approach.

The second reason is that games remain a pastime of greater interest to children than to adults. The average age of gamers in general (and these have been very broadly defined) tells us nothing about who are the most enthusiastic players, or who devotes the most time and energy to game-playing. It is more cogent to consider the evidence from the United States that game-playing peaks in the 11–14 age group (Rideout et al, 2010).

It is very difficult to understand the bizarre shape this debate has taken. Adult gamers of my acquaintance have been at pains to reassure me that they are not interested in playing any higher level material than is currently available, yet they argue passionately for the introduction of R18+. They do not particularly care what material would be available or otherwise in a new R18+ classification. It seems that adult gamers are primarily interested in having societal recognition that their pastime is appropriate and they see the introduction of a legal R18+ classification as a way – perhaps the only way – to achieve that.

Comparative classifications

The gaming lobby's assumption that higher-level MA15+ material would find its way into a legal R18+ classification is frequently defended on the ground that the same material is in an adults-only classification overseas. However, there is no reason to expect Australia to have a particular regulatory response just because another country has that response. Therefore, even if Australia had an adults-only classification, there is no reason to expect it to be populated by the same material as such classifications overseas.

The picture becomes richer if one looks at the actual regulatory structure in the comparator jurisdictions. For example, in the United States the classification system is an entirely voluntary, self-regulatory one. (In fact, efforts to introduce a statutory system in California have been successfully challenged in the Supreme Court under the US Constitution's freedom of speech guarantee: *Schwarzenegger and Brown v Video Software Dealers Association and Entertainment Software Association*). Therefore, no matter what the classification, all material is accessible by everyone in the United States.

There is little at stake for the industry in placing material in the highest category (M17+) as it does not entail legal restrictions on anybody's access to the material. If anything, it might only serve to bring about the "forbidden fruit" effect, making that material appear more attractive to consumers (Gentile, 2008). This is further reason to be sceptical of the use of overseas classifications as a basis to argue what the classification should be in Australia.

Parental responsibility

It is often said that the answer to the problem of children and violent electronic games is for parents to be more responsible. Obviously it is impossible to argue against the need for parental vigilance, but it is unrealistic and dangerous to leave parents to fend for themselves on such matters.

Normally when we invest one group with the responsibility to protect something or someone, there is one of two things: either a market mechanism or a regulatory backstop. Under a market mechanism, self-interest is sufficient grounds for confidence that the responsible person will do the job diligently and effectively. With a regulatory backstop, there is some kind of system for making sure, independently, that the job is being done to an appropriate standard.

Neither of these things applies to parenting the media. Parents' interests do not always coincide with those of their children and there would be no votes in the introduction of a "media-parenting police".

Furthermore, it is misleading to frame this issue as being about avoiding harm to individual children. There are implications for a child's whole community when violent games are played because exposure to violence will colour the way players interact with others.

There is a need to protect those others as well as the player – possibly more so. It is unfair and unrealistic to expect parents to shoulder the burden of protecting the broader community's interests in this sense.

For these reasons, parental responsibility, while desirable and to be encouraged, is not the answer to the need to limit children's exposure to violent games.

Possible reforms

The Ministers' current review of the criteria for MA15+ is expected to decouple the games classification system from that of films. This might be quite justified, considering the different nature of the two media.

However, if the two systems are to be decoupled, it is difficult to see why this should be limited to higher-impact material. Arguably all interactive material should be moved into a higher category. This suggestion is perhaps best illustrated with a table:

Table 2: A proposed classification for video game violence

Category	Current description (films and games)	Proposed description for games
G	Very mild violence, low sense of threat or menace, justified by context	No violence at all
PG	Mild and infrequent violence, justified by context	Very mild violence, low sense of threat or menace, justified by context
M	Moderate violence, justified by context	Mild and infrequent violence, justified by context
MA15+	Strong violence, justified by context	Moderate violence, justified by context
R18+	High impact violence permitted; not necessarily justified by context (films only)	Strong violence, justified by context
RC	Very high	High-very high violence, not justified by context

Such a system would give more general recognition to the concerns about interactive violence and about the levels of violence that can currently be accommodated at MA15+. It would also deliver to adult gamers the recognition they seem to crave. What it would not do, of course, is increase the profits of the IGEA's members, or ensure that inappropriate material really stays out of the hands of children.

Conclusion

This chapter has reviewed the regulatory scene in Australia in relation to sexualisation and violence, especially interactive violence.

In some ways the two areas are in contradistinction to each other: in sexualisation there is pressure on governments to increase regulation (or actually to introduce regulation); in violence the pressure is to liberalise the current system. In sexualisation the struggle is between advertisers and the public; in violence it is more complicated because the public appears to be split on whether there is any need for change. Of course the gaming industry is also involved in the debate, but it is questionable whether its interests actually coincide with those of the gaming public.

However there are some very significant points in common between the two debates. In both areas, there are apparent tensions between freedom of expression and the protection of children's interests. In both areas, the industry claims to know what is best for children and to be well-placed to protect children's interests. Most importantly, in both areas there is a body of cogent research evidence of media use having a negative influence on children's well-being. The question is how best to apply this evidence through the regulatory system for the protection of children's interests.

I have suggested some ways of doing so, notably by using a consumer protection paradigm in relation to sexualisation and by completely decoupling the games classification system from that used for films.

References

APA (American Psychological Association) (2010). *Report of the APA Task Force on the Sexualization of Girls*. Task Force on the Sexualization of Girls. Accessed 29 August 2011, <http://www.apa.org/pi/women/programs/girls/report-full.pdf 22 August 2011>.

ASB (Advertising Standards Bureau) (2010), *Community Perceptions of Sex, Sexuality and Nudity in Advertising*. Turner, ACT: ASB.

ASB (2007, February 13). *Case Report 20/07*. Canberra: ASB.

ASB (2008, August 13). *Case Report 287/08*. Canberra: ASB.

Australian Government (2009). *Government Response Inquiry into the Sexualisation of Children in the Contemporary Media Environment*. Canberra: Australian Government.

Black, S (2009). *FOI reveals DJs kids were supposed to be 'adult and sexy'*. Crikey.com, 1 June. Accessed 29 August 2011, <http://www.crikey.com.au/2009/06/01/foi-reveals-djs-kids-were-supposed-to-be-adult-and-s-xy/>.

Free TV Australia (2008) *Submission by Free TV Australia Limited, Senate Environment, Communications and the Arts Committee, Inquiry into the sexualisation of children in the contemporary media environment*. Accessed 29 August 2011, <http://www.aph.gov.au/senate/committee/eca_ctte/sexualisation_of_children/submissions/sub139.pdf>.

Gentile, DA (2008). The ratings systems for media products. In S Calvert and B Wilson (eds), *Handbook of children and the media*. Boston: Blackwell.

Lee, J (2008). *Campaign Interruptus: Watchdog Withdraws Ads*. Sydney Morning Herald, 26 August.

PRWire (2011). *Espresso Communications Snags a Highly Commended for R18+ Classification for Video Games Campaign*. Accessed 29 August 2011, <http://www.prwire.com.au/pr/20227/espresso-communications-snags-a-highly-commended-for-r18-classification-for-video-games-campaign-1>.

Rideout, VJ, Foehr, UG, & Roberts, DF (2010). *Generation M2: Media in the lives of 8-18 year olds*. Merlo Park CA: Henry J Kaiser Foundation.

SCAG (Standing Committee of Attorneys-General) (2010). Communiqué 10, December.

SCECA (Senate Standing Committee on Environment, Communications and the Arts) (2008). *Sexualisation of children in the contemporary media*. Canberra: Australian Government. (ISBN 978-0-642-71935-5).

Schwarzenegger and Brown v Video Software Dealers Association and Entertainment Software Association 564 US (US Supreme Court, Docket # 08-1448). Judgment delivered 29 July 2011.

Chapter 10

Media and social policy: Towards an evidence-based approach to content regulation

Danya Braunstein, Julia Plumb and Wayne Warburton

As shown in previous chapters, there are a number of well-researched ways in which media can impact both positively and negatively on children and youth. It is our view that policy-makers in Australia need to align media policy decisions with this evidence, in order to maximise the positive impacts and minimise the negative impacts of these effects on children. That is, media policies in Australia should be "evidence-based". However, despite more than half a century of comprehensive research with convergent findings around key media impacts on children, this evidence is still debated, at times denied, and all-too-frequently ignored in the policy room.

This chapter examines the state of evidence-based policy procedures in Australia and overseas. It also explores the discrepancies between what researchers have found about media influences on children and what policy-makers and the public understand and do about these media effects.

The first part of the chapter looks at the key issues in policy-making both in Australia and overseas, with a focus on the role of government regulation, the acknowledgement or otherwise of research evidence and the regulatory frameworks involved in balancing the needs of children with the preservation of adult freedoms. Secondly, the chapter explores media policies spanning both content and access-related concerns in five key areas related to child development and children's media use: physical health, alcohol and other drugs, sexualisation, television programming, and internet use (a sixth key area, classification systems, was discussed in detail in Chapter 9). In the final part of the chapter we discuss the importance of educating children and young people about the media and discuss ways in which future trends in media convergence will create an even greater need to educate children about media.

Policy and regulation

In general terms, media policies are important for media content-makers, broadcasters, publishers and content-consumers as they provide information, guidelines and recommendations about the appropriateness of media for various social groups (such as children). In doing so, they aid the design and implementation of regulations and inform media practice at a number of levels – either by individuals or collectives, by children themselves, or by parents, media industries, distribution networks and governments (Gentile et al, 2007). As noted in Chapter 9, there can be controversy when governments and regulators attempt to control media usage; nonetheless, putting all responsibility for media regulation onto individuals is also not a sufficient solution. Not only do children themselves lack self-regulatory control (see Chapters 6 and 8, this volume), but it is unrealistic to assume that all children will have parents who have the time, information and, in some cases, the motivation to constantly regulate their children's media use. In such an environment, media regulation from authorities such as governments and classification boards can and must play a role in protecting children. With this in mind, a key question is thus "how can effective policies be implemented to protect children from inappropriate media"? One vital criterion is that such policies be *evidence-based*.

What is evidence-based policy?

Evidence-based policy is "a process that transparently uses rigorous and tested evidence in the design, implementation and refinement of policy to meet designated policy objectives" (Productivity Commission, 2009). It is a concept frequently discussed by governments as underpinning the process of policy development. For example, in 2008 the then-serving Prime Minister Kevin Rudd addressed senior public servants by saying "[p]olicy design and policy evaluation should be driven by analysis of all the available options, and not by ideology. ... We're interested in facts, not fads" (Rudd, 2008).

However despite similar rhetoric being commonly put forward by media policy-makers, in many instances policy around media and children in Australia is not being adequately influenced by available research evidence. In particular, a large and convergent body of evidence linking violent media with aggressive and anti-social thoughts and behaviours seems to be too often ignored in classification and programming policy. Such policies seem more geared toward protecting public moral sensibilities concerning material thought "offensive" than to the protection of children from well-researched risks (such as those from media violence), which may be deemed less morally "offensive" but are clearly harmful. A stronger evidence base for Australian media policy would include more attention to the effects of violent media, at a minimum.

Many reputable groups agree that the evidence for potentially negative effects of media on children, and in particular the effects of violent media, is sufficiently strong to warrant warnings to professionals, along with suggested changes to professional practice. Such organisations include the American Academy of Pediatrics, the American Medical Association, the American Academy of Child and Adolescent Psychiatry, the American Psychological Association, the American Academy of Family Physicians and the National Institute of Mental Health as well as Australian organisations such as the Australian Psychological Society, the Royal Australasian College of Physicians, various government committees and a range of children's advocacy and research interest groups. Although policy statements from these peak bodies may be effective in slowly changing professional practice standards, the concerns expressed by such organisations do not seem to have filtered through to wider public policy, regulation, or social practices. Children continue to experience increasing levels of media exposure, much of which has the potential for harm (see Chapters 1 to 7, this volume), perhaps due to an overriding consensus in public opinion that media is merely harmless entertainment (Strasburger, 2009). Given this stark disconnect between scientific evidence and social practice, there is increasing concern amongst those with an interest in healthy child development that government-level policies may not be sufficiently addressing this gap.

Many governments promote the use of evidence and research to ensure that policies will be effective (that is, will have the desired outcome: Buckingham, 2009). However, a number of sources argue that even when research is available it is often not taken into account during the policy-making process (see Strasburger, 2009; Gentile et al, 2007; Blevins & Anton, 2008; Buckingham, 2009). A prime example of this may be seen in the US efforts to protect young internet users through the creation of an Office of Technology Assessment (OTA). The OTA was to provide research and inform congressional debate and policy-making in the attempted creation of Acts relating to children's internet access (*Communications Decency Act, Child Online Protection Act* and *Children's Internet Protection Act*). Although there is evidence that such Acts could have offered some level of protection for children, the OTA had little influence on the congressional hearings and was disbanded following the first creation of an Act. Further, two of the Acts were ultimately rejected by the Supreme Court for violating the First Amendment rights of adults (Blevins & Anton, 2008). The third Act was passed only when its scope was limited to internet filtering software in public funded libraries, thus protecting children in just one small area of internet access. Blevins and Anton (2008) argued that the OTA disbandment was politically motivated, as it failed to serve Congress members' short-term interests, and pointed out that it exposed an important issue – politicians may use scientific knowledge to promote their political agenda but will also endeavour to undermine objective research evidence if these findings conflict with their political interests.

Similarly, social commentators have argued that Australian governments have not necessarily acted in the public interest at times, but instead have promoted their own political aims and the commercial interests of media industry providers (Turner & Cunningham, 2002). For example, past governments have been accused of creating media ownership legislation and delaying key decisions, such as the introduction of Pay TV, in ways that appear to have favoured the financial interests of established media owners and producers (Turner & Cunningham, 2002). When purely commercial objectives dominate policy decision-making, the statements and narratives in the public arena often cloud the issues, rather than provide clarity, and research evidence is frequently ignored. Policies produced in such a climate are therefore less likely to produce real changes to practices and genuine protections for children, despite appearing to cater to public concerns.

The role of the government in Australian media policy

Australian government operates at three levels: the Commonwealth Government, State and Territory governments, and local governments such as municipal councils. Commonwealth laws govern certain areas and State legislation must remain consistent with the Commonwealth laws in these areas. Although States can define their own legislation outside of these areas, in some circumstances all States must be in agreement for an aspect of federal law to be reformed (for example, classification laws: see Chapter 9). Government can provide two broad types of intervention:

1. Subsidising the creation of media (for example, by providing funding to support media production through Screen Australia, or by providing public broadcast opportunities on the government-funded media outlets, ABC and SBS, which broadcast on television, radio and online); or
2. Regulating the distribution and exhibition of media products through various regulatory and self-regulatory bodies that monitor media production and audience responses to media (for example, the Australian Media and Communications Authority (ACMA), FreeTV Australia and the Australian Press Council).

Government policy also regulates media ownership in Australia, with the Australian Competition and Consumer Commission (ACCC) monitoring the amount of foreign investment in Australian media and preventing disproportionate control of media production. The government also creates content quotas to provide for public interest. This limits the amount of internationally-sourced media content available within Australia, as well as ensuring certain media are targeted towards appropriate audiences (for example the Children's Television Standards regulate children's television programming at specific times of the day). The Commonwealth Government has the biggest input into media policy creation and tends to set media policies around media production on a national scale. However, there are also Commonwealth policies regulated by the ACMA that relate to local content. For example, local television content quotas exist in regional areas to provide material of local significance, such as broadcasting local news bulletins rather than relying solely on national news and weather broadcasts.

The majority of Australian media is currently regulated by an independent statutory authority, the ACMA (ACMA, 2011), which is part of the federal government Department of Broadband, Communications and the Digital Economy (DBCDE). Comprised of a range of committees and consulting groups who work with representatives of industry, consumers, government and academia, the ACMA is responsible for the regulation of broadcasting, the internet (including mobile phone content), radio communications and telecommunications. The ACMA describes its responsibilities as being the promotion of self-regulation and competition in the communications industry, whilst protecting consumers and other users, and fostering an environment in which electronic media respects community standards and responds to audience and user needs. Within this regulatory framework, the ACMA also cites as one of its aims the protection of children from exposure to unsuitable media.

The Advertising Standards Bureau (ASB) regulates television and radio advertising in Australia, with ACMA regulating some aspects such as Australian content levels. The Australian Government Classification Board classifies films, computer games and some publications, and also provides classifications to the ACMA on Internet content. Non-broadcast advertising is regulated by the ASB and print media (including online outlets) is self-regulated by the Australian Press Council. The ACMA also shares regulation for online content with industry and the community, meaning that codes of practice for online content service providers are monitored, but the ACMA has limited powers for dealing with prohibited online content (Chapman, 2011). For example the ACMA may take action over online content classified by the Classification Board as being suitable only for those aged 18 years or older, or regarding unrestricted access to mobile content that is classified suitable only for those over 15 years old, but complaints for content not in these categories must be raised with the content provider.

Protecting children within the current regulatory frameworks

A key conundrum for policy-makers involves balancing the need to protect children on one hand with maintaining appropriate adult freedoms on the other (see also Chapters 8 and 9). In the digital media age, media content is accessible at all times of the day and from multiple platforms (for example, via mobile phone, mp3 player, netbook, tablet computer and laptop computer). These circumvent the traditional forms of regulation and control that may have once been available for traditional media such as television, print and radio, and make it harder to protect children from inappropriate content. However, when it comes to regulating content in a portable media environment, citizens of democratic countries; including Australia, the United States and the United Kingdom; commonly resent and push back against any perceived restriction to their freedom to access and use media (Lisosky, 2001; Dooley et al, 2009). For example, public outrage at being censored delayed the Commonwealth Government's proposed changes to the *Broadcasting Services Act 1992* (Cth) to mandate filtering software within Internet Service Providers (ISPs) to prevent access to sites classified as unsuitable (including to minors) by the ACMA.

Self-regulation and co-regulation policies

Rather than find the difficult balance between child protection and adult freedom in government-level policies and regulations, governments are increasingly moving towards a "bottom up" approach that emphasises less government involvement and more cooperation between self-regulatory bodies and co-regulatory bodies to establish industry best practices (Lievens, 2007). An example of this is the Council of the European Union's 1998 *Recommendation on the Protection of Minors and Human Dignity*, which was revised and adopted in 2006 and emphasised self-regulation via codes of conduct, parental control tools, hotlines, awareness actions, multi-stakeholder involvement and cooperation across borders (Lievens, 2007). This approach to self-regulation has some potential to be effective in terms of informing media consumers and protecting children from harmful content.

An Australian example of improved consumer protection in a co-regulatory regime is the Mobile Premium Services Industry Scheme which operates according to the ACMA rules for restricted access mobile phone premium content providers (for example, phone sex lines) and made effective revisions following community concerns about inappropriate access and accidental subscription. The ACMA determines the rules which currently require suitable warnings about the nature of the adult content, including a "double opt-in" regime for service subscriptions and age-verification tools to determine that the subscriber is aged over 18 years for R 18+ content (or over 15 years for MA 15+ content).

Self-regulation policies have the advantage that they are seen as more likely to be adopted by industry, especially when their use is not mandated by government, and consumers may feel they still have some degree of choice. However, as noted in Chapters 9 and 11, there are many issues for concern. The codes of practice that underpin such systems (that is, the self-imposed rules by which those bound by the code agree to operate) are notorious for having insufficient end-user input during development, resulting in "watered down" protections for users. In addition, such systems often have poor monitoring for breaches of the code and few sanctions for those who commit these breaches. Essentially, self-regulation offers little protection unless the codes themselves are well constructed, industry behaviour is policed and breaches are penalised in a way that can impact and change industry behaviour. A further weakness is that such systems often put significant responsibility onto the consumer or guardians, such as parents. For example, there have been recent calls for self-regulation in regards to media classification (that is, producers would self-classify their media products). Reclassification would be driven solely by consumer complaints, a process that puts full responsibility for identifying inappropriately classified media squarely on families, a group who may not be sufficiently media-savvy to identify risky material, may not be motivated to complain and may not be aware of the complaint avenues available to them.

The current Australian regulatory framework for media has two key problems in terms of children's access to inappropriate media. First, with multiple complaint bodies it is difficult for consumers of media to know where to go with concerns, complaints or inquiries. Secondly, the system is reactive rather than pro-active. Potentially harmful media is easily accessible by children until enough people complain about it to warrant a review of the content and/or there is action against the media producers or distributors who failed to comply with the relevant standards or Acts. These concerns have prompted the 2012 recommendation by the Australian Law Reform Commission to overhaul completely the current classification system to adopt a new Classification Board which would regulate all media content in Australia.

Policies relating to child development and children's media use

As the trend for media policies shifts towards industry self-regulation and responsibilities being shared by industry, communities and individuals rather than by governments, we as a society need to consider how such policies address key areas concerning children's development and whether they will be truly effective. The next section of this chapter explores five key areas related to child development and children's media use. It examines past policies and considers ways that future media policies can be made more effective.

Media policy and childhood obesity

Obesity is a serious and increasing problem in the western world. The World Health Organisation (WHO, 2008) estimates that a quarter of Australians are obese (that is, have a body mass index (BMI) over 30 kg/sq metre). Childhood obesity is a particularly critical issue and a number of authorities have attempted to hold media partly responsible for changing the messages children receive about food products, especially through advertising (RACP, 2004; AAP, 2006). In Australia there can be no more than five minutes of advertising per 30 minutes of programming during C (Children's) time zones, but this still means that an average child who watches 2.5 hours each day in this timeslot would end up viewing over 9125 advertisements every year (RACP, 2004). The American Academy of Pediatrics (2009) claims that of 40,000 ads per year watched by young people in the United States, half of these ads are for food, with the majority being high-calorie and sugared foods and only 3 per cent being healthy foods. In Australia, it has been estimated that one third of advertisements during children's television viewing times are for food, most commonly confectionary, fast food, soft drinks and snacks. This prompted the Australian Division of General Practitioners in 2003 to recommend a total ban on "junk" food advertising during children's television time zones (RACP, 2004). Similar policies have been adopted in other countries. In the United Kingdom, the Office of Communications (Ofcom) in 2006 banned advertising for high-fat/high-sugar foods to audiences under 16 years old and Sweden has imposed a complete ban on advertising to children under 12 years old for any product (Buckingham, 2009; Kleeman, 2007).

However, there are also problems with imposing bans on food advertising. These include defining "harmful food", deciding which television time zones should be affected by the bans and assessing the impact such bans will have on funding for programming (and thus on the funds available to produce quality children's television). To give a local example, the Australian Children's Television Foundation (ACTF) supported a South Australian government initiative to address this issue, but argued that the vague definition of junk food as "energy-dense, nutrient-poor" made the advertising ban unworkable in practice (ACTF, 2008a). Clearly, the future development of detailed and uniform nutritional standards for food advertising will be crucial to effective food advertising policy (see Knell, 2008).

The ACTF also identified a disconnect between the times typically set aside for children's television programming and the times when the majority of children are actually watching television: "peak viewing" time zones (see also Chapter 1). This forces a choice between banning advertising during programming designed for children, or during programming that actually captures a significant child audience along with its intended adult audience (ACTF, 2008a). Recommendations have been made to simply ban advertising during times when children are most likely to be watching (not just times designated for child viewing), as this would be simpler for consumers to understand and the most effective way of limiting children's exposure to food advertising (Handsley et al, 2009). Such an approach needs to also work in practice, however, and there can be revenue implications for children's programming. For example, ITV in the United Kingdom closed its children's production arm and dramatically reduced its free-to-air children's hours as a result of falling revenue following the Ofcom advertising ban (Kleeman, 2007).

Policy in this area must balance the financial viability of television stations and funding for quality children's programming with the research evidence which indicates that certain types of food advertising have a negative effect on childhood obesity rates and thus a high social cost. Australia is fortunate to have a partial solution – the creation of ABC3, which has provided government-funded, advertising-free children's television since 2009, as well as programming on other ABC channels in peak time zones that is also advertising free (although possibly less attractive to children than peak-time programming on commercial stations). More recently, ABC2 has dedicated its daytime programming to ABC4Kids, which has advertising-free content more suitable to young children than that of ABC3.

Media policy and alcohol, tobacco and drug use

Over the past few decades, research and policy directives have impacted considerably on media representations of illicit and adult-restricted substances. During this time, the media itself has been responsible for both the promotion and the reduction of substance use. In 1997, a US study found that alcohol, tobacco or illicit drugs were present in 70 per cent of prime time network drama, 95 per cent of top grossing movies and half of all music videos (RACP, 2004). In addition, 90 per cent of rap songs, 41 per cent of country music songs and 23-27 per cent of rock/hip hop/R&B songs referenced cigarette, alcohol or drug use, with up to 63 per cent of rap songs referencing illicit drug use. In popular music, 68 per cent of substance references were found to link substance use with positive consequences such as social acceptance, sex and parties, and only 16 per cent suggested negative consequences (Primack et al, 2008; Rideout et al, 1999). Research has shown that alcohol and cigarette advertising, including indirect methods (such as product placement in movies), causes people to adopt favourable attitudes to the substance or product and leads to increased consumption of the substance. Children and youth are particularly susceptible to these types of marketing (Strasburger, 2009; see also Chapter 6). For example, non-smoking teenagers whose favourite film stars smoked on screen are 16 times more likely to view smoking favourably (Tickle et al, 2001).

To reduce these negative media effects, the Australian government has focused since 2001 on a national drugs campaign, utilising print, broadcast and online media to target youth and people at-risk for tobacco, alcohol and illicit drug use. In addition, anti-tobacco advertising has been on Australian television since 1971, shortly after considerable research had linked cigarette smoking with cancer. By 1976 broadcast advertising of tobacco was banned and by 2006 Australia had completely banned sporting sponsorship by tobacco brands. However, these policies were only able to impact on media produced within Australia and were continually undermined by media created overseas, particularly from the United States. Despite voluntary bans on product placement within Hollywood films, research shows that tobacco product placement in films was higher in 2000 than in the 1960s, with 62 per cent of top-grossing films screened in Australia in 1999-2000 having at least one positively-depicted smoking scene (Soulos & Sanders, 2004). In 2007, 40 per cent of US television episodes rated TV-PG and TV-14 (that is, classified for parental guidance and aged 14 and over respectively) showed at least one depiction of tobacco use per episode, an exposure that is estimated to have reached over 1 million young viewers in the United States (Cullen et al, 2011) and countless more in other syndicated countries such as Australia. However, evidence does suggest that the anti-smoking campaigns in Australia, although targeted towards adult smokers, have contributed greatly to changed attitudes in younger people and are partially responsible for a reduction in the numbers of youth smokers (Wakefield, 2005).

There are clear links in the research literature between media exposure to depictions of alcohol use and the initiation of alcohol use by minors (see Kirsch, 2010; Strasburger, 2009 for reviews). Using this evidence to inform policy, however, is far from simple. Pervasive and positive attitudes toward alcohol in the media make regulation very difficult and may undermine the effectiveness of any policy initiatives. To give but one example, the line "I need a drink", which essentially suggests that alcohol is the appropriate response to even low levels of stress or anxiety, is ubiquitous in television, movies and music regardless of any other alcohol bans put into place.

One policy response in Australia has been to regulate alcohol advertising on television so that it occurs only during programs classified M (Mature), MA (Mature Audience) or AV (Adult Violence) (ADF, 2010). In addition, advertisers are instructed that alcohol advertisements cannot appeal directly to children. Although this regulation offers some protection to children, alcohol brands sponsor major sporting events and their signs are clearly visible during televised broadcasts. Moreover, admired athletes and sportspeople wear clothing clearly showing their alcohol industry sponsors (ADF, 2010). Alcohol producers also sponsor popular youth events such as the Big Day Out (BDO) music festivals (open to patrons aged 15 and over), thus providing an implicit association between alcohol use and immersion in cultural and social activities (ADF, 2010). For example, in 2010 BDO was sponsored by five alcohol brands. The Australian Drug Foundation argues that self-regulatory and co-regulatory advertising codes (such as the Alcohol Beverages Advertising Code) have failed to control alcohol advertising over the past two decades and recommend the withdrawal of alcohol advertising from sporting games where there is a high concentration of viewers under 25 years old (ADF, 2010). There is also growing pressure to ban any tobacco or alcohol advertising or product placement, both by broadcast and indirect methods, in all media (AAP, 2006; Soulos & Sanders, 2004).

Media policy and the sexualisation of children

Links between sexualised media and negative outcomes for children, such as body-dissatisfaction, eating disorders, self-objectification and child sexual abuse are well-documented and are described in Chapter 7 of this volume (see also Rush, 2009). In response to this research evidence, there is a growing concern among practitioners who work with children (and others) that such media not only provides children with access to sexual material that is inappropriate for their age, but also provides misleading and unrealistic sexual content that normalises sexual behaviours inappropriate for children (for example, wearing a bra and dressing provocatively as a six-year-old). It is noteworthy that over 75 per cent of prime time television shows in the United States have sexual content but only 14 per cent mention risks or responsibilities related to sex. Evidence from a variety of sources suggests that these depictions of casual sex, sex without contraception and sex without consequences have contributed to the United States having the highest rate of teenage pregnancies in the western world (AAP, 2010a).

Responses in the United States have included recommendations encouraging the media industry to include socially responsible content about sex and sexual relationships, improve effective communication about sex information and focus on interpersonal relationships with an emphasis on respectful and non-exploitative interactions (AAP, 2010a; Brown, 2000). However, these recommendations are yet to be enshrined in higher-level government policies that could regulate the behaviours of content producers, for whom "sex sells".

Similarly to the situation in the United States, in the Australian Commonwealth Government's response to the report of the '*Inquiry into the Sexualisation of Children in the Contemporary Media Environment'* (Australian Commonwealth Government, 2009), the government was reluctant to change regulatory systems already in place. Although the inquiry resulted in a series of practical recommendations, the government continued to endorse the current system whereby complaints about advertisements continue to be directed to the Advertising Standards Board (an industry-based body, independent from the government). The government also noted that the current classification system is adequate for screening of music videos and film and television content, and that billboards (such as the AMI erectile dysfunction billboards discussed in Chapter 9) are under the governance/jurisdiction of local councils or State and Territory governments rather than the Commonwealth Government. The government agreed "in principle" that more research into child sexualisation and media was needed, but noted that such research was beyond the scope of the National Health and Medical Research Council, necessitating the exploration of other avenues to conduct it. To date, such exploration has not eventuated. A stronger policy and regulatory response to these recommendations was hoped for by a range of groups with an interest in healthy child development (see also Chapter 9).

Media policy and children's television viewing

General television broadcasting in Australia, when compared with the industry in the United States and Canada, is regulated more by government than by industry, a situation arising as a result of the differing ideologies at play when each nation established its broadcast industry (Lisosky, 2001). For Australia, the importance of establishing a national identity, and a lack of faith in industry self-regulation, has led to increased governmental control over both public and commercial broadcasters since 1971 (Lisosky, 2001). Australian policy, like policy in Canada, has been influenced by advocacy groups and broadcast industry associations that have campaigned for changes to children's television policies (for example, the Australian Council on Children and the Media (ACCM) and the Australian Research Alliance for Children and Youth (ARACY)).

The most effective policies that have been implemented over recent years for protecting and promoting positive effects for children have been the regulation of both children's time zones and Australian-content quotas, and the formation of a dedicated children's channel (ABC3). Reforms to the Children's Television Standards were targeted at changing the commercial television stations' children's programming to complement the new ABC children's channel (ACTF, 2007). To this end, recommendations included retaining the quota of 260 hours of C (Children's) classified programs each year, but adjusting the time zones to provide greater durations of "blocks", such as weekend time zones between 9.00 am and 10.00 am when higher numbers of children are watching television (ACTF, 2007). One concerning outcome of this recommendation was an increase in the PG time zones, meaning that commercial free-to-air channels were able to schedule PG-rated programs at all times of the day, including between 6.00 am and 8.30 am, and 4.00 pm and 7.00 pm weekdays, and 6.00 am and 10.00 am on weekends. These were previously only for C (Children's), P (Pre-school) or G (General) programs (Free TV, 2010). By definition, PG programs are suitable for children but may have some content that requires parental supervision. This change in programming seems to require far greater vigilance by parents for monitoring the programs their children watch, rather than providing more suitable programming for children.

The introduction of ABC3, and the later dedication of ABC2 to ABC4Kids during daytime, has provided a child-friendly television destination and assisted parents with regulating the media content to which their children have access. Examples of European dedicated children's channels include CBBC and CBeebies (United Kingdom), Gulli (France), KiKa (Germany) and Barnkanalen (Sweden), and evidence from audience uptake of these channels supported the creation of a children's channel in Australia (ACTF, 2006). The introduction of digital television in 2009 made the ABC3 dedicated children's channel possible. The ACTF proposal supporting a dedicated children's channel was that 55 per cent of the programming would be Australian made, providing a stronger Australian identity for viewers and creating increased competition amongst programmers, which in turn would drive increased program quality (ACTF, 2007; ACTF, 2006). Additional licenses given to established networks allowed greater diversity of programs and an opportunity to attract greater advertising revenue across multiple channels, which increased funding towards programs. Research of digital programming supported these policies, showing commercial free-to-air broadcasters are actually exceeding Australian content quotas and children's content quotas as a result of multi-channel digital broadcasting (ACMA, 2010). Repeat broadcast of programming was not considered to be an issue, with evidence suggesting children enjoy re-watching programs (ACTF, 2006), thus assisting stations to budget for the need to fill broadcast time for 15- 24 hours per day.

Overall, Australia's digital television policies seem to have been effective in facilitating the regulation of times when children's programs are broadcast and the setting of minimum content quota requirements for Australian programming. However, they have not been able to address all the relevant issues, such as programming during 8-17-year-olds' peak viewing times (6.00 pm-9.00 pm) and the spread of PG programming into younger viewing zones. In addition, with up to 45 per cent of programming available on Australian television being imported from overseas (ACMA, 2010), attempts to regulate the content of imported television programs are fraught with difficulty. Although bodies such as the European Union's "Audio Visual Media Services Directive" have set a precedent for cooperative policies between EU countries regarding international content (Lisosky, 2001), there is as yet no global agreement on television content and classifications.

Media policy and the internet

The internet and technological developments in portable media have created an amazing opportunity for increased communication, interactivity and global dispersion of information, but have also led to increased risks for children in terms of cyberbullying, interaction with strangers and access to potentially harmful content (for example, sexual or violent material, or promotion of negative beliefs, attitudes and/or behaviours). The nature of the internet and the speed at which internet and broadband technology is advancing means this medium is difficult to regulate. However, the importance of introducing safety precautions for children's internet use is clear: based on US studies, the Royal Australasian College of Physicians (RACP, 2004) suggests that approximately 50,000 Australian children aged between 10 and 17 will be approached every year on the internet for sexual purposes.

Children's access to the internet also causes concerns about internet addiction and time spent online. Research suggests children are online up to three times as long as adults, with the key ingredients that stimulate children's interest being increased social interaction, uninterrupted access to entertaining activities (for example, games) and multimedia and interactive features (Aikat, 2005; Dooley et al, 2009). Because of the amount of time children spend on computers, there is growing concern among media researchers, psychologists and paediatricians about screen-based addictions (for example, internet, video game and online video game addictions; eg, see Gentile, 2009; Young, 2010). Indeed, such concerns have reached the point where screen-based addictions are expected to be appendicised in the forthcoming fifth version of the Diagnostic and Statistical Manual for Mental Disorders (DSM-V), in an effort to stimulate further research. Social networking brings additional issues and risks through processes of normalisation and peer group relationships, for example sites that promote suicide, eating disorders (pro-anorexia sites) or risky activities such as "planking". Amendments in 2004 to the Commonwealth *Criminal Code* have made it illegal to promote violent acts such as self-harm, suicide, and bullying (Dooley et al, 2009), but it is hard to control access to non-Australian sites and more research is needed to assist policy-makers to ascertain risks to children posed by the internet, along with ways to overcome them.

There have been difficulties with attempts by governments in the United States, United Kingdom and Australia to introduce internet filters and safety protocols because many people have seen them as restricting adult freedoms. Nevertheless, these countries have various bodies focused on research, public education and the development of policies for protecting children within the online environment: the UK Council for Child Internet Safety (UKCCIS), the Federal Communications Commission (FCC) in the United States and the Cybersafety initiative by the Australian government (managed by the ACMA). Initiatives have included restricting children's access via computers at schools and libraries, policing websites that violate codes of practice (specifically those that promote child sex exploitation) and promoting training programs for parents and children regarding media-literacy and safety precautions (Byron, 2008). Providing parents with more tools to protect children is possible through parental control software or technology, such as the Belgian government's identity card that regulates children's access to special child-friendly chatrooms and verifies that the user is aged over 12 via an online national database (Lievens, 2007). Such approaches have their limitations, however. For example, Lievens (2007) argues that use of the Belgian technology is limited, as it only currently provides for children aged over 12 and it violates certain legal and privacy safeguards by providing identification details on the card such as name, age and gender.

Educating children about the media

Research indicates that media literacy has many advantages for children (see Kirsch, 2010; Strasburger, 2009 for reviews). Because media literacy essentially involves the ability to understand and decode media messages, recommendations for parents include discussing with children the ways that media messages are constructed, and encouraging children to develop critical thinking and viewing skills and to make positive media choices (AAP, 2010b). When examining developmentally appropriate media education, there are some research findings that are potentially important to take into account. For example, whilst teenagers are most likely to be influenced by advertising strategies based on persuasive arguments, younger children are more likely to respond to celebrity endorsement, product placement and physical attractiveness, jingles and colourful images (Livingstone & Helsper, 2006). In addition, younger children (roughly under the age of eight), are more vulnerable to messages because they have difficulty distinguishing between advertising and other television programming, and this has led many countries to ban certain advertising to children under a certain age (for example, Sweden, Norway, Greece, Denmark, Belgium and the United Kingdom; AAP, 2006).

The model used by the UKCCIS may provide a helpful template for media education. The UKCCIS consists of a panel of members from senior government, industry, child safety organisations and voluntary participants (Byron, 2010). It has set a global precedent by assisting with the formulation and introduction of policies on classification systems and codes of practice, as well as raising awareness and providing resources to parents and children to deal with internet risks (Byron, 2010). This model provides a good example of cooperation between various legislators and action groups, and successful engagement with parents and children to promote media education, and may work well across broader media applications.

This approach was adopted in the development of the Australian Cybersafety initiative, which maintains an online website (Cybersmart), provides a helpline to resource and assist parents and children, and provides training programs to educate schools and teachers to deal with media issues, such as cyberbullying. The collaborative approach was also influential in the development of the Young and Well Cooperative Research Centre which connects young people with researchers, practitioners and reformers with the aim to develop positive ways of using media and technology to improve mental health for children. In the end, policy related to media education should aim to empower parents and children to understand media effects, to engage independently with information about media and to make informed choices about their media consumption (Reid, 2005). This requires the provision of access to high quality, current, and age-appropriate information and resources for media users (Reid, 2005).

The media-savvy child

The next generation of children is growing up in an environment where media is accessible via a multitude of platforms, where information data are easily transferable from one device to another and where converging information across multiple platforms contributes to a digital media environment that traditional policy-makers could never have anticipated. As digital media technologies become more integrated, the boundaries between media products and services become less and less distinct (for example, 3G mobile phones now operate as communication devices, internet access points, social networking tools and gaming consoles).

In this converging and increasingly portable media environment, limiting children's access to inappropriate materials becomes increasingly difficult. To address this, initiatives which empower children to self-regulate their media use align well with research evidence and seem to be particularly important. Most children from kindergarten on are taught about exercise and healthy eating, and "all the time" foods, "sometimes foods" and "never" foods. Given that even very young children have significant media exposure in Australia, similar teaching on which types of media are "mostly good to use", "sometimes good to use" and "never good to use" could be valuable. In other words, teach children that the "you are what you eat" principle espoused throughout this book applies to the mind as well as the body. To date, Australian education policy-makers have not taken media education to this level, although growing concerns over children's internet use may drive policy reforms in this area. It is crucial to note, though, that assisting children to develop self-regulation skills with media does not remove the responsibility of governments to properly monitor and regulate media, and to produce appropriate media policy that protects children.

Conclusion and the way forward

Australian policy-makers will need to respond to the current media environment in a way that factors in the emerging and converging media environment and provides genuine safeguards for children. In our view, a key element is making greater use of existing research, commissioning new research, and creating policies that factor in what we know about child development in a way that pays more than "lip service" to the findings. In particular, research about the effects of media should be taken more seriously during policy development, media content production should be driven more strongly by social factors than by financial gain, and media education should be more thorough and start at a younger age for children in Australian schools.

The current trend towards converging responsibility for media policy into fewer government agencies and regulatory bodies may turn out to be effective as the media environment itself converges. Some self-regulation regimes may also be well-suited to maintaining a regulatory framework that can respond to the rapidly changing media environment but, as discussed, these can also have significant drawbacks that undermine their ability to protect children. In particular, the underlying codes of practice can be ambiguous or provide weak protection, can put commercial interests ahead of consumer interests and may not be enforced adequately when media producers are in breach. Such problems need to be adequately addressed before self-regulatory regimes can be considered truly effective.

Clearly, there is a long way to go in the development of media policy approaches that effectively balance the commercial needs of producers, the freedoms of adults and rights of children to be protected from harmful influences in our civilised society. While international consensus about media policy will take more time to establish, Australia has a need to create effective policies for protecting children *immediately*. There are no simple solutions in the complex current media environment, but increased cooperation between media producers, media researchers, government and law enforcement agencies, professionals who work with children, child advocacy groups, parents and the children themselves is a good place to start. It is, however, only a start – within this collaborative process, it will be imperative that all parties pay more attention to the extensive research evidence concerning media effects. By basing policies firmly on scientific evidence, we stand the best chance of formulating effective regulations that simultaneously protect the right to freedom of expression, and prevent physical and psychological harm from coming to children in this media-saturated age.

Reference List and Bibliography

Aikat, D (2005). *"Click here for fun, games, friends...": Analyses of media content characteristics of children's web sites*. Paper presented at the annual meeting of the International Communication Association, Sheraton New York, New York City, NY. Accessed December 2010, <http://citation.allacademic.com/meta/p_mla_apa_research_citation/0/1/5/1/2/pages15127/p15127-1.php>.

AAP (American Academy of Pediatrics, Council on Communications and Media) (2009). Policy statement: Media violence. *Pediatrics, 124*, 1495–1503.

AAP (2006). Policy statement: Children, adolescents, and advertising. *Pediatrics, 118*, 2563–2569.

AAP (2010a). Policy statement: Sexuality, contraception, and the media. *Pediatrics, 126*, 576–582.

AAP (2010b). Policy statement: Media education. *Pediatrics, 126*, 1–8.

ACMA (Australian Communications and Media Authority) (2010). Media release: *Commercial television licensees exceed Australian content quotas in 2009*. Accessed May 2011, <http://www.acma.gov.au/WEB/STANDARD/pc=PC_312221>.

ACMA (2011). *The ACMA Organisation*. Accessed May 2011, <http://www.acma.gov.au/WEB/STANDARD/pc=ACMA_ORG_DIR>.

ACTF (Australian Children's Television Foundation) (2006). *Submission to Department of Communications, Information Technology, and the Arts in respect of the Discussion Paper: Meeting the Digital Challenge – Reforming Australia's media in the digital age*.

ACTF (2007). *Submission to the Children's Television Standards review*. Accessed December 2010, <http://www.actf.com.au/about_us/pdfs/CTS_Review_Submission.pdf>.

ACTF (2008a): Response to *Television Advertising and the Consumption of Unhealthy Food and Drinks by Children: South Australian Government Consultation Paper*.

ACTF (2008b): Submission to the Senate: *Inquiry into the sexualisation of children*. Accessed December 2010, <http://www.actf.com.au/about_us/pdfs/inquiryintosexualisation0408.pdf>.

ADF (Australian Drug Foundation) (2010). *Position statement on alcohol marketing*. Accessed April 2011, <http://www.adf.org.au/policy-advocacy/position-statement-on-alcohol-marketing>.

APS (Australian Psychological Society) (2000). Position Paper: *Media representations and responsibilities, psychological perspectives*. Accessed April 2011 from, <http://www.psychology.org.au/publications/statements/media>.

Australian Commonwealth Government (2009). *Australian Government Response to the Committee's Report*, Senate Committee on Environment, Communications and the Arts 'Inquiry into the sexualisation of children in the contemporary media environment'. Canberra: Commonwealth Government of Australia. Accessed April 2011, <http://www.aph.gov.au/Senate/committee/eca_ctte/sexualisation_of_children/gov_response/gov_response.pdf>.

Blevins, JL, & Anton, F (2008). Muted voices in the legislative process: The role of scholarship in US Congressional efforts to protect children from internet pornography. *New Media and Society, 10*, 115–138.

Brown, JD (2000). Adolescents' sexual media diets. *Journal of Adolescent Health, 27S*, 35–40.

Buckingham, D (2009). The appliance of science: the role of evidence in the making of regulatory policy on children and food advertising in the UK. *International Journal of Cultural Policy, 15*, 201–215.

Byron, T (2008). *Safer children in a digital world: The report of the Byron Review 2008*. Accessed August 2011, <http://www.dcsf.gov.uk/byronreview/>.

Byron, T (2010). *Do we have safer children in a digital world? A review of progress since the 2008 Byron Review*. Accessed August 2011, <http://www.dcsf.gov.uk/byronreview/>.

Chapman, C (2011). *The 'convergence phenomena' from a regulators perspective*. Speech to the Communication and Media Lawyers Association, Sydney, NSW. Accessed May 2011, <http://www.acma.gov.au/webwr/_assets/main/lib312076/chris_chapman_camla_speech.pdf>.

Cullen, J, Sokol, NA, Slawek, D, Allen, JA, Vallone, D, & Healton, C (2011). Depictions of tobacco use in 2007 broadcast television programming popular among US youth. *Archives of Pediatrics and Adolescent Medicine, 165*, 147–151.

Dooley, JJ, Cross, D, Hearn, L, & Treyvaud, R (2009). *Review of existing Australian and international cyber-safety research*. Perth: Child Health Promotion Research Centre. Edith Cowan University.

Free TV Australia (2010). Fact Sheet: *Revised Commercial Television Industry Codes of Practice: Extension of Parental Guidance (PG) Time Zones on Digital Multi-Channels*. Accessed May 2011, <http://www.freetv.com.au/media/Code_of_Practice/PG_Time_Zones_Fact_Sheet.pdf>.

Gentile, DA, Saleem, M, & Anderson, CA (2007). Public policy and the effects of media violence on children. *Social Issues and Policy Review, 1*, 15–61.

Gentile, DA (2009). Pathological video-game use among youth ages 8 to 18: A national study. *Psychological Science, 20*, 594–602.

Handsley, E, Mehta, K, Coveney, J, & Nehmy, C (2009). Regulatory axes on food advertising to children on television. *Australia and New Zealand Health Policy, 6*. Accessed December 2010, <http://www.anzhealthpolicy.com/content/6/1/1>.

Kirsch, SJ (2010). *Media and youth: A developmental perspective*. Malden MA: Wiley Blackwell.

Kleeman, D (2007, June 4). Don't starve kids TV. *Broadcasting and Cable*, 32.

Knell, GE (2008). Obese kids: Time for media to act. *Broadcasting and Cable*, 11 August.

Latzer, M (2009). Convergence revisited: Toward a modified pattern of communications governance. *Convergence – The International Journal of Research into New Media Technologies, 15*, 411–426.

Lievens, E (2007). Protecting children in the new media environment: Rising to the regulatory challenge? *Telematics and Informatics, 24,* 315–330.

Linebarger, DL, & Piotrowski, JT (2010). Structure and strategies in children's educational television: The roles of program type and learning strategies in children's learning. *Child Development, 81,* 1582–1597.

Lisosky, JM (2001). For all kids' sakes: Comparing children's television policy-making in Australia, Canada and the United States. *Media, Culture and Society, 23,* 821–842.

Livingstone, S, & Helsper, EJ (2006). Does advertising literacy mediate the effects of advertising to children? A critical examination of two linked research literatures in relation to obesity and food choice. *Journal of Communication, 56,* 560–584.

Primack, BA, Dalton, MA, Carroll, MV, Agarwal, A, & Fine, MJ (2008). Content analysis of tobacco, alcohol, and other drugs in popular music. *Archives of Pediatric and Adolescent Medicine, 162,* 169–175.

Productivity Commission (2009). *Strengthening evidence-based policy in the Australian Federation: Roundtable proceedings, Volume 2: Background Paper.* Canberra: Commonwealth Government of Australia. Accessed April 2011, <http://www.pc.gov.au/__data/assets/pdf_file/0020/96230/25-chapter1-volume2.pdf>.

RACP (Royal Australasian College of Physicians: Paediatrics and Child Health Division) (2004). Paediatric policy: *Children and the media: Advocating for the future.* Accessed December 2010, <http://www.racp.edu.au/index.cfm?objectid=D7FAA93E-E091-4209-15657544BA419672>.

Reid, AS (2005). Rise of third generation phones: The implication for child protection. *Information and Communication Technology Law, 14,* 89–113.

Rideout, V, Foehr, U, Roberts, D, & Brodie, M (1999). *Kids & Media: The New Millennium.* Merlo Park, CA: The Henry J Kaiser Foundation.

Rudd, K (Prime Minister) (2008), *Address to Heads of Agencies and Members of Senior Executive Service.* Great Hall, Parliament House, Canberra, April 2008. Accessed May 2011, <http://pmrudd.archive.dpmc.gov.au/node/5817>.

Rush, E (2009). What are the risks of premature sexualisation for children? In M Tankard Reist (ed), *Getting real: Challenging the sexualisation of girls* (pp 41–54). Melbourne: Spinifex Press.

Soulos, G, & Sanders, S (2004). Promoting tobacco to the young in the age of advertising bans. *NSW Public Health Bulletin, 15,* 104–107.

Strasburger, VC (2009). Children, adolescents and the media: What we know, what we don't know and what we need to find out (quickly!). *Archives of Disease in Childhood, 94,* 655–657.

Tickle, JT, Sargent, JD, Dalton, MA, Beach, ML, & Heatherton, TF (2001). Favourite movie stars, their tobacco use in contemporary movies, and its association with adolescent smoking. *Tobacco Control, 10,* 16–22.

Turner, G, & Cunningham, S (2002). The media and communications in Australia today. In S Cunningham and G Turner (eds), *The Media & Communications in Australia* (pp 3–20). Sydney: Allen & Unwin.

Wakefield, M (2005). *Anti-smoking advertising: lessons learned.* Accessed April 2011, <http://www.druginfo.adf.org.au/druginfo-seminars/mass-media-campaigns-seminar-wakefield>.

WHO (World Health Organisation) (2008). *Global database on Body Mass Index.* Accessed June 2011, <http://apps.who.int/bmi/index.jsp>.

Young, K (2010). *Internet addiction: A handbook and guide to evaluation and treatment.* New York: Wiley.

Chapter 11

A two-edged sword? The place of the media in a child friendly society

Alan Hayes and Carole Jean

While one could choose from a vast array of examples, the positive power of the media to influence opinions and shape behaviour is aptly illustrated by a recent event in Australia. Footage broadcast of Australian cattle, exported live to Indonesia, being inhumanely treated before slaughter led to a reaction that was swift and unanimous in its condemnation. Broadcast at prime time across the networks, in the print media and on the Web, the footage made the cruel manner in which the animals were treated evident to all who viewed it. The public outcry prompted a ban on all live cattle exports. The 24-hour news cycle could not have worked more powerfully.

We first consider the place of the media in a child-friendly society by briefly exploring the tension between their role in promoting the public interest and the power of the profit motive that underpins their commercial survival. The public interest motive was demonstrated clearly in the above example of the treatment of live cattle exported from Australia. As the chapters in this volume well illustrate, however, when it comes to the best interests of children the media can be a two-edged sword. On the one hand, news, commentary and social affairs content can powerfully serve the public interest by exposing society's problems in protecting children and young people from violence, sexual abuse or exploitation. On the other, the media can also disseminate material that is inappropriate for a young and vulnerable audience, and that results in trauma or de-sensitisation and/or antisocial behaviour.

While material positively highlighting problems of child abuse, neglect, sexual assault and domestic and other violence is to be applauded, it tends to be less prevalent than the steady diet of inappropriate material that carries the risk of deleterious impacts. Violent, sexualised or exploitative material that is directed at adults may either be not broadcast, because it is deemed too offensive or distressing, or be broadcast subject to classification standards that can be honoured more in the breach than the observance. As earlier chapters illustrate, children can be exposed to such material in the mainstream media and this is at odds with the aspiration to be a child-friendly society. And much material is now available in forms and on media that are increasingly difficult to regulate. The ubiquity of such content and the ease of access to it are indeed concerning.

The contributors to this volume bring a wealth of evidence and ideas on a topic that carries some disturbing messages. The areas discussed collectively go to the place of children in society. The rhetoric of a child-friendly society stands in stark contrast to the reality – media influences have impacts on children that can not only deleteriously affect their childhood, but can potentially span lives and cross generations. It is a disturbing contradiction that social concerns about the impact of violent and sexualised media on children coexist with the ever-increasing availability of violent, sexualised or exploitative material. The preceding chapters squarely focus attention on the cognitive, emotional and social residues of exposure to such material. They also explore the predisposing factors in individuals as well as the enduring developmental residues that flow from exposure to harmful experiences in childhood and adolescence.

The evidence to action gap: Obesity, advertising and the limits of self-regulation

The present volume also highlights the "evidence to action" gap that pervades many areas of public policy (see also Chapter 10). Much has been written about evidence-based policy (eg, Banks, 2009). The problem in many areas, however, is that while the weight of evidence is clear, converting it to policy and practice is an inherently complex process. Action requires as a pre-condition acceptance of the evidence as well as the mobilisation of community and political will to effect change. Rationality too often confronts self-interest and the seductive simplicity of the *status quo*. In the face of commercial, social and political pressures, the best that perhaps can be achieved is evidence-informed policy; the worst is that evidence is ignored or worse still distorted. Too often, heat tends to be more evident than light.

Again, using an Australian example, the media well recognise the extent of the problem of burgeoning over-weight and obesity both in the developed as well as in the emerging industrialised nations. Considerable media coverage and public policy focus are devoted to raising awareness of the topic and educating the public on the health risks that flow from inactivity and weight gain. The National Preventative Health Taskforce highlighted the problem and underscored the need to reduce the exposure of children to advertising of unhealthy foods at times when children are most likely to be in the audience. The industry peak body, the Quick Service Restaurant Industry (QSRI) initiated a welcome move to self-regulation of marketing to children. Recent research, however, shows that rather than a reduction in advertising of convenience foods during children's viewing peaks, the time devoted to such advertising actually increased (Hebden et al, 2011). Confronted with a choice between public interest and commercial reality the latter seems to have again prevailed, illustrating the limits of effectiveness of self-regulation (see also Chapter 10).

The violence paradox

The social and political discourse on violence also demonstrates the double-edged nature of the media and its influences. Violence, abuse, neglect and sexual assault emerged as prominent concerns in the second half of the 20th century. The horrors of the two world wars that marked the first half of the century were indelibly etched into the psyches of those who survived slaughter on an unprecedented scale. Events that took place over the last century continue to be critically analysed and communicated. As such, they continue to be experienced, albeit vicariously, with the media playing a vital role in educating about the events, their causes and consequences.

Accompanying this recognition has been the growing concern in many nations, both developed and developing, to address the problem of violence, especially as it impacts on women and children. As Tremblay and Nagin (2005) observe, "[c]oncerted effort to suppress aggression in human interactions is one of the major social historical transformations observed in countries in the Western world in the latter part of the 20th century" (p 84). They reflect on the sanctions against the use of physical punishment, observe that "there is now a strong movement to make these criminal acts" (p 84) and conclude that "we are slowly creating a social environment in which the physical aggression solution generally becomes a much less adaptive strategy than its alternatives" (p 101).

However, reflecting on one of the paradoxes of a century marked by violence on an industrial scale, they note that:

> [O]nly a small minority of the inhabitants of the wealthy countries will be among those victims. Paradoxically, the fortunate minority, who are less and less at risk of being physically aggressed by a parent, teacher, a spouse, a neighbor, a stranger, or a soldier, are using a large part of their financial resources and leisure time to consume fictive depictions of physical violence on television, in movies, and in electronic games. (p 85)

Like other countries, Australia increasingly recognises the personal, social and economic costs of violence and the ways in which violent behaviour blights lives with impacts that too often span generations. The Council of Australian Governments (COAG) is the forum that brings the leaders of the national, State and Territory governments together to address problems that confront the Australian federation. The priority that is given to addressing family and community violence is evident in two recent initiatives: the "National Framework for Protecting Australia's Children (2009–2020)" and the "National Plan to Reduce Violence against Women and their Children (2010–2022)".

The first of these prioritises child protection. The stimulus was community concern for the disturbing statistics on child abuse, neglect and sexual assault. Violence and emotional abuse profoundly affect the lives of too many children. Between 2004 and 2006, the leading cause of death among children aged 0–14 years was injury, which is broken down into three subcategories: road transport accidents, accidental drowning, and assault and homicide. In 2006, assault was the third most common type of injury causing death for Australian children aged 0–14 years. It resulted in the deaths of 27 children in 2006–2007, compared to 66 deaths of children from transport accidents and 46 drowning deaths (Australian Institute of Health and Welfare, 2009).

Child deaths are the tip of an iceberg of child abuse, neglect and sexual assault. In 2007–2008, there were 317,526 notifications of children and young people to Australian child protection authorities. Of these, 55,120 were substantiated (that is confirmed following investigation by child protection workers). Disturbingly, around 60 per cent of those substantiated instances of abuse, neglect or sexual assault applied to the same children, who were the subject of multiple events worthy of notification in a single twelve-month period. While there is some evidence of progress in addressing the problem – by 2009–2010 the number of children subject to a notification across Australia had decreased by 10 per cent from 207,462 to 187,314 and the number of children with a substantiated event of abuse, neglect or sexual assault had decreased by 4 per cent from 32,641 to 31,295 (from 6.5 to 6.1 per 1000 children) – child protection remains an area of policy priority given these unacceptably high, though albeit somewhat reduced, rates of substantiation.

The second – the "National Plan to Reduce Violence against Women and their Children (2010–2022)" – also focuses concerted policy attention on violence generally, but especially when perpetrated against women and children. Public willingness to acknowledge the scope and scale of the problem tends to be patchy. The words of the Hon Kate Ellis MP, Minister for Women, underscore the mood:

> There seems to be what I find a very concerning trend in this country for people both men and women to try to play down the statistics – to try to shy away from them – or shut down discussion on the matter, but it will be absolutely impossible to make inroads into these family and domestic violence figures if people continue to diminish their importance. (Australia, 2011)

Nationally, the Personal Safety Survey (ABS, 2006) collects data on physical assaults in the last 12 months. It indicates that 242 000 women representing 3.1 per cent of population of women aged 15 or older were the victims of such assaults. For men, 485,400, or 6.5 per cent of those 15 years or above, reported having experienced a physical assault. Physical violence, including both actual assaults and threats of violence since age 15 was reported by 33.3 per cent of women and 49 per cent of men. For women, the survey indicated that in the most recent incident during the last 12 months, and where the perpetrator was male, 15.7 per cent of instances involved a current partner, 22.2 per cent a previous partner, 34.4 per cent family or friends, 18.2 per cent a stranger and 15 per cent another person. Where the perpetrator was a male, men reported negligible current partner or previous partner violence and 11.2 per cent for violence perpetrated by family or friends, 11.7 per cent by other known persons and 73.7 per cent by strangers. The difference between the patterns reported by women and men is stark. The level of violence experienced by Australian Indigenous women is even more alarming, with a hospitalisation rate as a result of assault that is 35 times higher than that of other Australian women.

The personal, social and economic costs of this family violence (including to children) are unacceptably high. The economic cost alone in Australia is estimated at $13.6 billion per annum (National Council to Reduce Violence against Women and their Children, 2009). Violence also has major impacts on the physical health and wellbeing of victims and is a major contributor to relationship breakdown and homelessness. In 2010, the Australian Institute of Family Studies (AIFS) completed a comprehensive review of the 2006 family law reforms. Some of the most concerning findings of that large-scale evaluation related to the extent of family violence reported by couples involved with the family law system. Around two-thirds of separated mothers and over 50 per cent of separated fathers reported that they had experienced emotional and/ or physical abuse (Kaspiew et al, 2010). Following separation, one fifth of parents held safety concerns related to ongoing contact with the other parent. An unsafe society can hardly be seen as child-friendly.

The origins of aggression

With this in mind, the aetiology of aggression and violence needs to be considered in some detail to achieve a balanced perspective on media influence. Genetic predispositions, the influence of biology and hormones and the learning of social behaviours through influences in the environment are all linked to the development of aggressive behaviour (see Chapters 1 and 3). Adolescence is commonly perceived as involving a rapid increase in aggression, violence and antisocial behaviour. The "age-violent crime curve", a frequently cited criminological finding, seems to bear this out. The curve shows a rapid acceleration in the violent crime rate from early adolescence, peaking in early adulthood before declining with a rapidity similar to its rise (Tremblay & Nagin, 2005). The explanations for the rise typically involve social learning, including the influence of peers and exposure to violent behaviour;

hormonal changes related to puberty, especially increased testosterone and its impacts on physical strength (Dahl, 2004); as well as neurological changes related to risky judgment and decision-making, such as increased myelinisation of neurons and neural pruning (Blakemore & Choudhury, 2006; Hayes, 2007; Spear, 2000; 2004).

But age-violent crime curves carry problems. First, they are based on the statistics about juvenile offending and this reflects selectivity. In addition, the unit of measurement reflects the response of police and the juvenile justice system in arresting and incarcerating adolescent offenders (Tremblay & Nagin, 2005), rather than the occurrence of aggression, *per se*. Longitudinal data, as opposed to police and court statistics, actually show a decrease in physical aggression for both males and females across the years from 10–18 years of age (Cairns & Cairns cited in Tremblay & Nagin, 2005, p 88). Only around 4 per cent of adolescent boys show an accelerating trend and these were more likely to have shown higher levels of aggression from early childhood on (Nagin & Tremblay, 1999).

This squares with the re-analyses by Sampson and Laub (2005) of the Gluecks follow-up study of 500 male delinquents and 500 matched male non-delinquents, first tested at 10–17 years and followed up 14, 25 and 32 years later. Their analyses demonstrate across time the scope for divergence in the pathways of delinquents, despite their "shared beginnings". Only a small percentage of those who offended in adolescence and early adulthood went on to become repeat offenders (Sampson & Laub, 2005). They argue that the changes that take place in adulthood relate to the stabilising effects of work and family factors, which explained the patterns of desistance or persistence with delinquency that they observed in the life courses of the juvenile offenders studied.

The second problem with age-violent crime curves is that they do not capture the incidence of aggressive behaviour earlier in life (Hay, 2005). Longitudinal studies commencing in infancy tell a very different story – humans are actually at their most violent as toddlers (Tremblay, 2003; 2004; Tremblay & Nagin, 2005). The period from 9–30 months shows increasing levels of physical aggression (Tremblay, 2004) before starting to decrease from that point onwards. And children who are not physically aggressive in early childhood are unlikely to become so with age (Côté et al, 2006). As such, we are socialised out of violence, rather than socialised into violence.

Trajectories of aggression: behaviour change and individual differences

As physically aggressive behaviour decreases with socialisation it tends to be replaced by indirect aggression (Vaillancourt et al, 2007). Examples of such indirect aggressive behaviours include manipulating dislike of a peer, befriending a person who is disliked by another to exact revenge, maliciously betraying confidences, impugning a person's reputation, or ostracising a member of the group. The incidence of indirect aggression increases across childhood and adolescence and is predicted by: being female, exhibiting more pro-social or more physically aggressive behaviour than peers at age two years, coming from a lower socio-economic status family and having experienced lower levels of parental support in early childhood than other children (Vaillancourt et al, 2007). For boys, increased levels of indirect aggression related to inconsistent parenting practices and greater conflict, particularly with their mothers. As Vaillancourt and colleagues suggest, for girls, the rise of indirect aggression may occur in parallel with greater sophistication in social skills, including their higher facility with prosocial behaviour: "perhaps girls have learned at a very young age that nice **and** mean work" (p 324, emphasis added).

Just as there are sex differences in the patterns of aggressive behaviour, there are also differences in the trajectories of aggression that have been observed, longitudinally. Using data from a nationally representative sample, Côté et al (2006) followed 10 cohorts of approximately 1000 Canadian children over 6 years. They found that around a third of children showed low levels of aggression in early childhood that continued to decline with age and labelled this group *low desisters*. Around half were labelled as *moderate desisters*, showing moderate levels of aggression early in life that declined from preschool and across the school years. A sixth of children showed trajectories of aggression that were labelled *high stable* reflecting more frequent aggressive behaviour in toddlerhood that continued at a high level across childhood. Of this last group over 60 per cent were boys. These results reflect the variation in patterns of aggressive behaviour at any point in development as well as their variability, over time (Tremblay & Nagin, 2005).

Genetic and environmental influences

The sources of individual differences in aggression are complex. They include genetic differences in neurotransmitters that underpin impulsivity and the propensity to aggressive reactivity, such as serotonin (Pihl & Benkelfat, 2005; Rhee & Waldman, 2011). Hormonal differences, in levels of testosterone or the stress-related hormone cortisol, are also thought to underpin aggressive behaviour (van Goozen, 2005). While the biological contributors to aggression are progressively becoming better understood, there is still much more to be learned about the complex interplay of genetic and environmental factors (Rhee & Waldman, 2011).

The environmental influences on aggression are similarly complex and multiple. Parental behaviour, especially harsh and inconsistent parenting, and a range of other factors from maternal alcohol, tobacco and other drug misuse before birth, perinatal complications, and peer influences in childhood and adolescence, are but some of the factors that have been linked to an elevated propensity for aggression (Tremblay & Nagin, 2005). A link between witnessing inter-parental violence and subsequent violent behaviour in intimate relationships in early adulthood has also been observed, (Cui et al, 2010; Usculan & Fuhrer, 2009); though the relationship is at best modest (Black et al, 2005). Analysis of prospective longitudinal birth cohort data from the Christchurch Health and Development Study also showed a link between witnessing inter-parental violence and subsequent relationship violence perpetrated by young adults, once socio-demographic context factors had been controlled, although this was again modest in size (Fergusson et al, 2006). Just as the rates of aggressive behaviour decline across development, exposure to violent behaviour does not necessarily portend a life of violence. However, exposure to abuse or neglect early in life can lead to neurological and endocrinological changes that influence reactivity and responsiveness and thus aggressive behaviour. Again, the effects are not necessarily immutable – environmental risk is about an increased likelihood rather than a guaranteed destiny.

Nor is DNA destiny. Rather, there is an interplay between environmental factors and genetic pre-dispositions that is much more complex than nature versus nurture. Some of these interactions are epigenetic (literally *above the genome*). A ground-breaking new field, epigenetics, highlights the importance of environmental influences on the expression of genes. Such influences can span generations as indicated by research that shows how famine in one generation followed by abundance of food for another can influence risk of obesity and heart disease across generations (Pembrey et al, 2006). To this extent you are what your grandparents and parents ate. The marks of experience of previous generations are written on the genome and act to influence the expression of genes. But for each individual it is experience that throws the genetic switch. To that extent, you are what you eat.

Differential susceptibility

Susceptibility to complexly interacting genetic and environmental influences is not a simple process. Like epigenetics, differential susceptibility is a rapidly developing field of research, with wide implications across several disciplines. Susceptibility to environmental influence varies considerably among children. Those with difficult temperaments, for example, have been shown to exhibit more behaviour problems when experiencing low quality child care and fewer problems when high quality care is available (Pluess & Belsky, 2009; 2010). As such, they are more likely to be influenced for good or ill depending on the quality of their developmental context. Children with difficult temperament have also been shown to be more susceptible to negative maternal discipline and to show fewer externalising behavioural problems if exposed to positive maternal discipline (van Zeijl et al, 2007). Bakermans-Kranenburg and van Ijzendoorn (2007) have also provided support for the differential susceptibility hypothesis in a study of attachment security in children who show insecurity, distress and avoidance (characteristic of disorganised attachment). Such children are more susceptible to unfavourable care environments but responding positively to favourable ones. This study demonstrates the link between the genetic substrate and differential susceptibility to environmental experiences.

A relationship has also been established between a specific gene that underpins differential susceptibility to childhood maltreatment and the propensity to move from being a victim to a victimiser (Caspi et al, 2002). Those with high levels of expression of the *monoamine oxidase A* (MAOA) gene were shown to be less likely to victimise others than those with low levels, despite both groups having experienced maltreatment. In part, this illustrates the value of differential susceptibility in explaining why risk is not destiny.

Differential susceptibility also underscores why care needs to be taken in terms of the "diet" of media material generally available to children and young people. Just as the link between diet in earlier life and adult overweight and obesity has been well established, so too has the link between early experience and development, health and wellbeing, across life.

From sole cause to salient causal factor

For the current consideration of the impacts of the media, a focus on differential susceptibility also moves the discussion beyond the simplistic binary consideration of whether the media has impacts or not. Like many other public health problems, combinations of factors complexly cause outcomes related to health and wellbeing as well as to behaviours such as aggression and violence. Strasburger (2009a) observes that "the media are not the leading cause of any paediatric health problem in the United States ... they do [however] make a substantial contribution to many health problems" (p 2265). It is not appropriate to argue that the media are a sole cause, but the evidence suggests that they "may represent one of the single most important influences on adolescent attitudes and behavior" and that "the evidence that media contribute to adolescent behavior is substantial, and can no longer be ignored" (Strasburger, 2009b, p 203).

Again, the influences can be positive or negative, reflecting the double-edged nature of media impacts. On the one hand, the media can powerfully influence development of pro-social attitudes to non-violent problem solving, understanding of difference and diversity, altruism and civic engagement along with the attitudes, values and behaviours that underpin respectful relationships. On the other, the media can exert negative influences on attitudes, values and behaviours in a diverse range of areas related to sex, drugs, eating disorders, school performance and violence (Strasburger, 2009b).

In considering media influences, the difference needs to be clearly understood between being the sole cause as opposed to a salient causal influence among others. A medical example illustrates the argument. Around 10 per cent of lung cancers occur among those who have never smoked, as opposed to those who have smoked for a considerable time. There are multiple causes of this outcome for non-smokers other than the obvious one – passive exposure to tobacco smoke – including exposure to other environmental carcinogens and genetic pre-dispositions to the disease. The existence of these other causes, however, does not obviate the need to take seriously the causal role of smoking in the majority of cases of lung cancer. While the media may not be "the leading cause" of the problems discussed in this and other chapters, media influence cannot be ignored. Differential susceptibility explains the variation in the extent of influence of the media. Those who are most susceptible may not always be identifiable before the fact and this is the basis for the prominence of broad-spectrum prevention, risk management and harm minimisation in public health approaches.

Concluding thoughts

This chapter has focused on the impacts of the media – for good or ill – focusing particularly on current insights into the developmental course of aggressive behaviour, given that this is an area of such contemporary public policy concern. The material discussed highlights that human aggression peaks in toddler-hood, has multiple physiological and environmental causes, and decreases across the lifespan in most people as they become more and more "socialised" into resolving conflict and expressing their urges in ways that are socially acceptable. This process becomes more volatile in adolescence, as hormones, neural changes and powerful external pressures coincide. In addition, adolescence is also a time of both identity formation and increasing exposure to mass media. Indeed, for modern Australian children, mass media influences are an important factor in identity formation. Problems arise when the one has a maladaptive effect on the other.

The exploitation, desensitisation, objectification, sexualisation and adultification that flow from exposure to violent and sexualised material could be seen as processes that override this crucial developmental process of socialisation out of violence, and reinforce reversion to the behaviours of an earlier stage of development. That is, media with such content has important developmental impacts on children and adolescents.

Media also has a role in what might be called the violence paradox, whereby victims are more likely to become victimisers. Cultural stories, mores and values set the context for this process and mass media is a powerful mediator of culture. In the sweep of history one thing is clear, however: cultures can correct. We are not bound by inexorable destiny: rather, we can reverse processes of decline and dysfunction.

That said, the frequency of contact, ease of access and pervasiveness of new media are unparalleled in history. We live in an age where abundance of choice and ready availability of products and information have created their own problems. Media is portable, pervasive and linked to powerful commercial interests whose simple message is "consume". As such it is the wallpaper to many Australian children's lives and a key driver of child consumer behaviour. The widespread accessibility and repeatability of exposure to media-based violent and/or sexualised material for children could be seen as the democratisation of dysfunction, in a culture that engenders confusion and desensitisation, and where the previously private has now become the pervasively public.

Truly child-friendly societies should seek to reduce risk, respect vulnerability and ameliorate the scope for harm. They should also recognise the individual differences in susceptibility to desensitisation, objectification, adultification and sexualisation. While there remains much to learn about the mechanisms that differentially drive risk and vulnerability, the links between early experience and later outcomes have become progressively clearer.

So what can we do? The juvenile offending literature points to the prime importance of adult and parental monitoring, as does the literature on child protection. We also have much to learn about how we can educate the community to exercise greater discernment in the choice of material that children and young people access. Passive acceptance and learned helplessness need to be countered by vigilance and agency. There is also a need to promote substitution of positive, pro-social alternatives. Finally, more research is needed on the psychological mechanisms that underpin neurological priming, desensitisation and susceptibility to the triggering mechanisms for violent behaviour and automatisation of response. As such, we need more research focused on vulnerability and resilience and how these change with time and experience. Experimental and longitudinal methods will further our understanding of the causal pathways and evaluation of interventions will extend the evidence base to inform public policy and professional practice.

In a broad sense, while there is still much to learn, sufficient evidence of the toxic effects of a diet rich in violence and sexualised material is available, as the earlier chapters in this book have convincingly demonstrated. The jury is not out. What is also clear, however, is that the perennial problem in public policy – the gap between knowledge and action – applies to this area, as it does in many others. Sustained behaviour change requires first that the evidence is available to those who frame policy and oversee regulation. Second, all those in the "village" that raise our children need to be better informed about the factors that can have toxic impacts on children's development, health and wellbeing. Finally, events such as the civil disobedience in the United Kingdom (during August 2011) oblige us to consider the causes of such antisocial behaviour. As argued, the media is but one influence, among many, though having said that, its salience cannot be minimised. The media are pervasive and influential – for good and ill. We are what we eat – and what our children consume has impacts that can extend across their lives. While individuals need to learn to make appropriate choices and exercise control, our collective responsibility cannot be overlooked as we aspire to a child friendly society.

Notes and Acknowledgments

1. The views expressed are those of the authors and may not reflect the views of the Australian Institute of Family Studies or the Australian Government.
2. We acknowledge the contributions to this chapter of the following colleagues at the Australian Institute of Family Studies, Nancy Virgona, Antonia Quadara, Alister Lamont and Liz Wall. Their assistance is greatly appreciated.

References

ABS (Australian Bureau of Statistics) (2006). *Personal Safety Survey 2005* (reissue). Canberra: Australian Bureau of Statistics.

Australia House of Representatives (2011). Debates Volume: vol HR 6 (26 May), pp 4803–4806.

Australian Institute of Health and Welfare (2009). *A picture of Australia's children*. Canberra.

Bakermans-Kranenburg, MJ, & van IJzendoorn, MH (2007). Genetic vulnerability or differential susceptibility in child development: The case for attachment. *Journal of Child Psychology and Psychiatry, 48*, 1160–1173.

Banks, G (2009). *Challenges of evidence-based policy making*. Canberra: Australian Public Service Commission.

Black, DS, Sussman, S, & Unger, JB (2010). A further look at the intergenerational transmission of violence: Witnessing interparental violence in emerging adulthood. *Journal of Interpersonal Violence, 25*, 1022–1042.

Blakemore, S-J, & Choudhury, S (2006). Development of the adolescent brain: Implications for executive function and social cognition. *Journal of Child Psychology and Psychiatry, 47*, 296–312.

Caspi, A, McClay, J, Moffitt, TE, Mill, J, Martin, J, Craig, IW, Taylor, A, & Poulton, R (2002). Role of genotype in the cycle of violence in maltreated children. *Science, 297*, 851–854.

Côté, SM, Vaillancourt, T, LeBlanc, JC, Nagin, DS, & Tremblay, RE (2006). The development of physical aggression from toddlerhood to pre-adolescence: A nation wide longitudinal of Canadian children. *Journal of Abnormal Child Psychology, 34*, 71–85.

Cui, M, Durtschi, JA, Donnellan, MB, Lorenz, FO, & Conger, RD (2010). Intergenerational transmission of relationship aggression: A prospective longitudinal study. *Journal of Family Psychology, 24*, 688–697.

Dahl, RE (2004). Adolescent brain development: A period of vulnerabilities and opportunities. In RE Dahl & LP Spear (eds), *Adolescent brain development: Vulnerabilities and opportunities, Annals of the New York Academy of Science, vol 1021* (pp 1–22). New York: New York Academy of Science.

Fergusson, DM, Boden, JM, & Horwood, LJ (2006). Examining the intergenerational transmission of violence in a New Zealand cohort. *Child Abuse and Neglect, 30*, 89–108.

Hay, DF (2005). The beginnings of aggression in infancy. In RE Hartup, WW Hartup, & J Archer (eds), *Developmental origins of aggression* (pp 107–132). New York: The Guilford Press.

Hayes, A (2007). Why early in life is not enough: Timing and sustainability in prevention and early intervention. In A France & R Homel (eds), *Pathways and crime prevention: Theory, policy and practice*. Cullompton, Devon: Willan Publishing.

Hebden, LA, King, L, Grunseit, A, Kelly, B, & Chapman, K (2011). Advertising of fast food to children on Australian television: The impact of industry self-regulation. *Medical Journal of Australia, 195*, 20–24.

Kaspiew, R, Gray, M, Weston, R, Moloney, L, Hand, K, & Qu, L (2010). *Evaluation of the 2006 Family Law Reforms*. Melbourne: Australian Institute of Family Studies.

Nagin, D, & Tremblay, RE (1999). Trajectories of boys' physical aggression, opposition, and hyperactivity on the path to physically violent and non-violent juvenile delinquency. *Child Development, 70*, 1181–1196.

National Council to Reduce Violence against Women and their Children (2009). *The cost of violence against women and their children*. Canberra: Commonwealth of Australia.

Pembrey, ME, Bygren, LO, Kaati, G, Edvinsson, S, Norhtstone, K, Sjöström, M, Golding, J, & the ALSPAC Study Team (2006). Sex-specific, male-line transgenerational responses in humans. *European Journal of Human Genetics, 14*, 159–166.

Pihl, RO, & Benkelfat, C (2005). Neuromodulators in the development and expression of inhibition and aggression. In RE Hartup, WW Hartup, & J Archer (eds), *Developmental origins of aggression* (pp 261–280). New York: The Guilford Press.

Pluess, M, & Belsky, J (2009). Differential susceptibility to rearing experience: The case of childcare. *Journal of Child Psychology and Psychiatry, 50*, 396–404.

Pluess, M, & Belsky, J (2010). Children's differential susceptibility to effects of parenting. *Family Science, 1*, 14–25.

Rhee, SH, & Waldman, ID (2011). Genetic and environmental influences on aggression. In PR Shaver & M Mikulincer (eds), *Human aggression and violence: Causes, manifestations, and consequences* (pp 143–163). Washington, DC: American Psychological Association.

Sampson, RJ, & Laub, JH (2005). A general age graded theory of crime: Lessons learned and the future of life-course criminology. In D Farrington (ed), *Integrated development and life-course theories of offending: Advances in criminological theory* (Vol 14; pp 165–181). New Brunswick, NJ: Transaction Publishers.

Spear, LP (2000). The adolescent brain and age-related behavioural manifestations. *Neuroscience and Biobehavioral Review, 24*, 417–463.

Spear, LP (2004). Adolescent brain development and animal models. In RE Dahl & LP Spear (eds), *Adolescent brain development: Vulnerabilities and opportunities, Annals of the New York Academy of Science, vol 2021* (pp 23–26). New York: New York Academy of Science.

Strasburger, VC (2009a). Media and children: What needs to happen now? *Journal of the American Medical Association, 301*, 2265–2266.

Strasburger, VC (2009b). Why do adolescent health researchers ignore the impact of the media? *Journal of Adolescent Health, 44*, 203–205.

Tremblay, RE (2003). Why socialization fails?: The case of chronic physical aggression. In BB Lahey, TE Moffitt & A Caspi (eds), *Causes of conduct disorder and juvenile delinquency* (pp 182–224). New York: The Guilford Press.

Tremblay, RE (2004). The development of human physical aggression: How important is early childhood? In LA Leavitt & DM Hall (eds), *Social and moral development: Emerging evidence on the toddler years* (pp 221–238). New Brunswick, NJ: Johnson and Johnson Pediatric Institute.

Tremblay, RE, & Nagin, DS (2005). The developmental origins of physical aggression in humans. In RE Hartup, WW Hartup & J Archer (eds), *Developmental origins of aggression* (pp 83–106). New York, The Guilford Press.

Uslucan, H-H, & Fuhrer, U (2009). Intergenerational transmission of violence. In U Schonplflug (ed), *Cultural transmission: Psychological, developmental, social and methodological aspects* (pp 391–418). New York: Cambridge University Press.

Vaillancourt, T, Miller, JL, Fagbemi, J, Côté, S, & Tremblay, RE (2007). Trajectories and predictors of indirect aggression: Results from a nationally representative longitudinal study of Canadian children aged 2–10. *Aggressive Behavior, 33*, 314–326.

Van Goozen, SHM (2005). Hormones and the developmental origins of aggression. In RE Hartup, WW Hartup & J Archer (eds), *Developmental origins of aggression* (pp 281–306). New York, The Guilford Press.

van Zeijl, J, Mesman, J, Stolk, MN, Alink, LRA, van Ijenendoorn, MH, Bakermans-Kranenburg, MJ, Juffer, F, & Koot, HM (2007). Differential susceptibility to discipline: The moderating effect of child temperament on the association between maternal discipline and early childhood externalizing problems. *Journal of Family Psychology, 21*, 626–636.

Index

addiction
  media, to 13
  video games, to 59–60

advertising 129–30
  AMI billboards, case study 180–3
  automatic influences on the consumer 133–6, 167–8
    on attitudes 134–6
  childhood obesity and 205–7, 221–2
  consumer research 130–1
  The Hidden Persuaders 129
  mental contamination 137–8
    sexualised images used in 138–40
  'persuasion knowledge' 130–1
    age children acquire 130–1
    whether has any effect 132
  legal and regulatory responses to, sexualisation of children 178–81
    Australian Association of National Advertisers (AANA), code 178–9
    Government's response to Senate inquiry 180–1
    Senate inquiry 178–80
      recommendations of 179–80
  mental contamination 137–8
    sexualised images used in 138–40
  'persuasion knowledge' 130–1
    age children acquire 130–1
    whether has any effect 132
  sexualised images used in 138–40
  'Tween' market 148–9

aggressive behaviour 42
  acquisition of knowledge and ideas of 73–4
  correlational research, viewing violence and 39–40
    longitudinal studies 40–2
  development of 225
    age-violent crime curve 225–7
  early experimental studies 36–7
  General Aggression Model 75–7
    repeated playing of violent video games 76

aggressive behaviour (*cont*)
    genetic and environmental influences on 228-9
        differential susceptibility 229-30
        identifying with characters who display 70-1
        imitation of 69-70
        learning of 72-4
        media impact 230-1
    media violence, links to 18-24, 42-3
    music videos, links to 101-3
    neurological basis of 46-9
    repeated playing out of 70-1
    research approaches to 9
    reducing the risk of 24-5, 78, 89, 90, 108-9
    risk factor approach to 2
    song lyrics, links to 94, 97, 98, 104-7
    sexual 99-100
    trajectories of 227-8
    video games, links to 61-9
    violent music , links to 101-7
    violent and, differentiated 62

Anderson, Distinguished Professor Craig 64-5, 67-9

Australia
    boys daily media consumption 5
        girls, compared with 5
    children daily exposure to media 1, 4
        computers, time on 4
        increases with age 6
        mobile phones, time using 4
        music, time listening 4
        television viewing, hours 4
        United States, comparison 3
        video games, hours playing 4

Australian Association of National Advertisers (AANA), code 178-9

Australian Communications and Media Authority (ACMA) 202
    Children's Television Standards 183-4
    policy regulation 203
    study of children's media habits 2007 4
    study of television content quotas 2010 212

behavioural effects of viewing violent television 34
    classes of 42
    early research 35-6
    experimental studies, first 36-7
    US research 37-9

Breikvik, Anders Behring 78–9
Broadcasting Services Act 1992 (Cth) 184–5
Canada
    television viewing by children, survey of motives 9
    television regulation policies 2010
character-based ethics 162
children
    abuse, neglect and sexual assault 223–4
    advertising and *see* advertising
        'Tween' market 148–9
    boys (Australia) daily media consumption 5
        girls, compared with 5
        increases with age 6
    boys (US) daily media consumption 5
        girls, compared with 5
        increases with age 5
    Children's Television Standards 183–4
    daily exposure to media 1–4
        black and Hispanic compared with white 5
    ethics, application to recurring issues
        'childhood' understandings as to what constitutes 170–2
        consequences of children's access to media, interpretation of 164–6
        freedom of expression v protection from harm 168–70
        media regulation or education of children 166–8
    media
        effects of, on 9
        motives for using 9
        protecting children from negative impacts 24–5
    parental controls, time and/or content 5
    policy
        childhood obesity, relating to 205–7
        children's television viewing and 210–12
        sexualisation of, relating to 209–10
    psychological processes of learning from media 22–4
    sexualisation
        child protection and 155
        developmental impact of 149–50
        media and industry practices contributing to 176
        mental health and 150–1
        premature of children 145–6
    television timeslots, most popular 4
    violence
        how impacts on 22–4
        number of acts exposed to 3

Children's Television Standards 183–4
classification 187–9
    adult gamers and 191–2
    civil liberties, consideration of 191
    comparator jurisdictions 192–3
    criteria for classifications, impact levels 188
    Guidelines for the Classification of Films and Computer Games 2005 187–9
    MA15+, reconsideration of guidelines for 190
    National Classification Code 185
    R18+ classification for computer games 189–90
    reform, proposed classification for video games 194
    refused classification, criteria 187
Competition and Consumer Act 2010 (Cth) 186–7
    Australian Consumer Law 186–7
computer
    children, daily exposure to 2–4
    games
        adult gamers and 191–2
        civil liberties, consideration of 191
        classification under the National Classification Code 185
        comparator jurisdictions 192–3
        MA15+, reconsideration of guidelines for 190
        R18+ classification for 189–90
        reform, proposed classification for 194
        refused classification, criteria 187
    ownership per household and location 8
    ownership rates 4
        tablet computers, of 4
    parental responsibility 193–4
consequence-based ethics 161
correlational research
    viewing and aggressive behaviour 39–40
        longitudinal studies 40–2
Cultivation Theory 22
cyberbullying 119–20
Cybersafety 213, 215
desensitisation 42, 49
DVD players
    ownership per household and location 8
education of children 214–15
    media literacy 166–7
    media-savvy child 215–16

ethical relativism 163–4
ethics
    application to recurring issues
        'childhood' understandings as to what constitutes 170–2
        consequences of children's access to media, interpretation of 164–6
        freedom of expression v protection from harm 168–70
        media regulation or education of children 166–8
    content of 159–60
    perspectives of 160, 172
        character-based 162
        consequence-based 161
        ethical relativism 163–4
        principle-based 161–2
    vulnerability and 169–70
exposure
    media, daily by children 1
        Australian and US comparison 2–4
    violence, acts of seen by children 3
Facebook 7
fear 15, 42
films
    classification under the *National Classification Code* 185
    refused classification, criteria 187
General Aggression Model 75–7
    repeated playing of violent video games 76
gratification theory 7
the Gruel brief 20
    Millett brief, comparison of signees 21
internet
    access rates 4, 118
        broadband 4
    children, daily exposure to 2, 3
    cyberbullying 119–20
    emerging issues 124
    exposure, average daily 4
    mobile, penetration rates 4
    online marketing 123–4
        advergame 125
    parents, advice for 124–7
        government websites 126
    policy relating to 212–14
    sexual exploitation by use of 120–1

internet (*cont*)
    sexually explicit material, viewing by youth 121–3
    traditional media, as medium for viewing 116–17
    ubiquity of 117–18

i-pod
    viewing on, increase in 6

media
    accessed from, change 6
    aggression and, links 19–22
    aggressive behaviour and *see* aggressive behaviour
    appeal of 7
        gratification theory 7
    Broadcasting Services Act 1992 (Cth) 184–5
    Children's Television Standards 183–4
    daily exposure to
        average internet user 4
        children 1
    incidental exposure to 1
    literacy 166–7
    motives for using 9
    National Classification Code 185
    negative impacts of
        addiction 13
        advertising, susceptibility 16
        attention deficit and education problems 13
        family relationships, detriment to 16
        fear, anxiety and phobias 15
        mental health problems 13
        physical activities curtailed 12
        poor health, links with 11
        prejudice and misogyny 17
        premature sexualisation of children 18
        protecting children from 24–5
        sleep deficits 12
        unhealthy lifestyle choices 14
    portability, increase in 6
    positive impacts of
        education 10
        pain management 11
        pro-social and helping behaviour 10
        social networks 11
        spatial cognition, coordination and fine motor skills 11
    violence, acts of seen by children 3

INDEX

media literacy 166–7
    education of children about media 214–15
    media-savvy child 215–16
media policy 198
    alcohol, tobacco and drug use, relating to 207–9
    Australian government role in policy 201–2
    childhood obesity, relating to 205–7
    children's television viewing and 210–12
    development 216–17
    education of children about media 214–15
        media literacy 166–7
        media-savvy child 215–16
    evidence-based policy 198–200
    gap between policy and reality 220–2
    internet and 212–14
    self-regulation and co-regulation policies 203–4
    sexualisation of children and 209–10
media violence
    aggressive behaviour, links to 19
    behavioural effects of viewing 34
        correlational research 39–40
            longitudinal studies 40–2
        early research 35–6
        experimental studies, first 36–7
        US research 37–9
    children, exposure to 4
    classification of 187–9
        Guidelines for the Classification of Films and Computer Games 2005 187–9
        refused classification, criteria 187
    Cultivation Theory 22
    impact on youth and children, how 22–4
    interactive greater than passive 187
    key impacts of 19
    Media Violence Exposure Index 47
    protecting children from 24–5
    studies in 19
Media Violence Exposure Index 47
meta-analysis and what evidence it provides 64–8
    Anderson, Distinguished Professor Craig 64–5, 67–9
    Ferguson, Dr Chris 64–5
the Millett brief 20
    Gruel brief, comparison of signees 21

mobile phone
    children, daily use of 2–4
    ownership per household and location 8
    viewing of, increase in 6
movies
    children, daily exposure to 2, 3
mp3 players
    i-pod viewing of, increase in 6
    ownership per household and location 8
music
    children, time spent daily listening to 2–4
    importance of 86–7
    negative effects of
        anti-social behaviour 98
        genres with violent/anti-social themes 93–6
        misogynistic attitudes 99–100
        rap, heavy/death metal 93–6
        sexual behaviour 98–9
        substance use 96
        suicide 100
    positive effects of
        ceremonies, festivals, dancing 92
        clinical benefits of 90
        educational effects 92
        games using 92
        mood and pro-social behaviours 88–9
        pain alleviation 90
        peers, identity formation and relations with 91–2
    research, application by parents and professionals 107–9
    time spent 88–9
        age 88
        ethnicity 88
        gender 88
    videos, sexualised 153
    violent and anti-social 101
        song lyrics and tone 104–7
        videos 101–3
National Broadband Network (NBN) 6
National Classification Code 185
    adult gamers and 191–2
    civil liberties, consideration of 191
    comparator jurisdictions 192–3
    criteria for classifications, impact levels 188

MA15+, reconsideration of guidelines for 190
R18+ classification for computer games 189–90
reform, proposed classification for video games 194

neurological effects 43–4
    brainmapping, beginnings of 44–6
    desensitisation 49
    prefrontal cortex, exploring 46–9
    video games, of 48

obesity
    policy relating to childhood 205–7
    reality and policy, gap between 220–2

online
    audio or video, rates of access 4
    marketing 123–4
        advergame 125
    policy relating to 212–14
    viewing, increase in 6, 116–17

Packard, Vance 129
    The Hidden Persuaders 129

persuasion knowledge 130–1
    children, age acquire 130–1
    whether has any effect 132
        automatic influences on the consumer 133–6

policy 198
    aggressive behaviour and *see* aggressive behaviour
    alcohol, tobacco and drug use, relating to 207–9
    Australian government role in policy 201–2
        creation of media, subsidising 201
        regulating distribution and exhibition 201
    childhood obesity, relating to 205–7
    children's television viewing and 210–12
    current regulatory framework
        protecting children within 202–3
    development 216–17
    education of children about media 214–15
        media literacy 166–7
        media-savvy child 215–16
    evidence-based policy 198–200
    internet and 212–14
    priority areas
        child abuse, neglect and sexual assault 223–4
        women, violence against 224–5

policy (*cont*)
    reality and, gap 220–2
    self-regulation and co-regulation policies 203–4
    sexualisation of children and 209–10
principle-based ethics 161–2
psychological processes
    children learning from media 22–4
publications
    classification under the *National Classification Code* 185
    refused classification, criteria 187
regulation
    advertising, sexualisation of children 178–81
        Australian Association of National Advertisers (AANA), code 178–9
        Government's response to Senate inquiry 180–1
        Senate inquiry 178–80
            recommendations of 179–80
    Broadcasting Services Act 1992 (Cth) 184–5
    Children's Television Standards 183–4
    classification *see* classification
    Competition and Consumer Act 2010 (Cth) 186–7
    current regulatory framework
        protecting children within 202–3
    National Classification Code 185
    self-regulation and co-regulation policies 203–4
    State legislation, enactment 183
relationships
    sexualisation, impact on 153
Schwarzenegger and Brown v Video Software Dealers Association 20–4, 193
sexual exploitation by internet use 120–1
sexualisation
    advertising, use of sexualised images in 138–40
        'Tween' market 148–9
    Broadcasting Services Act 1992 (Cth) 184–5
    child protection and 154
    Children's Television Standards 183–4
    Competition and Consumer Act 2010 (Cth) 186–7
        Australian Consumer Law 186–7
    defining 146–9
        American Psychological Association 147–8, 175–6
            negative consequences identified 176

developmental impact of 149-50
freedom of expression v protection from harm 168-70
legal and regulatory responses to, of children 178-81
    Australian Association of National Advertisers (AANA), code 178-9
    Government's response to Senate inquiry 180-1
    Senate inquiry 178-80
        recommendations of 179-80
media and industry practices contributing to 176
    ribald adult humour 176
    sexification 177-8
mental health and 150-1
National Classification Code 185
policy, media and 209-10
premature of children 145-6
relationships, impact on 153
sexual identity and, impact on 151-3

social networking
children, time spent daily on activities 5
needs met by 7

substance use
music, references to 96-7
policy relating to alcohol, tobacco and drug use 207-9

television
behavioural effects of viewing violent 34
    classes of 42
    early research 35-6
    experimental studies, first 36-7
    US research 37-9
children, daily exposure to 2-4
Children's Television Standards 183-4
ownership per household and location 8
policy and children's viewing 210-12
time-shifted viewing, increase in 6
timeslots, most popular seen by children 4
viewing by alternate modes, increase in 6
violence acts of seen by children 3

United States
boys daily media consumption 5
    black and Hispanic compared with white
    girls, compared with 5
    increases with age 5

United States (*cont*)
    children 8-18 daily exposure to media 1, 2
        Australian children, comparison 3
        computer use, hours 2
        listening to music, hours 2
        mobile phones, time using 2
        movie viewing, hours 2
        television viewing, hours 2
        video games, hours playing 2
    media saturation 2
    policies for internet restrictions 200
United Kingdom
    Council for child internet safety 213, 214
    television advertising bans 205–6
video games
    behaviour, link to viewing and violent 61–3
        meta-analysis and what evidence it provides 64–9
        researching 62
    Breikvik, Anders Behring 78–9
    children, daily time spent playing 2–4, 56
        age 56
        gender 56
    consoles, ownership per household and location 8
    effects of interactivity 71–2
    effects of repetition 71
    fictitious versus real violence 74
    General Aggression Model 75–7
        repeated playing of violent 76
    negative effects of
        addiction to 59–60
        attention deficits 60
        increased aggression 61–3
        school performance 61
    neurological effects of viewing violent 43–4
        brainmapping, beginnings of 44–6
        desensitisation 49
        Media Violence Exposure Index 47
        prefrontal cortex, exploring 46–9
    positive effects of
        coordination and spatial cognition 58
        education 58–9
        exercise 59
        pain management 57
        pro-social behaviour 58

psychology of effects of violent on children 69
    aggressive models, acquisition of 73–4
    associative learning 72
    identification 70–1
    imitation 69–70
    interactivity 71–2
    lack of negative consequences 72
    repetition 71
self-regulation, teaching children 77–8
underage children, sale to 20
violent
    content, amount of 57
    effect of 19–21
    fictitious versus real 74

violence
    aggressive behaviour and, differentiated 62
    behavioural effects of viewing 34
        classes of 42
        early research 35–6
        experimental studies, first 36–7
        US research 37–9
    child abuse, neglect and sexual assault 223–4
    children, number of acts witnessed by 3
    definition under *Guidelines for the Classification of Films and Computer Games 2005* 187–9
    development of aggressive behaviour 225
        age-violent crime curve 225–7
    fictitious versus real 74
    General Aggression Model 75–7
        repeated playing of violent video games 76
    genetic and environmental influences 228–9
        differential susceptibility 229–30
        media impact 230–1
    neurological effects of viewing violent 43–4
        brainmapping, beginnings of 44–6
        desensitisation 49
        prefrontal cortex, exploring 46–9
    media *see* media violence
    music *see* music
    paradox 222–5, 232–3
    video games and *see* video games
    women, against 224–5

You Tube 7